Man and God

Xavier Zubiri

Translated by Joaquín Redondo

**Translation critically revised by
Thomas Fowler and Nelson Orringer**

This translation was made possible by a grant from the
Spanish Ministry of Culture

University Press of America,® Inc.
Lanham · Boulder · New York · Toronto · Plymouth, UK

B
4568
.Z83
H6613
2009

Copyright © 2009 by
University Press of America,® Inc.
4501 Forbes Boulevard
Suite 200
Lanham, Maryland 20706
UPA Acquisitions Department (301) 459-3366

Estover Road
Plymouth PL6 7PY
United Kingdom

All rights reserved
Printed in the United States of America
British Library Cataloging in Publication Information Available

Library of Congress Control Number: 2009927843
ISBN-13: 978-0-7618-4702-1 (paperback : alk. paper)
ISBN-10: 0-7618-4702-2 (paperback : alk. paper)
eISBN-13: 978-0-7618-4703-8
eISBN-10: 0-7618-4703-0

Co-published by arrangement with
the Xavier Zubiri Foundation of North America

∞™ The paper used in this publication meets the minimum
requirements of American National Standard for Information
Sciences—Permanence of Paper for Printed Library Materials,
ANSI Z39.48-1992

Man and God is a translation of *El hombre y Dios*, published by Alianza Editorial/Fundación Xavier Zubiri, Madrid, 1985. This translation is published by agreement with the publisher and copyright holder of the Spanish original.

CONTENTS

Translator's Introduction	1
Editor's Introduction	9

Man and God

Author's Introduction	19
Part I: Human Reality	**21**
Chapter 1. What Is It To Be Human?	23
§1 Reality	24
§2 "Human" reality	32
Chapter 2. How Can One Be A Human Being?	63
§1 What is a human being according to these actions?	64
§2 How does a human being make itself a relative person in its actions?	66
Appendix 1. The power of the real	73
Part II: Divine Reality	**89**
Chapter 3. The Unfolding of the Problem: I. The Reality of God	91
§1 The point of departure for the problem	93
§2 Justification of the reality of God	104
§3 Some characteristics of the reality of God	125
Chapter 4: The Unfolding the Problem: II. Human Access to God	135
§1 What do we understand by "access?"	136
§2 God, accessible reality	140
§3 The access of human beings to God	146
Appendix 2. Personal causality and morality	154
§4 The formal root of the access of human beings to God	157
Part III: Human Beings, Experience of God	**221**
Chapter 5. God, Experience of Human Beings	223
§1 Experience with respect to God	231
§2 Different forms of donation	232
§3 Dimensions of the experience of God	234
Chapter 6. Human Beings, Experience of God	237
§1 What is experience of God?	238
§2 Modes of the experience of God	240

§3 Individual, social, and historical dimensions of the experience of God 244
§4 Other attitudes with respect to the experience of God 250
Chapter 7. Unity of God "and" Human Beings 253
§1 Generic characteristic of the unity of God "and" human beings 255
§2 Type of unity between God "and" humans 257
§3 Experiential unity of God "and" human beings 260
§4 Unity of human beings "and" God as transcurrence of religation 265

By Way of Conclusion 269
The Theological Problem of Human Beings 270
Index 281

TRANSLATORS' INTRODUCTION

This book is the first of three major works by Xavier Zubiri (1898-1983) on the subject of theology. All three books are posthumous, based on lectures given by Zubiri, which in some cases he had begun to edit for publication. The details for *Man and God* are given in the Editor's Introduction. Zubiri felt compelled to make this major incursion into theology because he was driven to it by his philosophical reflections. Some general background on his philosophy is therefore appropriate.

Background on Zubiri's Philosophy

Zubiri's last private conversation with Heidegger in 1930, just before leaving Freiburg im Breisgau for Berlin, had important consequences for both philosophers, as he later mentioned to his wife, Carmen Castro de Zubiri in 1931. He also told her that in his opinion Heidegger would never publish a continuation to *Sein und Zeit* (*Biografía de Xavier Zubiri*, Carmen Castro de Zubiri, Madrid, 1992). Heidegger's metaphysics had not fully satisfied Zubiri. At the last moment before saying good bye to Zubiri, Heidegger said to him, "Why, *Herr Kollegue*, did you not mention all this before?" Zubiri had already started on a different metaphysical quest. Years later Zubiri would write: "Fundamentally, the entire philosophy of Heidegger is a commentary to this idea that man is the one that comprehends being... *Being*, then, is the possibility that things show themselves and that man may comprehend them. With this, the radical characteristic of man becomes the comprehension of *being*. This, however, cannot be upheld: first, because the primary function of man is not to comprehend *being*, but to confront the reality of things sentiently and, second, because *to be* lacks the note of substantivity; *being* is only *respectively*, and this respectivity is not the respectivity to man, but to the reality of everything. Therefore, it is reality and only reality that has substantivity." ...."Reality and *being* are two different and distinct moments of the real, but not because reality is a type of *to be*, as Kant and Heidegger assert, but quite the reverse, because being is a *further* moment or actuality of the real, a moment which has nothing to do with intellection" (*Sobre la esencia*, Madrid, 1962, pág. 453) [*On Essence*, tr. by A. Robert Caponigri, Washington, DC, 1980, p. 407].

In a special prologue Zubiri wrote (1980) for the English translation of *Naturaleza Historia Dios* [*Nature History God*, tr. by Thomas B. Fowler, University Press of America, 1981], he elaborated further:

> Indeed, Is metaphysics the same as ontology? Is reality the same as *to be*? Well inside phenomenology, Heidegger glimpsed the difference between things and their being. This led him to affirm that metaphysics was grounded upon ontology. My reflections followed an opposite course: being is grounded upon reality. Metaphysics is the ground of ontology. What metaphysics studies is not objectivity, or being, but reality as such.

Zubiri argued that modern philosophy rests unconsciously on four concepts that correspond to incorrect substantivations: space, time, consciousness, and being:

> Space, time, consciousness, being, are not four receptacles for things, but only characteristics of things which are already real, they are the characteristics of the reality of things, and things, I repeat, are already real in and by themselves. Real things are not in space or time, as Kant thought (following Newton), but rather real things are spatial and temporal, something quite different than being in space and time. Intellection is not an act of consciousness, as Husserl thought. Phenomenology is the great substantivation of consciousness which has been current in modern philosophy since Descartes.

Rejecting this infrastructure, Zubiri sought a new path:

> Facing these four gigantic substantivations of space, time, consciousness, and being, I have attempted an idea for the real prior to them. This is the theme of my book *Sobre la esencia* (Madrid, 1962): philosophy is not philosophy of objectivity, or being, it is not phenomenology or ontology, but rather philosophy of the real *qua* real, it is metaphysics. In turn, intellection is not consciousness, but the mere actualization of the real in the sentient intelligence. This is the theme of the book which has just been published, *Inteligencia Sentiente: Inteligencia y Realidad*, (Madrid, 1980) [*Sentient Intelligence: Intelligence and Reality*, tr. by Thomas B. Fowler, Washington, DC, 1997].

Man and God is divided by Zubiri into three parts. The first serves as an essential introduction to the core of the work. This first part together with the excellent translator introductions by Dr. Thomas B. Fowler (*Nature History God*; *Sentient Intelligence*) and Dr. A. Robert Caponigri (*On Essence*) should provide the attentive reader with the necessary preparation to enjoy the philosophical riches of this book. The following will only give a summary idea of the content of Zubiri's thought. Nothing can substitute for a close reading of what Zubiri has written.

Basic ideas of the work

When dealing with the philosophical problem of God, Zubiri embarks on a rigorous metaphysical examination that leads him to reflect on the many perspectives taken in the past to reach an understanding of the existence of God as an intellective goal. In the end, he considers they do not have sufficient precision to reach God *qua* God. In large measure, this is because they start from an intellectual framework that is either inadequate or just plain wrong. Zubiri's solution in this case, as in all of his thought, is to penetrate one level deeper than other thinkers, in order to reach the most fundamental issues.

For Zubiri the philosophy of "being" is not sufficient to deal with the reality of God. God is not a modified "Being," not even when festooned with "infinity." After all, we obtain the concept of "being" from everything that exists in our cosmos, and God is not just one more being "in" this cosmos, even if we call Him "infinite being." God *qua* God is more than infinite being. As Zubiri puts it, "being" is the second moment of reality. Moreover, previous attempts to base theology on proofs of the existence of God have failed because such proofs, such as the Five Ways of St. Thomas, invariably assume a particular philosophical framework, and thus are only as convincing as that framework itself. Rather, we must base theology and such "proof" of the existence of God as is possible on something much closer to our fundamental experience of reality. For Zubiri, that is the *power of the real*. We have to reach the ground of the power of the real, that which grounds our notion of "being." All human life is fundamentally an experience of the power of the real. To reach the real God *qua* God we have no alternative but to proceed intellectually through our personal experience of the real, for He is the ground of the power of the real. The "and" of the title reminds us that for Zubiri God is already a structural essential part of the reality of all human beings.

Consequently the intellectual justification of God is not accomplished by Zubiri as a demonstration because God is not an object whose existence can be demonstrated. God is not a reality *object*, but a reality *ground*. This is the fundamental error of all earlier attempts to prove the existence of God. Instead, Zubiri explains that each person encounters God by realizing him- or herself as a person. We realize ourselves with things. Each real thing brings its own power, and the power of reality itself. This power is not grounded upon another concrete reality, because that yields an infinite regress. Since reality itself must ground my relatively absolute reality, reality itself has to be an "absolutely absolute" reality. This is the metaphysical essence of God. God is the One who is grounding the power of reality.

Eschewing philosophical frameworks, Zubiri bases his theology on an analysis of human reality, which lead us to its grounding reality, something ultimate, possibilitating, and impelling. Because reality is grounding, it serves as the *real ultimate support* of my life. It will also serve to *make my self-realization possible*, and to *impel me towards my realization*. These three characteristics have an intrinsic unity; they form the ground of reality. On our human side this consists in being "religated" (fr. Latin re-ligare, re-tied)) to my ground in order to be. From the side of reality to be a ground means that it has power over me. The power and strength of the real as a dominance moves me to realize myself as a person. This dominance of the real is a seizing or laying hold of, and in this dimension man is "relatively absolute." He needs both the power of, and the religation to, fundamental reality.

The atheist, the agnostic, and the believer: the will to truth

Zubiri disagrees completely with Nietzsche: the key characteristic of humans is not the *will to power* but the *will to truth*. This has an especially profound meaning in the context of Zubiri's thought, because of his notion of *real truth*: that truth we possess as a result of our direct contact with reality through primordial apprehension. The will to truth extents to our quest for truth through use of reason as well. The will to truth aids us in understanding the three attitudes toward belief in God: agnostic, atheistic, and theist.

The agnostic searches for the ground of his or her own belief, but this searching intelligence defends the proposition that said ground is not really knowable. This leads to frustration in the intellectual order. Instead, for the agnostic what is finite possesses complete satisfaction. His or her god is the finite, and nothing alien to finite reality can be accepted as existing. The attitude of indifference is just the will to the bare desire to live. It is the will to truth as just living, affirming that no proof can lead to the conclusion that God exists. To this intellectual indifference there corresponds a mode of appropriation called unconcernedness. There is no search here; the one who is unconcerned "feels" that underneath his or her lack of concern there is the mute beating of a presence which is ignored. Consequently, Zubiri affirms, such a person is being directed towards God surreptitiously. Because of this he or she has to justify intellectively indifference to reality.

For the atheist life rests upon itself, and that is why such a person has no will to grounding. The atheist considers life and the reality of man as pure facts. An atheistic life means a life lived without any God, "outside" of God. The atheist is not against God, merely outside of Him. When the atheist appropriates being as pure fact he is living a life of self-sufficiency; he does not need grounding. For him self-sufficiency by itself is the absolute.

Finally we have the attitude of religation which consists in the human will uniting "this" reality, which ties all real things, with "the" divine reality through the transcendental reality. With his way of religation Zubiri wishes to unite the cosmic and anthropological ways, and supersede them in their way towards God, since neither reaches God as a personal reality, ground of the cosmos and of humankind.

Transcendence does not mean "outside," but rather something distinct, the ground of things. Certainly there is a distinction between God and things, but what we do not have is separation. God does not consist in being the ground, but his presence in it is fundamental. God is formally in things, but making them be in God as realities distinct from God. God is present in things with a fontanal presence, as fountain of their reality. The manifestation of the divine in things is called "deity." "Deity" is not God, but is the manifestation of God by His presence "in" them. This is the intellective justification of God according to Zubiri.

The access of man to God is in the form of a surrender, and this surrender is formally "faith." Faith is not a problem of authority, but of admission of the personal reality that is being donated to me. Faith formally consists in surrendering myself to the transcendent depth of my person, and not abandoning it. This personal surrender to God is carried out, therefore, in a concrete way, in my person. Indeed, faith is concrete, above all because each one of us has an idea of God by reason of the terminus. For each one of us God is "his" God. And this occurs in a very precise manner in the History of Religions. Because of all of this God is a concrete God: individual, social, historical.

The fontanality of God in man takes on the form of donation. God is an "absolutely absolute" reality, and man in this donation is a "relative absolute," therefore, it is in the moment of "absolute" where God is present as personal donation. The "absolute" is the point of convergence between human beings and God: humans are endowed with many of the divine attributes, including free will. But they are not God, hence they are only relatively absolute.

Other forms of experience of God are, besides the experienced absolute, the presence of God in the form of "grace," the Incarnation, and the actual presence of Christ in the Eucharist. We may take note of the tensive presence of God in the person of Christ. Christ, as reactualization of the person of the Word, is a form of experiencing God. In Christ the experience is also present, although in a subsisting way, between God and humans. Christ is true God and true man. In Christ we can say: while more divine, more human, and while more human, more divine.

The intellection of God is sentient. At the level of grounding this experiential intellection is also determined by the senses. Through the sense of kinesthesia we apprehend this implication or personal tension between God and human beings. Thanks to the intelligent sense of kinesthesia we apprehend the "towards" or "tensiveness" existing between human beings and God. For this reason the unity between human beings and God is a unity of donation and experientiality, this is the type of unity which constitutes the unity of theological tension. The enigma of life is inscribed in the enigma of reality—an enigma that adopts the form of restlessness as expression of the "tensive unity" between human beings and God. We must keep in mind that the problem of religation is resolved in the problem of this experience between human beings and God, where both are experiential aspects of each other. These thoughts should provide the reader with some preparation as he or she encounters the profound meditations of a master philosopher. More details about the genesis and organization of the book can be found in the next section, the Editor's Introduction.

A Note on the translation

This translation is the product of three experts in the thought of Xavier Zubiri, with the final revision given here that of Dr. Thomas Fowler. We have sought to render the original text into a natural and readable English, while maintaining fidelity. But as any student of philosophy is aware, there are hard limits to this task, especially in the case of a philosopher whose ideas are very radical and original, and who consequently must utilize many neologisms and employ words in an almost poetical fashion with respect to their meaning.

Because this book, *El hombre y Dios*, is well-known in English through references to the translation of its title, *Man and God*, we have decided not to change the title. However, to avoid charges that Zubiri was "sexist" or anything of the type (he was not), something that would distract from understanding of the work, we have translated *hombre* as "human being" or "human" throughout the text itself. Concerning other terms, Dr. Diego Gracia, Director of the *Fundación Xavier Zubiri* in Madrid, Spain, gave valuable advice on translation of the Spanish *teologal* by the English "theological." For Zubiri the term "theologic" (*teológico*) deals primarily with knowledge about God himself, and "theological" to the knowledge of God through all the reality of which He is the ultimate transcendent ground. The Spanish word *fundamentar* and its various forms have been translated by the English *ground*, in the appropriate form, both because the idea behind *fundamentar* is that of grounding, and because English expressions such as "to fundament" sound peculiar without meaning anything substantially different than "to ground".

Finally, to facilitate reference to the original Spanish edition, the pagination of that original is indicated by numbers in curly braces, e.g., {25}.

{i}

EDITOR'S INTRODUCTION

This is the first of Zubiri's posthumous books. It has some special characteristics here presented to the reader, to ease reading and interpretation.

First, this is the book that Zubiri was preparing for the press when he died rather suddenly. Therefore it belongs to his last period, although we shall soon indicate the extent to which it represents his thoughts at that time. It is a book which he was very eager to publish. The general scheme of the work and its first version had been finished to his own satisfaction, at least with respect to fundamentals, although as was his custom he planned to continue working on the texts.

Second, it is a book which Zubiri did not complete. Before entering into further details, let the reader be advised that this book contains three different revision levels. The First Part was finished and revised by Zubiri; the Second Part was composed but it surely needed for a new treatment which would have provided it perhaps with a better form and enriched it significantly; the Third Part is in an earlier stage, as it consists of the transcription, corrected by Zubiri, of three oral lectures.

These circumstances posed two alternatives {ii} to the editor: (1) produce a critical edition that would reproduce the text scrupulously as it had been left, inserting as notes any correcting observations; or (2) to try to introduce a minimum of obvious corrections, so that the book would come out in the same form as previous ones of the author, and as the author would have wanted it to appear. The second alternative has been chosen for three principal reasons: first, this option does not preclude that, if Zubiri research so demands, a critical edition may be published at a later time; second, the corrections to be incorporated were minimal; third, it seemed most appropriate to produce a book similar in its form to the author's previous works, as he really desired.

That said, it is useful to explain the history of this book as well as the history of its composition.

The problem of God, the philosophical problem of God, had been a permanent concern of Zubiri since his youth. He used to say that there were three main themes that concerned him from adolescence. Even in those early years, he had begun to think and write about them. They are intelligence, reality and God. Concerning the first two, he had published definitive works before his death: *Sobre la Esencia* (On Essence, 1962), *Inteligencia Sentiente* (Sentient Intelligence), comprising three parts: *Inteligencia y Realidad* (Intelligence and Reality, 1980), *Inteligencia y Logos* (Intelligence and Logos, 1982), and *Inteligencia y Razón* (Intelligence and Reason, 1983). Indeed, in the days before his death, he happily remarked that he also had near completion a book which he had already entitled *El Hombre y Dios* (Man and God). Therefore, this book is his answer to one of his basic vital and philosophical concerns and is, consequently, a book that has a long history. {iii} During 1935 and 1936, in Madrid and Rome, Zubiri wrote the famous essay, often republished and studied, "En torno al problema de Dios" ("In regard to the problem of God") (*Naturaleza, Historia, Dios*, 5a. ed., Madrid, 1963, pp. 361-397)[1]. During his exile in Paris while the Spanish Civil War was raging, he dealt with the problem of God in several seminars, one of which is reflected in his "Note sur la philosophie de la religion" ("Note about the philosophy of religion") (*Bulletin de l'Institut Catholique de Paris*, T. 28, no. 10, 1937, pp. 334-341). Dating from this same period (although it has its roots in a seminar given in Madrid about Helenism and Christianity (1934-1935), is the theologico-philosophical essay: "El ser sobrenatural: Dios y la deificación en la teología paulina" ("Supernatural being: God and Deification in Pauline theology," NHD, 399-478).

During the time of his oral seminars whose two phases extend from 1945 to 1976, the problem of God appears several times. The theme of the 1948-1949 seminar is *El problema de Dios* (*The problem of God*), with thirty three lectures. After the publication of *Sobre la Esencia* (*On Essence*), the seminars concerning the problem of God multiply: *El problema filosófico de la historia de las religiones* (*The philosophical problem of the history of religions*, six lectures), followed by two more lectures about *El problema de Dios en la historia de las religiones* (*The problem of God in the history of religions*), all of them presented during the seminar of 1965. In 1968 he gave a new seminar about *El hombre y el problema de Dios* (*Man and the problem of God*, six lectures), with an incursion into strictly theological problems, to which in 1967 he had already dedicated an extensive seminar *Reflexiones filosóficas sobre algunos problemas de teología* (*Philosophical reflections about some theological problems*, ten conferences). However, it was in the 1971-1972 seminar that he outlined and developed the problem; this was the seminar entitled *El problema teologal del hombre: Dios, religión, cristianismo* (*The theological problem of man:*

God, religion, Christianity, twenty-six lectures), where its three sections appear well defined: man and God, the {iv} history of religions, and that singular religion which Christianity is. Finally, Zubiri again revisited the first of those three subjects in his Rome seminar (Gregorian University, 1973), under the title of *El problema teologal del hombre: el hombre y Dios* (*The theological problem of man: man and God*, twelve lectures).

During the course of these years he had also published two articles on the same subject: "Introducción al problema de Dios" ("Introduction to the problem of God") which appeared in 1963 (NHD, 341-360), and "El problema teologal del hombre" ("The theological problem of man") published in 1975, which presents the main points of the Rome seminar, *Teología y mundo contemporáneo, Homenaje a Karl Rahner*, Madrid 1975, pp. 35-64 (*Theology and the contemporary world, Homage to Karl Rahner*). In addition he had published a few other studies in NHD covering the same theme, some prologues, and an important work concerning the Eucharistic Mystery written for his investiture as *Doctor honoris causa* in theology at the University of Deusto, Spain.

All this history ends, for our purposes, at the Rome seminar. This seminar, set down in writing by his wife, Carmen Castro de Zubiri, its text corrected by Zubiri himself, is the one he used as the basis for this book. He considered that everything pertaining to the philosophical problem of God, as dealt with in his previous seminars or essays, had been collected and superseded by the Rome seminar. In fact, I repeat, he was still working on it, and it was the only text on his desk at the time of its last revision. All this, then, gives us an idea of the history of the text; but we now need to know more about the history of its composition. Let us return then, to the three revision levels mentioned at the beginning of this Introduction.

We have, above all, the First Part entitled "La realidad humana" ("Human Reality"). This section had already reached {v} the final stage of writing, done by its author during the last months of his life. This revision was begun in the spring of 1983 and concluded at the beginning of the summer of the same year. Only the transition between the First and the Second parts dissatisfied him; he wondered if he should move some pages from the end of the First Part to the Second Part. But he never did. For this reason the editor has decided to leave them where they are with only a slight reordering, which takes into consideration the marginal notes written by Zubiri himself. Consequently, this Part is one where everything is by Zubiri, completely satisfied with the existing revision.

The situation is different with respect to the Second Part. When Zubiri returned from Rome, he began the revision of this part of the book, then titled "La marcha intelectiva hacia Dios" ("The intellectual way to God"). He found that the First Part was under better control and duly perfected, while this Second required further elaboration. To it he ardently dedicated himself during the end of 1973 and almost all of 1974; he nearly completed it. He did not do so; upon reaching the section concerning the formation of faith, he felt that he should make a small digression about the formation of the human person. This digression, as was normal in his way of working, was longer than expected, and grew to more than 200 pages—a disproportionate amount compared to the approximately 150 that he had written on the issue of the intellective route of the human being towards God. He decided to exclude these pages about the formation of the human person; and he wished them to be included in another book, which he indicated should be published and would incorporate a set of anthropological studies. Thus, we find ourselves faced with a {vi} text left at a level of revision differing from the First Part, preceding it by ten years. Secondly, it does not take into account terminological and even conceptual changes brought about by the passing of time and his lengthy research on human intelligence, which occupied him at least six years. Thirdly, the text itself is full of notations, a good number of which are due to discussions he had with me towards the end of 1974 and the start of 1975, with some of the conclusions he was planning to incorporate into the text, written on the margins of the pages I was passing on to him.

The question then became what to do with a text left in this incomplete state.

The possibility existed of presenting it just as Zubiri had left it, with all its marginal notations and without any editing. This had the merit of bringing to the reader a sample of Zubiri's agonizing struggle with truth, together with his ceaseless changes of conceptualization and formulation in the search for more accurate expressions of what he understood to be the reality of the case. But it was necessary to consider that some of that text had already been included in the First Part and, moreover, that some of its formulations had been developed more precisely in that same First Part. On the other hand, it would have been possible to begin a thorough restructuring of this text, since Zubiri left behind the scheme for a new arrangement. But this would have required a delicate transplanting operation, and some important formal corrections. After weighing all the pros and cons, the solution chosen was that of reproducing fundamentally the textual order of 1973-1974, changing only expressions which he himself {vii} had rejected in his previous writings, eliminating from this text elements already presented as a first Appendix to the First Part, and introducing those developments of the content which were clearly composed in the margins of his text.

The Third Part presented a different set of problems. As indicated above, of this part we have only the transcription, corrected by Zubiri, of the Rome seminar given during the autumn of 1973. Zubiri agreed fundamentally with what he had said in that seminar, although it is certain that if he had reflected again on the text he would surely have enriched and polished it. On the other hand, it is evident that without the presentation of the Third Part, the book would be unfinished. Therefore, the decision could only be to convert into written language the corrected transcription of the oral language. This was already been done for the final pages of the Second Part since, as noted above, Zubiri did not finish them with respect to the formation of faith.

The change from oral to written language is a task upon which I had already embarked on the text of the seminar *El problema del hombre* (*The problem of Man*), which Zubiri had already approved for the preparation of his *Estudios Antropológicos* (*Anthropological Studies*). All that was necessary was to follow the same criteria with respect to the Rome seminar. However, this presented a special difficulty, since the seminar had been given in a Faculty of Theology and of Catholic Theology at that, and Zubiri had used a great number of theological examples referring to the Christian faith. The greater part of these examples had been removed by him from the First and Second parts of the book, because at the time he wanted to produce a strictly philosophical book. But this removal was not an easy task in the {viii} Third Part, because here the examples belong to the structure of his discourse. Zubiri himself was aware of the problem and apologizes in the text, adducing as the reason the place where he was lecturing and the importance of showing that he was not talking in a vacuum. Consequently, the examples have been retained just as examples and not as strict philosophical reflections whenever those examples are, at least, non-contradictory thinkable possibilities. Such occurs with the case of grace and the hypostatic union of Christ, which in this last Part appear repeatedly and emphatically. We warn the reader about this, to preclude any misunderstanding of the reasons for these examples, and the mistaken impression that Zubiri has introduced specific elements of the Christian faith into philosophical discourse. We have already pointed out that in the overall plan of the work, Zubiri considered that this book should be completed with another one referring to the history of religions, and a third dealing with the specific problems of Christianity.

Finally, the possibility remained of completing this book with other Zubiri texts recorded from previous seminars. That did not seem appropriate because he himself was not using them in his revision of this text which we now offer the reader. This approach does not preclude that at a later date, if circumstances warrant, an edition may be made of some seminars or parts of those seminars that deal with the problem of God. Of course, all those who study Zubiri will be able in due course to have access to all the necessary manuscripts in order to compare some texts with others and thus appreciate the evolution of a thought that was ceaselessly improving upon itself.

{ix} However, an exception has been made with respect to a text previously published, which formally belonged to this seminar. Zubiri had written it with the aim of making it the Introduction of the book. But he later discarded it, and composed another Introduction, which is the one that has been preserved. The text in question is "El problema teologal del hombre" ("The theological problem of man"), dedicated to Karl Rahner, to which we have already alluded. It is included in the present book as a kind of conclusion, because it synthetically gathers together the principal points of the work, and paves the way for extending Zubiri's ideas towards the history of religions and Christianity. Since we offer it as a conclusion, we have removed from it the last lines naming the three Parts of the book.

Thus we offer a book which is wholly Zubiri and only Zubiri. The elimination of some phrases and examples—nothing has been suppressed in the First Part, very little in the Second, somewhat more in the Third—does not alter the text at all, but on the contrary makes it fully Zubiri's at the level of 1984, just as he himself would have wished. In the rare instances where, for the reasons indicated above, words have been substituted, this has been done by taking his literal phrases, used by him to formulate his concepts. The purely compositional substitutions obey only the need to reduce oral to written language, in exactly the same way as Zubiri himself had done on multiple occasions.

Therefore, although this is not a critical edition, it can be said that it is a purely Zubirian edition, made with the same spirit in which he wanted his unpublished books to be put out, and made as closely as possible to his own {x} wording. Thus a new Zubiri book has come into being. Strictly considered, it is a book conceived by him as such, with three fourths of the total developed by him. It is a Zubiri book from cover to cover, subjected only to minimal editorial revision.

The reader, once advised about the different composition levels of the work, has the key to come to his own conclusions. Further studies will be able to identify points that Zubiri himself would have wished to clarify. There is no doubt that he would have improved his own text, had he had the time and energy. Thus, it remains an open work upon which others will be able to build, as was his wish, incorporating new developments that will bring us closer and closer to the true reality of things.

March 24, 1984

Ignacio Ellacuría
"José Simeón Cañas" University
Central-American University
San Salvador, El Salvador, Central America

---

[1] *Nature, History, God* (tr. by Thomas B. Fowler, Washington, DC: University Press of America, 1981), hereafter NHD. Text available online at www.zubiri.org.

MAN AND GOD

AUTHOR'S INTRODUCTION

The title of this book may lead readers to think that in it I am going to deal with God understood in a particular way, for example, the God of Christianity. But this is not the case. I shall deal only with God in the sense of divine reality, without regard to my particular set of beliefs. Only for the sake of clarity and ease of expression shall I refer almost indifferently to "God" and "divine reality", unless indicated otherwise.

"God" is the title of a great problem. This problem can be solved in different ways: positively (theism), negatively (atheism), or by suspending belief (agnosticism). But often overlooked is the fact that in all three cases there is but a single problem. The atheist thinks that since God is not an immediate reality, it is the believer who has the responsibility of justifying his affirmation of God's existence. But the case is the same for the theist: he lives immersed in his faith in God and consequently presumes that it is the atheist who must provide reasons to deny God. To convert God into a problem is appropriate for the atheist; but the believer, in this view, has no problem. Neither atheist nor believer thinks that their atheism and theism, respectively, are solutions to any underlying problem. The problem is someone else's; but just what is it?

Today people are characterized not so much by having a positive idea of God (theist), or a negative one (atheist), or an agnostic one, but by a more radical attitude: that of denying the existence of a true problem of God. For the theist, the one who has the problem of God is the atheist; for the atheist it is the believer. Therefore, the heart of the matter is to discover that God is problematic for all. The believer has to give reasons for his belief and the atheist also has to give reasons for his denial of God, just as the agnostic too must give reasons for his agnosticism. Atheism and agnosticism are no less beliefs than theism. The three need to give the basis of their respective attitudes, because in the final analysis the firmness of one's state of belief is not enough, and its intellectual justification is necessary.

What kind of problem is here? Not the type of problem that one may or may not choose to pose, as if it were a problem of science, one which is fundamentally arbitrary. In that case, God would be just another object, though perhaps the most important that humanity must confront. In other words, the problem would be to determine whether, besides human beings and things, God is real. Rather, the truth is just the opposite: we are dealing with a problem that we *must* pose to ourselves. Indeed, it is already posed to us by the mere fact that we are human beings; it is a dimension of human reality as such. Consequently, this problem must be called "theologic" [*teologal*]. "Theologic" does not mean "theological" [*teológico*]. It means that there is a human dimension formally and constitutively involving the problem of divine reality, of the *Theos*. The theologic is such by involving the dimension that opens onto the divine. The theologic is, consequently, a strictly human structure accessible to immediate analysis. We must attend to this analysis. The clarification of that dimension is the true proof that the problem of God is a problem. The problem of God, *qua* problem, is not one arbitrarily posed by human curiosity; indeed, it is human reality itself in its constitutive problematic quality.

Thus it turns out that the title *Man and God* is not an addition of two "objects", man or human being "and" God; but the analysis of human reality insofar as it constitutively involves "turning" (let us call it that) towards divine reality. The "and" of man *and* God is an empirical *constitutive* turning. And it is the same for the atheist, agnostic and theist, applying equally to all human beings.

Full analysis will be undertaken in three steps that will be the three parts of this study:

> Part I. Human Reality.
> Part II. The Problem of Divine Reality.
> Part III. The Human Being, Experience of God.

These three steps constitute an intrinsic, formal unity. In this unity consists the ultimate structure of the theologic dimension of the human being. The making of the reality of the human is what, in a synthetic way, must be called *theologic experience*.

PART I

HUMAN REALITY

The human being is a type of reality incorporating two essential aspects. It is, moreover, a reality with well-determined characteristics. Thanks to them their possessor is human. But these same characteristics pose an important problem. The human being not only has characteristics different from those of other realities, but in virtue of their very nature, is a reality that essentially must go on creating or inventing itself. In other words, we must examine two questions: What is it to be human? And, how can one be a human being? These are not two independent questions; but neither are they identical. They must be studied successively, and this study will take place in the following two chapters:

Chapter 1. What is it to be human?
Chapter 2. How can one be a human being?

CHAPTER 1

WHAT IS IT TO BE HUMAN?

First we must determine the essential characteristics of the human being. The human being is, above all, a *human reality*. Of what, we ask, does human reality consist?

This simple formulation of this question involves two terms: *reality* and *humanity*. Although the general theme of the book does not strictly demand explanation of what is understood by "reality," I cannot but repeat, in the interest of precision, some concepts explained in detail in my book, *On Essence*. The reader need not dwell too much on them, because if I bring them to mind now it is only to sharpen the philosophical outlining of the main theme. Subsequently I will enter into what more directly concerns the theme of this book: the human characteristics of this reality.

The present chapter is therefore divided into two sections:

§1. Reality.
§2. The human aspect of this new reality.

§1

REALITY

Everything real is constituted by certain *notes*. I shall use this term and not "properties" for reasons that I will explain later. It is a simpler term than "property", and has the double advantage of denoting two moments of the thing. On the one hand a note belongs to a thing; on the other, it advises us what the thing is in accordance with this note. Thus, heat is a note of some particular thing, and at the same time tells us what the thing is in accordance with this note.

I understand by the reality of something the fact that these particular notes may belong to the thing *in its own right*,[1] that is to say, they may not be just signs of a response. Thus, for a dog, heat is something that "heats"; in other words, it imposes on him a type of behavior: to approach, to flee, etc. But for us, as human beings, heat above all else "heats." Its characteristics belong to it in its own right. And that is why, by being apprehended this way, heat has in its own right what I shall call the *formality of reality*. It is not merely a stimulant. "Reality" does not mean existence here, and still less something beyond my apprehension; it is the formality according to which that which is called "heat" is apprehended as something in its own right, or in other words, in accordance with the formality of reality. Existence itself belongs to the *content* of reality and not to the *formality* of the real. All notes, in addition to their content and their existence, have a formality of otherness depending on the one who apprehends. For an animal the formality of what is apprehended is mere stimulation; for human beings what is apprehended is in its own right, is reality.

This *in its own right* has to be taken in a strict way, i.e., as a formality of something strictly apprehended. And that is not particularly obvious. Hence, I never strictly apprehend a table, some walls, etc., in their own right. What I apprehend in its own right is a thing, a constellation of notes (a thing that has such form, such color, such weight, etc.) but I never apprehend a "table". The table is not in its own right a table; it is a table only in so far as it forms part of human life. What is apprehended as a moment or part of my life is what I have called a "meaning-thing" to distinguish it from "reality-thing". It is that which, with respect to a different set of problems, I expressed by saying that a real thing is what acts on other things or on itself, formally, in virtue of the notes that it possesses in its own right. The table acts on other things, not as a table, but as something heavy, colored, etc. A table is only a "meaning-thing". However, a meaning-thing is not independent of a reality-thing. A meaning-thing is but a reality-thing which has the capacity to be a meaning-thing. Water has no capacity to be a table. That capacity is what constitutes the "condition". Condition is the articulation of a meaning-thing and a reality-thing.

1. Real things have a multitude of notes and this multitude forms a unity. But the unity is not simply additive: a thing is not green, plus heavy, plus warm, etc., but an intrinsic unity. It is what we call a *system*. What constitutes a systematic unity?

Every note in a thing is a "note-of". Of what? Of all the rest. Glucose has a reality proper to itself; but insofar as it is in my organism it is "glucose of" this {20} system we call an organism. This moment of the "of" is not a conceptual moment but a real one; I say that it is a physical moment in the sense of real, as differentiated from conceptual. Thus the "of" expresses the unity of the notes. And this unity is just what constitutes the system. In the "of" consists the system as such. The ultimate and primary reality of a thing is to be a system of notes. This "of" imposes on each note a way of being "of" for all the rest of them. It is what we express by saying that each note has a perfectly well-defined position inside the system. Thus, the system has a systematization. This systematization is cyclic and not lineal. If it were lineal, the final note would not be a note "of" for all the rest of them. The system comprises all the notes in a cyclic way, that is, in an inclusive way. And now is the time to repeat that this "of" is a physical thing and not a conceptual moment of the real thing. The "of" belongs to a thing in its own right; it is therefore a moment of its reality.

2. These notes of a real thing are of two types: some stem from the activity of certain things upon others. These I call "adventitious notes." Others do not proceed from such activity, but belong to the thing by virtue of what it already is in its own right. They are "its" notes. For this reason I call them "formal notes". This character of "its" constitutes the proper mode of how a thing is "one." The unity is modalized in each thing. And this mode, in accordance with which each thing is one, is what I call *constitution*. Therefore, all the notes of a system are *constitutional*. So, in virtue of this constitutional character of each real note, the sys-

tem of notes possesses what I have called *constitutional sufficiency*. {21}

3. A real system whose notes have constitutional sufficiency possesses, by virtue of this, a certain autonomous character with respect to constitution: this is what I call *substantivity*. Constitutional sufficiency is the formal reason for substantivity.

Substantivity is not Aristotelian substantiality. For Aristotle, a substance is the subject of properties, especially essential properties. But here, real things are not substantial *subjects*, but substantive *systems*. For Aristotle, what I here call "notes", are accidents, that is, non-substantive realities. But, what Aristotle never realized is that there can be non-substantive substances. And they exist; for example, the numerous substances which comprise my organism. In an organism there is no more than one substantivity, proper to the organism as a system. And all its substances, for example, the glucose, have in themselves and by themselves what has been called their own substantiality. However, this same glucose, ingested into my organism, has preserved its substantiality (I ignore metabolic transformation), but has lost its substantivity, in order to convert itself into a mere "note-of" my organic system. It is there as a non-substantive substance. Precisely because of this, I do not call notes "properties" but "notes". They are not properties inherent to a subject but coherent notes among themselves in the unity of the system.

4. Among these constitutional notes there are some that are grounded in others. But there are some that are not grounded in others, and because of being ungrounded, rest upon themselves. That is why these notes are more than just constitutional; they are *constitutive*. For example, all white cats with blue eyes are deaf. These notes are certainly constitutional, but are not constitutive because they are grounded in the notes of the genes, {22} which then would be constitutive, unless they in turn are grounded in others; that is a biological problem which does not concern us here. The constitutive notes comprise the radical subsystem of substantivity: they are its *essence*. Essence is the structural principle of substantivity. It is not the correlate of a definition. It is the system of notes necessary and sufficient so that a substantive reality may have its remaining constitutional notes, including adventitious notes.

5. The unity of the system, I said, is its "of". That is what is primary in a real thing, what constitutes its "inwardness" so to speak, its "in". But then different notes are its "outward" projection, its projection *ad extra*, its "ex". This projection is just what I call *dimension*: it is the projection of the whole "in" into the "ex".

This projection may have different modes. Each one of them is a dimension. I call them so because in each is measured the total unity of the system. These dimensions are dimensions of the constitutional sufficiency; they are dimensions of the substantivity.

6. Because they are real notes, these notes qualify the system itself, that is to say, the real thing, in a peculiar way. The notes are not simply of this or that content, but each note is a form of reality. The color green is the green form of reality. And taking the entire system as a constituted reality, this unity is what I call *form of reality*. Thus, the notes which a living being has are reduced to physico-chemical elements. However, the living being has its own form of reality because it is different from the one belonging to a star or a stone. Life is a form of reality, not a force or an element. {23} On the other hand, in virtue of this form of reality, the system belongs to reality in its own modality. This is the *mode of implantation in reality*. Thus, personhood is a way of being implanted in reality differently from the mode in which, for example, a stone or a dog is implanted. Let us not confuse, then, form and mode of reality, even though I may use the two indiscriminately when what I wish to say does not require that distinction.

In summary, everything real, be it an elementary note or substantive system, has two moments. There is the moment of having those notes; this is suchness. And there is the moment of having form and mode of reality; this I shall call "transcendental", a term used to denote not a concept, but a physical moment, as I shall soon explain.

7. Each real thing, through its moment of reality, is "more" than what it is by virtue of the mere content of its notes. The moment of reality in fact is numerically identical when I apprehend several things as a unit. This means that the moment of reality is, in each real thing, an open moment. It is "more" than the notes, because it is open to everything else. This is the *openness* of the real. The openness is not of conceptual character. Nor is it the case that the concept of reality can be applied to several real things; rather, reality is a moment physically open in itself. That is the reason why transcendentality is not a mere concept, common to everything real; transcendentality is not *community*. It is actually about a physical moment of *communication*.

8. The last thing I must add is that everything real, both in its suchness and in its reality, is intrinsically respective. This is the *respectivity*[2] of the real. {24} *Respectivity* is not *relationship* because relationship presupposes the things related. Rather, respectivity is a moment of the constitution of each relationship.

Respectivity refers each real thing to another; therefore, it has a referring dimension. But in order to be able to refer the real to other realities, each real thing must begin by being *constitutively* open. Because of this, in order to be what it really is, the real is constituted in this openness, in accordance with which the form and mode of reality are in their own right. They have to be so because the openness of reality means that each real thing is so in a determinate form and mode. Insofar as this occurs, we say that a real thing has a form and a mode of reality grounded in openness: the ground of this "its-own-ness" of the real is precisely the respectivity. Nothing is real if it is not "its own" reality, and nothing is "its own" reality unless it has to be, by virtue of being constitutively open. This openness, and consequently, this respectivity, affects the real in its two moments of suchness and of reality. The result is that every real thing is open "toward" other real things, and each form and mode of reality is open to other modes and form of reality.

9. The unity of reality is not the product of some type of external grouping by a *táxis*, as Aristotle thought. As I see it, this is not the case. We are concerned with what each reality is in itself. If we imagine the creation of a reality, plucking notes out of nowhere, we would have to say that in this production, the respectivity to other realities comes in as a formal element.

To be sure, these realities can be quite diverse. They may be other already constituted realities; and in that case their intrinsic unity and respectivity is that which, without going into more detail, we call the *cosmos*. But this is not the {25} radical respectivity, because in fact there could be, and apparently there seem to be, several diverse *kósmoi*. The radical respectivity in question is the respectivity not to other real things, but to another reality, whatever it may be (even though it might not exist) inasmuch as it is real. Reality as such is respective. Hence I shall no longer call this respectivity "cosmos"; I shall call it *world*. There can only be one world. For me, the world is the respective unity of all realities insofar as they are realities. World, then, is not the same as cosmos.

And so, precisely because respectivity is not relationship, even if there were only one real thing, this thing would be intrinsically and formally respective in and by itself. It would be in and by itself cosmic and worldly.

10. Due to its respectivity any real thing is present in the world. Being thus present is what I call *actuality*.[3] Classical philosophy understands by "actuality" the character of act which something has, understanding by "act" that which is opposed to

potency, that is, the plenitude of being of which the act consists. But I prefer to call this character not "actuality" but *actualness (actuidad)*. When talking of actuality in our day-to-day language, we do not refer to the character of act but to something different. Thus, for example, we say that viruses have a great deal of actuality today, but lacked that type of actuality a century ago, despite the fact they were then realities in act. One and the same reality can have several actualities, either simultaneously or successively, and can acquire new actualities or lose some, without changing the notes of its actualness. In this sense actuality does not equal actualness, but includes a moment of mere presentness. Nonetheless actuality does not {26} consist of this presentness; it consists of *being here-and-now* [*estar*] present.[4] Not presentness, but being present *qua* being here-and-now is what constitutes actuality. This being present here-and-now can be of many different kinds. In the example of the viruses, their way of being present in our century is extrinsic to them. But there are cases in which being present is an intrinsic moment of the real itself, for example, when we say that a person presented himself (showed up) in some place; this is the being present of the real from itself. There are modes of actuality which concern the notes of a thing. But there is an actuality that does not concern the notes; rather, it concerns the moment of reality of the thing itself. Everything real, merely by being real, is intrinsically and formally respective, i.e., it is present, it is actual in the world. It is actual not only from the standpoint of itself, as it is according to the notes—but is actual in itself. It is actual, not only intrinsically but formally. And so, this actuality of the real *qua* real is intrinsically and formally what constitutes *being*. Being and reality are not the same. Being is always of reality and as such presupposes it; this is the *subsequentness*[5] of being. And this subsequentness is precisely actuality. What is primary with respect to things is not to be *entities*, but *realities*. The actuality of the real, inasmuch as it is real in the world, is being; being is being here-and-now present in the world, *qua* being here-and-now. What remains open is the question of the different modes of this intrinsic and formal actuality.

11. Whatever is real because of its respectivity is real as a function of other real things. This is the *functionality* of the real. Thus, the luminosity of a star depends on its temperature. Functionality is not necessarily causality. Causality is only a mode of functionality, but {27} not the only one. Mere succession, for example, is also a type of functionality. A law is a type of functional dependency, but not necessarily causal. Now, the real is not a

function just of what other real things are according to their suchness; rather, everything real, in its own moment of reality, depends upon other realities through its own moment of reality, because this moment of reality is intrinsically and formally respective. This functionality of the real *qua* real is the fullest concept of the respective dependence of substantivities and their notes. Functionality is not production, i.e., cause; but indeed as I said, causal production is just a mode of functionality of the real *qua* real.

12. Finally, *real*, we say, means *in its own right*. But this "in its own right" has in its turn three different formal moments. It has a moment according to which a thing is what it is in its own right, in and by itself, as it is. This is what I call *naked reality*. It is not identical to the "in its own right"; but in the course of this book, for obvious reasons, I have taken "in its own right" and "naked reality" as synonymous. The "in its own right" also has that moment which we express in Spanish when we say that such and such a thing happens or has to happen by the force of the things.[6] Here "force" is not what is meant in Newtonian mechanics; rather it is the *forcefulness* or necessity that a thing be thus *de suyo*. This necessity belongs to the "in its own right", to the real. Furthermore, the "in its own right" has the moment of *powerfulness*. The reality of the real is, as I said above, "more" than its content of suchness. This "more" signifies that reality dominates its content. This dominance is what is proper to powerfulness. Clearly it is not forcefulness. All forcefulness {28} can be powerfulness; but not all dominance is forcefulness. Powerfulness is the dominance of the real.

Naked reality, forcefulness and powerfulness come together in a certain way, as is obvious, in every sentient intellection. But as moments of the "in its own right" they are not identical. That is why they have been the source of different concepts. I do no more than refer to some examples to clarify the ideas I have been expounding. Thus, the "in its own right" as naked reality is what the Greeks conceived in the concept of "nature", *phýsis*. The forcefulness was expressed in the concept of the necessary, *anánke*. Clearly, not everything natural is necessary, nor is everything necessary natural (when it is not a necessity of naked reality). The powerfulness conceived explicitly and formally as real is not simply dominance, but dominance of the real *qua* real. But each one of these three moments is tangential, so to speak, to the other two. There is no force from things, there is no necessity that in some way does not touch on, more or less, naked reality; and there is no power which may not tend to be necessariness or compulsoriness,[7] and reach naked reality in some way. The predominance of one of these moments over the other two may even constitute different types of intellection; but the other two are always present. The predominance of the moment of naked reality constituted the beginning of our knowledge. However, compulsoriness had always been present in Greek thought. So, Aristotle tells us (*Met.* 984b10) that the first pre-Socratics were compelled (*anankatsómenoi*) by the truth. The predominance of compulsoriness is what underlies, for example, Egyptian and Assyro-Babylonian mathematics. They discovered, for example, what we call the Pythagorean theorem. But their {29} necessity is mere compulsoriness; it does not have the character of the necessity proper to the elements of Euclid, founded on naked reality and not on compulsoriness. The problem of power was the occasion for the animist interpretation of power. Powerfulness does not mean *anima* or *animism*; rather, animism is a conceptual development of powerfulness. Inchoatively, so to speak, each moment, I repeat, is tangential to the other two. This intrinsic unity is formally constitutive of all sentient intellection. Perhaps this unity of the three moments is what comes through expressly in the meaning, so much debated, of the *arkhé* of Anaximander.

Our knowing, rooted in naked reality, has forgotten the other two moments of compulsoriness and powerfulness. It is urgent that we recover them.

* * *

Before proceeding, I repeat what I indicated at the beginning of Part I. If a reader is not especially interested in philosophical rigor, he may begin to read the book at the Second Part, and have recourse to the First, if in the course of reading he finds that necessary. If, when reading the First Part, everything is not sufficiently clear, he may refer to my book *On Essence*, where I have explained in detail almost all the concepts just set down.

This understood, we shall continue. Of what does the human part of reality consist? What is the human being as reality?

§2

"HUMAN" REALITY

Like any other reality, the human being is a system of notes in accordance with which he has a particular form and mode of reality. The question about human reality has two aspects: determination of the notes which constitute the human, and the elucidation of its form and mode of reality.

I

The notes of human reality

What is human reality from the point of view of its notes? Of course, I am only going to concern myself with the notes considered globally, so to speak. The human being is a system of notes that we can collect into three groups.

1. First and foremost, the human being has a group of notes in accordance with which we say that it is alive: this is *life*. Each living being is constituted by a certain independence from its surroundings, and by specific control over them; but these two moments express something more radical. Indeed, independence and control express (in their active or passive actions) that a living being acts not only through the notes it possesses, but also with respect to the system they constitute. Certainly any substantivity, even something which is just mineral, may involve the totality of the system in its activity; but a mineral does not act with respect to the totality of the system as such. This moment is the radical and formally exclusive moment of life. One lives for and to be oneself. In other words, the living being is a "self", an *autós*. This does not refer to a moment of "reflection" from the notes towards the self, because reflection as such consists of taking the self as an object. In addition to all the other objects, the living being would then have one more: itself. This is clearly the idea which Aristotle had. But here we do not refer to that; rather, we are seeking the nature of the *autós*. Only because the living being acts as an *autós* can it in some cases carry out reflection. To be

oneself is prior to any reflection, and is the foundation for its possibility.

This is what is formally constitutive of a living being: to be an *autós*, to be oneself. Life is not just the passing of time. Passing of time is the manner of self-possessing. Naturally, one could ask, Is one cell a self? Fully and completely as the human being is, certainly not. Indeed, there are degrees of life, degrees of being a self. In the most elemental living beings there is something like a rudimentary, primordial *autós*, which increases in the biological series until we reach man. These degrees are precisely the different types of living beings. To live is to have self-possession, and the passing of time associated with life is the manner of possessing the self.

2. The human being is a living being which has a special character: it is animated, it is a living animal. Among life's functions is that of *sensing*. This is what is formally essential to the animal: to sense is to have *impressions*. Now then, any impression has two moments: a moment of *affecting* the living being and a moment of formal *pointing* to something else, something *other* that affects the animal. Referring to the first {32} moment we say that the impression has a *content*: color, weight, sound, etc. Referring to the second moment we shall say that this content is something other than the living being; this is the moment of *otherness*. The intrinsic unity of these two moments is the impression: being affected makes us sense the other through an impression. Each sense has its own form of otherness. Sight presents, hearing announces, kinesthesia orients, etc. There are, thus, different forms of otherness in a living animal. But all these forms inhere in a radical form of otherness which I shall call *formality*.

In the case of non-human animals, the formality of the impression is *pure stimulation*. The animal senses the "other" only as stimulus. A stimulus is a sign for the animal to respond: the heat heats and is a sign that the animal should approach or flee, etc. But other than being a sign to respond, the stimulus is felt only as a stimulant. And this "only" is what comprises pure stimulus. The "other" belongs to the response itself as a type of signing or pointing; it is the pointing or signitive moment of the response. More than just a stimulus, it is something apprehended, but apprehended only as stimulant. The "other" exhausts its otherness in this articulation; this is the *formality of pure stimulus*.

3. But the human being has a third note besides life and the capacity to sense: *intelligence*. What is intellective knowing?[8] It is

usually remarked that intellective knowing is to conceive, to judge, to reason, etc. Certainly, the intelligence performs all these acts. But this does not enlighten us about the essence of the act of intellective knowing, what it formally is, what intellection is. I consider that intellection formally consists of apprehending things as real, that is, "as they are in their own right; {33} it consists of apprehending that their respective characteristics belong properly to each thing itself; and that they are characteristics that the thing has in its own right. Everything that the human being intellectively knows is known as something in its own right. This is the formal essence of intellection. I shall clarify this idea further. "Being in their own right" is the mode of things being present to the human being when it confronts them through its intellection. To conceive and to judge (logos), and to explain rationally, are nothing but modalizations of the apprehension of something as in its own right. If one wishes to speak about faculties, I will say that human intelligence is the faculty of the real, the faculty of the "in its own right." It is not the faculty of "being," because being is always something subsequent to reality. If we say of something that it "is real," this is due to the structure of our languages, since there is no "real being" but "reality in being," actual reality in the world.

This faculty of the real has a precise structure. To understand it, we will take another look at sensing.

The human being, just like the animal, senses heat, sound, weight, etc., as impression. But there is an essential difference between the human being and the animal. What is *same* is the *content* of an impression; but what is *different* is in the line of otherness. The human being senses "the other" not merely as something that is a sign to reply; it senses not only that heat *heats*, but senses that heat *is hot*. Its characteristics are characteristics that characterize what heat is "in its own right". The content does not consist only of affecting the human being, but of being something "in itself", be it affecting the human being or not. The animal senses the stimulus only in a stimulating manner. In an animal, otherness is just a *formality of pure stimulus*. But the human being senses this {34} stimulus as a different formality: as a *formality of reality*. Certainly, the great majority of human impressions are, as in any animal, merely stimulative. If one had to apprehend, for example, synaptic transmission of enzymatic reactions as realities, the life of the human animal would be impossible. But there are some special receptors that sense the impressions as otherness of reality. And this is specifically human. Human sensing is something different from animal sensing. The human being senses what is sensed not purely as stimulus but as real. Due to this moment of otherness, due to this moment of formality, in impression the human being senses a mode of otherness different from that sensed by an animal. The human not only senses heat, not only senses that heat heats, but it senses impressively that heat "is hot"; i.e., the human senses reality. Because of this the human being senses reality impressively; it has what I call *impression of reality*. The human being has the capacity to sense reality. This impression of reality is not a second impression added to the impression of heat. Rather, it is just a moment, the moment of formality of a unitary and unique impression: the impression of hot reality. But since we are not going to be concerned with heat, or weight, etc., but only with the moment of reality, I shall call this moment, although somewhat inadequately, the "impression of reality".

The impression of reality is characterized by great complexity, because each sense senses the formality of reality in a different way. The senses are distinguished one from another not only by the *content* of the sensed note, but also by the *mode* of sensing reality. Vision presents the real as *eidos*; hearing presents it as announcement; taste as {35} fruition (let us not forget that "wisdom" is, etymologically, taste[9]), tact as probing, smell as tracking. Kinesthesia presents to me, in dynamic tension, the reality, not "before" me, but as a "towards"; it is not "towards reality" but reality itself as "towards". And the enumeration could be extended to cover orientation, balance, etc. We are not dealing with different impressions of reality synthetically gathered together, but with different moments of the singular impression of reality. Because of this, those moments overlap. In particular, the moment of the "towards" overlaps all the senses; this is the *directional presence* of reality.

Now, this impression of reality poses a most serious problem. Insofar as it is impression, it is an act of sensing: to sense "the other" in impression is what formally constitutes sensing. But insofar as that which is sentiently apprehended is formally reality, apprehending it is, as we have seen, the formal act of the intelligence. And this means that the impression of reality, in virtue of being an impression, is an animal-type sensing; but inasmuch as what is sensed is reality, it is an intellective act. And both aspects are aspects of a single act. The impression of reality is not two acts, but only one. Therefore, this act is an *intellective sensing*, or what comes to the same thing, a *sentient intellection*. It is not the case that intelligence is turned towards that which is sensed; that would be a *sensing intellection*. We are dealing with a structural unity: the intelligence itself senses reality. This is *sentient intellection*. Assuredly, one can sense without intellection, but one cannot intellectively know without sensing. To sense is the primary and radical form of intellection. This is not sensualism. Sensualism pretends to reduce everything known intellectually to {36} the contents of impression. That is absurd. It is rather about a *sensism*: reality is always the "in its own right"; and the primary and radical form of sensing the "in its own right" is intellective sensing. Thus, the act of intellection, in contradistinction to the act of sensing, is not a complete act by itself, independent of the act of sensing. Not *what* is sensed, but *sensing itself* is that which is intrinsic to intellective knowing as such. Not by reason of object, but by formal structure as a faculty, do intelligence and sensing constitute one unique faculty *qua* faculty; a faculty which carries out the sentient apprehension of reality, i.e., the impression of reality. There are not two acts, one of sensing and one of intellective knowing, each complete in its own order, and synthetically converging; rather there is but one complete act of a single faculty, the faculty which I call *sentient intelligence*. This is the unity of the apprehension of reality as formality of things.

Clearly intelligence is essentially irreducible to that which is sensed. But what is essential to this irreducibility? Is it a difference between faculties? That is the question. The Greeks used the word *dýnamis*, which the Latins converted into *potentia seu facultas*. But, to my way of thinking, potency and faculty are not the same. The word *dýnamis* thus becomes ambiguous. Potency is "a" mode (among others) of making something possible. But it does not simply mean that this potency is ready and prepared to carry out its activity. Clearly, intelligence as potency is essentially irreducible to pure sensing. There is no doubt that pure stimulus, however enriched and complex, will never be reality. Formality of pure stimulus and formality of reality are essentially {37} irreducible. However, this does not mean that the intellective potency is capable *by itself* of producing its action. It is only able to do so *insofar as it constitutes an intrinsic and formal unity with the structure of sensing*. Intelligence is the potency to confront things as realities; but it is not a faculty. To be a faculty it must be intrinsically united with sensing. Therefore, as a faculty of intellective knowing of the real as real, it is a faculty intrinsically and structurally composed of two potencies: the potency of sensing and the potency of using one's intelligence. It is not the concurrence of two faculties, one sensible and the other intellective. No. The human being has only one faculty for intellective knowing, viz. sentient intelligence, in which he really senses reality in the form of an impression.

So what is reality and what is intellection?

Above all, reality (as I pointed out in the previous paragraph) is formality of the "in its own right". Consequently, (1) reality is not mere objective independence. The more perfect an animal is in the zoological scale the less it will confuse what is perceived with mere organic affection; it will not confuse food with its hunger. In its moment of otherness there is an objective independence. The more perfect it is zoologically, the more of an objectivist it will be. But it will never be the most rudimentary *realist*. On the other hand, the most modest child of a few weeks surely has no use of reason, but has the use of intelligence; even if the child is mongoloid, oligophrenic, etc., he has a reduced but real use of intelligence, and indubitably is a realist. Within his modest sphere he senses stimulating realities, stimulants which are "in their own right". The independence proper to sentient intelligence is not an *objective* independence, but a *real* independence. {38} (2) Reality is not mere objective independence, but neither is it just existence. Indeed, nothing real is non-existent, but it is not real because it *exists*, but because that *existence belongs to it in its own right*. If what is apprehended had existence but did not have it in its own right, it would not be a reality but a *specter*. The same must be stated about its notes: they are not real unless they constitute a system "of". A work of fiction is not a system of notes without existence; what is feigned[10] has neither existence nor physical essence. A system is real not only because of its notes and because of its existence, but because both notes and existence belong to the content of the thing apprehended. On the other hand, the moment of reality is constituted by the formality of otherness of the "in its own right". Reality is formality of otherness, and formality of the "in its own right". Existence and notes are moments of the content. The moment of formality is something prior to existence and to the notes.

And this moment is a physical formality and not a conceptual one, because it is a character of the openness of the real as real; reality is always physically and formally respective. It is a moment of an intellectively sensed thing. And because of this, the moment is formally non-specific. When I apprehend several things sentiently in one simple act of apprehension, I apprehend several distinct contents, but in one single impression of reality.

Reality is not, then, objective independence or existence. Still less is it something beyond what is sensed. To be sure, there is an infinite number of things beyond what is sensed; but we are brought to admit them, we are brought to them, by a sentient intellection of what is apprehended in its own right. Their notes, therefore, are real, but {39} this does not mean that they are real "outside" of perception. In the apprehension of a real thing in the world, to make of the real something beyond apprehension can be a serious type of error, as it has been millions of times in history. Reality is not existence beyond apprehension. The last two are two zones of the real; but reality is neither the one nor the other. Reality is nothing but pure "in its own right", not a zone within things. This is why the division of things into perceived and beyond perception is founded on the sentient impression of reality and not the other way around.

To this concept of reality there is coupled the parallel concept of what intellection is. Intellection is not to represent, but simply to have that which is apprehended present as in its own right. It is the mere being present of the *in its own right*, that is to say, it is mere *actualization of the real as real in the sentient intelligence*.

4. Clearly, the human being has three types of notes: it lives, senses and intellectively knows sentiently. And the intrinsic and formal unity of these notes constitutes the system of human substantivity. What is this substantivity from the point of view of its notes? This is essential.

The human substantive system has an unusual character: it is a system which encompasses what we might call two partial sub-systems, where "sub-system" means "quasi-system". We are not dealing with two unified systems, but of only one "single" system, the system of human substantivity, the only one which has strict constitutional sufficiency—something the "sub-systems" lack. These subsystems are what we call "body" and what should be called "psyche".

A) First and foremost is the sub-system called "body". It is a sub-system of physico-chemical notes that have three moments. {40} Each note has a very precise *functional position*. Each note discharges its own proper function—if I may be permitted this expression—with respect to the functions of the rest. And in virtue of this, the physico-chemical notes constitute, as a positional sub-system, what we call an *organism*. But "body" is not synonymous with "organism". The "of" not only determines the functional unity of the notes, but makes them a *well-ordered integrated set* of physico-chemical notes. In virtue of this moment, the body is not an organism but a principle of *solidarity*. Each note has repercussions with respect to all others; i.e., they are interdependent notes. But beneath this solidarity there is a still more radical moment: the organized and solidary notes express the *actuality* of the human being in the universe. This is the somatic function: it is the body as a principle of actuality in reality, the principle of being present in the cosmos and in the world. The intrinsic unity of these three moments: organism, solidarity, and actuality is what constitutes *body*. What is radical about the body is to be a principle of actuality. Body is, consequently, something more concrete than *matter*, because we are dealing with corporeal matter but not matter as opposed to spirit.

B) And yet the human being has other notes, and another partial sub-system, which I call *psyche*. But it too is only a partial sub-system. I do not call it "spirit" for the same reason I have not called the body "matter". And neither do I call it *soul*, because this term is burdened with a special, rather debatable meaning, namely, a substantial entity which makes its home "inside" of the body.

Because of this situation I prefer to call this aspect simply "psyche". Psyche is not a substance, not even in the popular understanding of the term (this is clearly evident); but {41} neither is it so in the metaphysical sense. The psyche is only a partial sub-system of notes within the total system of human substantivity. Certainly, this sub-system possesses some characteristics irreducible to the corporeal sub-system; and in many aspects (though not all) has a certain dominance over it. But, despite this, psyche is only a partial sub-system. The human being then, does not "have" a psyche and an organism, but rather "is" psycho-organic, because neither organism nor psyche by itself has any substantivity. Only the "system", the organism has it. Therefore, I believe, one cannot talk of a psyche without an organism. Let me clarify that I use the word "organism" here through linguistic license in order to facilitate reading of the text; strictly speaking, I should call it "body". The human being is not psyche "and" organism; rather, its psyche is formally and constitutively "psyche-of" this particular organism, and this particular organism is formally and constitutively "organism-of" this particular psyche. Therefore the psyche is of itself organic, and the organism is of itself psychic. The moment of the "of" is identical in the psyche and in the organism, and possesses a physical character. This numerical and physical identity of the "of" is what formally constitutes the systematic unity of human substantivity, which is a structural unity. Human substantivity is thus "one" by itself and of itself. What is the formal characteristic of this substantivity in which the human being consists by reason of his notes? That is what we have to examine next.

C) The moments of this substantive system co-determine themselves, but not as potency and act (as the Aristotelians would say) of a hylemorphic substantial unity; rather they do so as real moments in act and *ex æquo*, whose {42} co-determination consists of each being "of" all the rest. As I see it, the "of" is a unity of a higher metaphysical type than the unity of potency and act. And this "of" comprises not only the radical unity of human substantivity, but also its selfness throughout life, a selfness essentially distinct from any numerical persistence of all its notes—something which does not happen anyway. The human being is, then, a psycho-organic substantivity.

Due to this, the characteristics which I expounded with respect to the body strictly speaking belong to the entire psycho-organic system. The functional position encompasses the complete psycho-organic system. Sensing has a very precise position in the human system, for example with respect to intelligence, which is an intellective sensing. We shall soon see the enormous importance of this unity. It is a very different position from that which it has in a mere animal. And the same is true with respect to solidarity and interdependence. The psychic moment transfuses itself into each corporeal note, and conversely corporeity, as principle of the being here-and-now present, as principle of actuality, is a moment which concerns psychism itself. This can be seen in such phenomena as "expression", "physiognomy", etc.

In order to understand this psycho-organic systematic unity, it will be sufficient to take a brief look at human activity. Each note of human substantivity acts systematically, that is, no note acts alone and by itself, so to speak; and even though it acts through its own properties, it also acts always as a "note of"; that is, its actuation is only a moment of the "activity-of" the rest of them. Just as all the notes, by being "notes-of", constitute {43} but one substantive system, so this, what we call the activity of each note, is "activity-of". All its activities constitute one activity only: the activity of substantivity. This is what I express by saying that human activity is "at one and the same time" organic and psychic, otherwise one might infer that there are two activities, one psychic and another organic. I affirm the exact opposite, to wit, that there is but a single and self-same activity of the entire system in each and every one of its notes. The activity always has the character of system. To be sure, such activity is complex on account of this fact, and in it some characteristics are more dominant than others. But always, even in the act which appears to be most physico-chemical, they are in reality an activity of the entire system with all its physico-chemical and psychic notes.

And, I repeat, that the main point is not that the *subject* of all of these activities is one thing, be they organic or psychic; but that the *activity* is formally one. It is a systematic activity in itself by virtue of being proper to the entire system, which in every one of its acts is in activity at all its points, but with variable dominance of some points over others. The situation is analogous to the different levels and undulations of an entire liquid surface. Everything organic is psychic and everything psychic is organic, because everything psychic takes place organically and everything organic takes place psychically. On account of this, there is never actuation of a psychic note on an organic note or *vice versa*, for there is nothing other than the actuation of one psycho-organic state on another. The substantive reality of the human being {44} is thus a system in which each note is always a "note-of" all the rest, in which each note is but one moment of the primary coherential unity in which the substantivity consists.

Given this, what is, formally, the substantive reality of the human being?

We have already seen that the human being lives and senses, and that it is, like any other animal, an animated living being. The animal does not exhaust itself in sensing stimuli through the formality of pure stimulus. This formality, in fact, is not limited to being the formality of an impressive apprehension, but constitutes an environment, the environment of pure stimulus in which the diverse animal acts unfold. It is the proper role of formality to constitute an environment, the environment of everything animal. Each act of sensing, in fact, has three moments: a receptor moment, a tonic moment, and a motor impulse moment. I leave aside more complex aspects of animal life, because all such are found to be not merely based upon the act of sensing, but made up of to its three moments: receptor, tonic and motor impulse. Reception is a reception of stimuli; all reception is formally *stimulation* and only stimulation. What is stimulated? Each stimulus modifies the vital tone of the state of the animal; the tone becomes affected through stimulus. The stimulation is at this point mere affection (I use this term here, not in the general sense of something that affects the whole animal organism, but in the narrow sense of affections, of sensing states like anger, like hunger, etc.). This modification sets in motion the *tendency* or impulse to affection, which is nothing but the reply directed to a new situation, {45} constituted in stimulus fashion. The intrinsic unity of these three moments (stimulation, affection, tendency) is what formally constitutes sensing.

In the human being, the formality of what is apprehended

through impression is not pure stimulus, but reality; that which is apprehended through impression, as we saw, is apprehended as something "in its own right," as an intellective sensing. And this formality is not limited to being formality of an act, but constitutes the *environment* in which all human acts unfold. Above all, the character of the vital tone modification has changed. The animal vital tone, we said, is "affection", it is the way of sensing oneself through stimulation generated by the stimulus. On the other hand, the human being senses tonic modification in a different way: I feel not only contented or disgusted, but I sense myself one way or the other in reality. The tonic affection changes now into a way of sensing myself as a reality in reality; this is *feeling* or *sentiment*. Affection is not the same as *feeling*. There is only feeling when the affection formally involves the moment of reality. Furthermore, the apprehension of this real thing, when it modifies my feelings, impels me to respond. In what way? No longer is it the case of tending through stimulation to a new animal situation, but of tending to place oneself really in reality, though in a different way. To do this, one has to choose. Tendency and appetite give way to *volition*. Volition has essentially one moment of reality: a desire to be now in reality in a certain way. With this, the animal process unity, that is, the merely stimulation-based unity of stimulation, tonic affection and tendency, turns into a "human" process unity; that is, into a process of realization (apprehension of the real, feelings of the real, volition of the real). {46}

Now, these two unities, the unity of sensing and the properly human unity, are not two unities juxtaposed—as if the second were added to what is animal, or as if human unity were merely based upon animal unity. Rather, animal unity is an intrinsic and formally "constitutive" moment of the human unity; intelligence is in itself formally and constitutively *sentient*; feeling is in itself formally and constitutively *affecting*; the will is in itself formally and constitutively *tending*. Now, the biological unity of sensing is the essence of animality. Whence it follows that the human as such is in itself formally and constitutively animal. Consequently, the human being is an animal which confronts reality though its animal nature: *it is an animal of realities*. Here is the essence of the human reality, the essence of human substantivity. The constitutive environment of the human being is "reality": we are located in reality. From the point of view of notes, that is, from the point of view of suchness, the human being is an animal of realities.

But the human being, thanks to being precisely an animal of realities, has its own proper form and its own proper mode of reality. In virtue of this we have to consider the human being, not only from the point of view of its notes, but as a form and mode of reality.

II

Form and mode of human reality

Human reality does not exhaust itself just in its system of notes, that is, in being an animal of realities. Indeed, {47} precisely in virtue of these notes it has a more radical structure. In the first place, these notes make the animal of realities a form of reality and a way of being implanted in it. And in second place, this human reality, according to its form and mode of reality, is actual in the world, in the respective unity of reality as such; i.e., the human being has its own proper being. We must then examine the problem of human reality in accordance with these two moments: first, the form and mode of human reality in itself; and second, the actuality, i.e., the being of human reality in the world. Finally, we must confront the unity of being and human reality.

1) *Form and mode of reality.* The system of notes of the animal of realities is not identical to the form and mode of reality that the human animal has in virtue of them. So, let us see what is the form of reality of human substantivity, and what is its mode of reality.

A) The set of physico-chemical properties of a molecular edifice is one thing, and the fact that this edifice may have, because of its molecular structure, the form of reality we call life, i.e., possession of oneself, is quite another. Now, the human being has those talitative corporal and psychic notes which constitute its substantivity as animal of realities. Precisely because the human perceives things as realities, it behaves in a certain way with respect to them and himself; and it does so, not only on account of the properties that *it* really possesses, but also, and above all, on account of *their* character of reality. A stone falls due to the law of gravitation, due to the gravitational properties that it really has. But among those properties there is none {48} that denotes "to be reality"; that is, we presuppose it to be real, and gravitation acts as one of the properties comprising the real stone. In none of the equations is there a parameter or a variable "reality". But in the case of human beings it is not that way. A man who falls does so in conformity with the law of gravitation, exactly like the stone.

But there is a difference, *viz.*, it is necessary that we be told the form of reality of the man's fall: Has he committed suicide? Has he fallen by chance? Has he been murdered? In his fall the man behaves and acts with accordance with his character of reality, and not just in accordance with the physico-chemical and psycho-organic qualities which he possesses. Here, reality is not just a presupposition, but something in view of which the actions are carried out. And the case is that, indeed, human reality is for me not just a simple system of notes that constitute me "in my own right," but above all, it is the reality which is *proper* to me *qua* reality, that is to say, it is my reality, my own reality. And in virtue of that I am a reality that, as form of reality, not only is "in its own right" (in this I coincide with all other realities), but in addition I am "mine". I have a reality which is mine, something that does not happen to a stone. The human being has, as a form of reality, this that I have called "its-ownness",[11] being "its-own", or "self-possessing." This does not occur in the case of other realities. All other realities have the properties they have in their own right; but their reality is not formally and explicitly "their own". On the other hand, the human being is *formally* its own self, is *self-possessing*. Self-possessing is neither an act nor a note or system of notes, but the form of human reality *qua* reality; whether carrying out its own {49} actions or not, human reality is, as reality, something formally antecedant to such carrying out.

Therefore to my way of thinking, self-possessing constitutes, the formal explanation of *personhood*. Let us not confuse *personhood* with *personality*. I use the word "personhood", and not "personality" as used in classical terminology for reasons that I will discuss later. Morphologically the situation is not so unusual. Just as in the case of being *per se* it has been usual to speak of *perseity*, or in that of being *a se* of *aseity*, so also to be a person as form of reality, I use *personeity* or the more familiar English term, *personhood*.

Personhood is formally constituted, to my way of thinking, by "self-possessing". To be a person, clearly, is not simply to be a free, intelligent reality. Neither does it consist in being a subject of its acts. The person can be such a subject, but is so because he already is a person, and not the other way around. It is also commonly said that the formal explanation of the person is subsistence. But I do not think so: a person is certainly subsistent, but is so because he is his own or self-possessing. Self-possessing is the root and formal character of personhood as such. It is inexorably the character of a subsistent reality insofar as this reality is *its own*. And if its structure as reality is subjectual, then the person is a subject and will be able to have characteristics of will and freedom. This is the case of the human being.

If we call this characteristic that human reality has *qua* self-possessing "personhood", then the concrete changes that this personhood undergoes are what we call *personality*. *Personhood* is the form of reality; *personality* is the figure in accordance with which the form of reality molds itself in its acts {50} insofar as it does mold itself in them. I add this last precision because personality is not constituted by a sense of psychic characteristics (foolish, smart, slow-witted, irascible, introverted, etc.). All these characteristics belong indubitably to personality, but they are personality not as psychic and organic characteristics, but as determining and modifying the form of reality, the personhood. Personality as such is a question not of psychology or of empirical anthropology, but of metaphysics. That is the reason for the profound nature of personality. One is a person, in the sense of personhood, by the mere fact of being a human reality, that is, by having intelligence. To be sure, the human embryo acquires intelligence and thus personhood at a moment almost impossible to define; but once that moment arrives, the embryo has personhood. The entire genetic process prior to this moment is, for that reason, only a process of hominization. When the moment has arrived and it has this form of reality, the embryo certainly does not yet perform personal acts; and one might think that the personhood still lacks personality. However such is not the case because personhood does not configure itself only by performing acts, but also by passively receiving the structure that the genetic processes pour into that personhood, processes exercised in the human living being in its process of hominization. When the embryo acquires intelligence, it develops personality passively.

In summary, from the time the human embryo has the form of reality which is personhood, that personhood is always molding itself throughout its entire human life. The personhood remains always the same; the personality is formed {51} through all of the psycho-organic processes from the time the human embryo possesses intelligence until the moment of death. That is why a human being is always the same but never the same: by reason of its personhood it is always itself, by reason of its personality it is never the same.

These two moments of personhood and personality are not like two layers or strata of a human being; rather, personality is the moment of concretion of personhood. Therefore, we are not dealing with two strata but two moments of a single reality, viz., the concrete human person. From the point of view of his form of reality, the human being is a person, a *personal animal*.

B) Now, in order to be even more precise about the character of this form of reality, let us recall what was said with respect to the human being as a living being. Such a being is characterized by an independence and control with respect to its surroundings; this is its mode of implantation in the cosmos. Such independence from the surroundings varies according to the degree of life involved and the form of the living being. In the case of the human being there is something more than mere independence when facing the environment of its life. A living being is implanted in reality in a very precise way: namely, as forming part of it. But the human being is its own, its "own" reality with respect to all reality, whether real or possible, including, if we chose to admit it, divine reality. And in this sense, its reality, as its own, has a unique mode of independence: to be set apart from real things *qua* real. Its mode of implantation in reality is not to form part of it, but to be itself as a reality confronting all of reality. It is not to form part of reality but something else: an absolute mode of reality, an *ab-solute* mode of reality. In the case of the human being, its mode of reality, its {52} mode of implantation in reality, is to be a *relative absolute*. It is *absolute* because the human being itself confronts all possible reality; but it is *relative* because this mode of absolute implantation is an acquired character. In its life, and in the most modest of its actions, the human being not only realizes a series of personal acts, according to the properties it has and the situations in which it finds himself; but in each one of them the human person defines, in a precise and concrete way, the mode according to which its reality is relatively absolute. Therein lies the seriousness of each act. A real thing apprehended as such forces us, upon confronting it, to fix a concrete way of being absolutely. This seriousness, as a trait of my person, is what I have usually called the *restlessness of life*. It is not just the uncertainty proper to life as an adventure; rather, this restlessness consists of not knowing well the concrete mode of being absolute. The human being not only realizes a series of acts through the properties it personally has; but defines in each of its acts that precise and concrete mode by which, in each instant of its life, it is a relative absolute. Restlessness is the problematism of the absolute.

In virtue of this, the human being, as a mode and form of reality, is in the world, i.e., is actually in the world as a person and as absolute reality. And the human being, by virtue of this being here-and-now in the world, has there its own being. The question thus becomes, In what does this being of relatively absolute reality consist?

2) *The being of human reality.* A) First, let us say what being is as differentiated from *reality*. For this, let us remember what I presented at the beginning of this study: everything real is intrinsically and formally respective to everything {53} else. This "else" refers to the other things which constitute the cosmos. But "else" is not only the other things but also—and most importantly—the moment of reality itself, be there other real things or not. Reality itself, as such, is respective because by itself it is open; the impression of reality of multiple things, when they are apprehended as a unity, is physically and numerically the same. Therefore, the moment of reality is in each real thing a moment open by itself as reality. And precisely because of this, the reality of each real thing is intrinsically and formally respective. Nothing is real except in respect to all other reality as reality. In this respectivity is founded the unity of all the real. The unity of respectivity with respect to the notes of a thing is the unity we call "cosmos". Now, the unity of respectivity of everything real, not with respect to its notes, but with respect to its moment of reality, is what constitutes the *world*. World is not the total set of real things, but the unity of respectivity of reality *qua* reality. It is the unity of every form and mode of reality *qua* reality. Because of this, I pointed out, even though there were but one real thing, this single one thing would be formally worldly just because reality is an open moment.

Now, real things as real are in the world. In virtue of this, *they are actually present* in it. To be actually present, as far as it is an "is", is what constitutes *actuality* as differentiated from *actuity*. The actuality of the real in the world is what, to my way of thinking, constitutes *being*. Being is not the same as reality. If we consider the properties or notes which constitute, for example, silver, {54} these properties are not the being of silver but the argentuous reality itself, in its form and mode of reality. And the form and mode of reality are not being. If silver were able to speak it would say, "With all these real properties, I am really this way in the world". This is being: the "this way in the world".

Classical philosophy said that reality is the supreme mode of being, the real being, the *esse reale*. But this is not the case. It is not the case that there is reality because there is being; rather, there is being because there is reality. Therefore, there is no *esse reale* but *realitas in essendo*, "reality in being". Because of this, one cannot talk about the substantive being of something, because being by itself has no substantivity. There is no *substantive being*, but only *being of the substantive*. To understand this, let us enunciate some of the characteristics of being.

a) Being is actuality, mere actuality: it does not consist in the presence or the being here-and-now present of the real in the world; but in "being" present *qua* being actually. To be is worldly *actuality*. Reality, on the other hand, before being actual and precisely in order to be so, begins by being a system of notes in activity, in the character of act.

b) Actuality is founded on reality; being is founded on reality. Being is, consequently, subsequent to reality, and has the character of *subsequentness*. All actuality is subsequent to activity. To be sure, this is not a chronological subsequentness—that would be absurd. It is a structural subsequentness: being actually founded on reality.

c) This actuality is actually founded on reality, but reality is not extraneous to it, nor to being, because the difference between being and reality does not mean that being is something like a mere adjunct, more or less accidental to reality. That would be completely {55} absurd. Reality is the "in its own right." Now, a real thing is worldly in its own right. Being therefore belongs to it really, belongs to it in its own right: it really "is". It is just "reality-being". The gerund "being" was originally a present participle. When making of reality a mode of being, philosophy since Parmenides thought that the real is formally "entity": this was the *entification of reality*. And I think that this is unacceptable. Nothing is primarily entity. Not even God himself is primarily the Supreme Being: He is Supreme Reality. What is primary is reality. There is being only because there is reality. Real things certainly "are", but they are because they are "real". Reality is not *esse* but *in essendo*, "reality-being". "Reality-being" expresses the complete character of what constitutes a real thing whose being is founded in the moment of reality. "Reality-being" is not the same as "entity". Something is an entity when it becomes subsumed in being; therefore, each entity is "a being". But when we speak of "reality being", reality does not become subsumed in being, but rather the being is founded on reality because the real is present in the world by the mere fact, and only by the mere fact, of having reality. This being present is just the gerundial participle "being.". It is not a cursive present, which to my way of thinking, is a present of actuality and not of actuity. Therefore, "reality being" is radically different from entity. We shall see almost immediately the capital importance of this observation.

Thus far we have conceptualized the form and mode of human reality in and by itself: the animal of realities and the personal animal. Now we must conceptualize the actuality of this form and {56} mode of reality in the world, that is, What is the being of human reality, What is the being of the human?

B) *The being of the human.* The being of human reality is the worldly actualization of a personal substantivity, that is, of its person as mode of reality, relatively absolute. Here "person" denotes not just personhood but personality. Person is the concrete unity of personhood through one's personality; it is the person configured modally. This person is, as a mode of reality, a reality that is *relatively absolute*. And so, the worldly actuality of this relatively absolute reality we call "I". The "I" is not human reality. The "I" is the worldly actuality of that relatively absolute reality, that is, the "I" is the being of the person, the being of the relatively absolute reality. The "I" does not consist of being a subject of its own acts, but rather is a mode of being, a mode of worldly actuality of the relatively absolute. It is not the case that I am relatively absolute, but on the contrary, that the relatively absolute "is" I. The subject of its acts is not I; though perhaps improperly utilizing these predicative phrases, I shall say rather that "I" is not a subject but a predicate: this reality am I. This is what we express when we say "I myself". This is the being of the person. Because of this, the "I" is the being of the relatively absolute, and can be called "relatively absolute being".

The human has this absolute mode of being even in the most modest forms of confrontation with the real, because with each thing it deals, a person is self-possessing; in this consists life. Consequently, each thing imposes a mode of self-possession, a mode of configuring one's own relatively absolute reality. By virtue of this, that configured mode {57} is a worldly way of being relatively absolute. Because I am open to the apprehension of the real as real, I have to do something that, before becoming a person, would have been impossible for me. Until now, as an animal, I was hungry and would eat an apple. Now, on the other hand, I sense both hunger and the apple as realities. And eating the apple I "myself" eat an apple. This moment of the "myself" is an actualization of my reality with respect to all reality as such; it is a mode of worldly actualization of my personal reality, the first manner of formal openness, openness in "intermediate" form, openness to the absolute of being. But a moment arrives in which this obscure "myself" acquires a more precise and strong character, and my substantive reality does not act in an intermediate but in an active form. The being thus determined is now not only a "myself" but something more radical: it is a "my". It is *my* hunger, *my* apple, *my* act of eating, etc. Now the person actualizes absolute being in a worldly way, in a more express and radical form: *I* am "my" with respect to everything else. But matters do not end here. A moment arrives when the "my" acquires a new and even more precise character: *I* am not just "my" but something else, I am *I*. Here, my personal being actualizes itself with maximum explicitness inasmuch as my reality is relatively absolute. This is the fullness of determining in a worldly fashion my relatively absolute being.

And thus, "myself, my, *I*"[12] are three distinct ways of worldly actualization of my substantive reality, but they are not unrelated. In the first place, each is grounded upon the previous one. *I* could not "be my" reality if that were not grounded on the *I* am "myself". *I* am my own, *qua* being, with respect to everything that "*I* myself am", so to speak. Similarly, no one could be an *I* without being a {58} "my" and grounded on being this. That is why the expression "I myself" has been created. In the second place, not only is each of these ways grounded on the previous one, but this previous way is preserved in the next as an intrinsic and formal moment of its own character. The "*I*" is always the "*I* of *my*", of a "my which *is itself*". A potiori, I will call the being of my substantive reality *I*.

The *I* is not only the being of my personal substantivity; in addition this *I* has, at each instant, a particular form. This form is just what until now we have been calling "personality". Personality is not only a form of reality but at one and the same time, the form of absolute being. *I* am *I* and the mode of how *I* am *I* is what personality is. For this reason I mentioned above that personality is not a matter of the study of the *psyche*, but is a metaphysical question. To understand this let us take as an example the case of repentance. It is usually said about a person who has committed a crime and repents of it that he "has erased the crime". No, he has not erased the crime; how could it be possible to erase it? The crime had a reality and not even Divine Omnipotence—except for some nominalists—can make things such that what happened never was. The crime continues "being" as a moment of my reality. In what does repentance consist? In others not imputing it to me? That would be an act of forgiveness, it is not repentance. Repentance consists of incorporating the past *reality* into a different figure of *being*. *I am* still the criminal who has committed a crime, but now I am so, penitently; I am a thing which I was not when I committed the crime. Repentance aims not exactly towards the *mode of reality*, but towards the *mode of being* of the criminal act. {59} From this it follows that the *I* is neither a logical nor a metaphysical subject, but purely and simply the worldly actualization of the personal *selfness*. That is why it must be said (against all of idealism) that not only is reality not a position of the *I*, but on the contrary the *I* is posited by reality. It is my own substantive reality which posits (if one wishes to talk about positing) the worldly actuality of my person, the one that posits the *I*.

The *I* is not what is primary; what is primary is the reality. And precisely because of that the *I* flows back over my own reality and constitutes that unity of being and reality which we call "*I* myself". This is precisely the "reality-being".

We must now confront the structure of this unity of the "human reality-being".

3) *Unity of human being and reality*. We have examined human reality and then the worldly actuality of this reality, its being culminating in *I*. *I* is the being of human reality. But to this being, to this *I*, naturally, human reality itself is not a stranger. Human reality "being" is the human being *being I*. To enter more directly into the theme of this book, henceforth I shall refer not to the reality and being of the human separately, but rather to the human reality-being. And to avoid complications I shall call *I* not only the being of human reality, but this reality formally being, that is to say, to human reality "I-ized", if I may be permitted the use of this barbarous expression for just one instant. Unless explicitly mentioned *I*, and whatever I may say about the *I*, will refer to this unity of reality and being, to the human reality-being.

This is not a mere *conceptual* problem but a problem posed by the *physical* structure of human reality because the human being is relatively {60} absolute reality: absolute not only with respect to things, but above all, with respect to other personal realities if they exist. Indeed these other absolutes do exist, not only in fact but necessarily in virtue of an essential character of human substantivity as such: its nature as a species. What is a species? How are persons co-determined in the species?

A) A species is not the real correlate of a definition. For classical philosophy, species is a moment of unity of multiple realities. The starting point would be the existence of many "animals of realities." There would be a species because there are many human beings. But species is not that. If it were so, what we call "species" would only be a natural class. And a species is much more than a class. As it happens, this concept of species is merely conceptual. But "in reality" is an intrinsic and formal moment that belongs to each human animal, a moment in accordance with which it multiplies itself. The species does not unify but pluralizes. The species only exists "speciating". Because of this there is not merely a multiplicity of animals, but a constituting multiplication. This is just what we call "genesis". Human reality is constitutively genetic. And this genetic moment comprises what is specific about reality, and consequently the very principle of the co-determination of persons, of the constitution of the *I* of each person.

This specific moment does not pluralize itself in all the notes of human reality in their detail, but only according to a schema of structural replication. This schema is a constitutive moment of each animal (I leave aside non-animal living beings, which do not concern us here). Genetic multiplication in accordance with a schema is what formally constitutes a *phylum*. A species then is {61} the phyletic unity of the individuals. To be of each particular species is to belong to such-and-such particular *phylum*. Realities which are not phyletic do not constitute species.

The schema, we see, is not a moment added to my reality; rather, my own reality involves some characteristics which constitute the schema of a possible replication: this is the genetic code. Whence follow three important consequences.

a) Since each replicate is an animal of realities, it follows that the replicate is *eo ipso* a personal animal; that is to say, my schema is a schema of a personal animal, of "another" human person.

b) Since the schema is not something marginal to substantivity but is a constitutive moment of it and thus of its own life, it follows that my substantivity is constitutively and vitally poured out from itself to other persons. The "others" are not something added to me but something towards which I am constitutively poured from myself; I am *in my own right* schematically the other persons.

c) As a consequence of this, my own reality, in a schematic but real mode, is affected by its own schema and also by other persons. Thanks to the schematic structure of my substantivity the "others" flow back over me. This flowing back takes place in two respects. In the first place, by reason of the replicated organism: the schema affects me as a schema of another psycho-organic organism, the psycho-organic organism of the generated being. But in second place, the schema affects me by its presence with respect to me. The schema is not only a schema of psycho-organic constitution but at one and the same time a schema of corporeal actuality. The "other" is schematically not only another animal of realities, {62} another person, but something corporeally present to me. The schema is at one and the same time a schema of organic function and schema of somatic function. Whence it follows that each person has two sides. On one side is a reality which is "his own", determined as absolute with respect to every reality as such. But on the other side, my person is a reality whose absolute character is in some way co-determined by flowing back, by other persons, by other absolutes. My psycho-organic reality, when determining my absolute reality-being, when determining my *I*, determines it not only with respect to "the" reality but also with respect to other relatively absolutes. How?

B) *Co-determination of persons*. The constitutive notes of my particular genetic scheme belong to my own substantive system. The flowing back of this schema into my substantive "reality-being" is therefore the projection of the unity of my entire system onto the notes of the schema. This projection is what I have called "dimension" in this problem. Since the schema *qua* schema is quite complex, this dimension is also complex, and has different dimensional aspects. To simplify I will also call these dimensional aspects "dimensions". Strictly speaking they are only *interpersonal dimensions*. These dimensions are determined, then, by the schematic flowing back of the "others" over my reality. These dimensions are three.

a) *First dimension*. As animal of realities the human being, I repeat, does not multiply genetically except in a schematic mode. This clearly means that in each member of the human *phylum*[13] there are traits and characteristics which do not belong to the other members {63} of it, or to the rest of the members of the species. In other words, the members of the human *phylum* in one form or another are different. But an observation has to be made about this difference, namely, that the rest are not simply "different". They are something else: the rest are "diverse". They are different but within the same *phylum*, that is, within the same species. The diverse members are different but of the same "version": they are diverse. Diversity is different within the same version. A dog and a man are different but not diverse. Diversity is not a merely numerical and qualitative distinction, but a distinction within the same species. And since human beings are animals of realities it turns out that one who is diverse from me is not only one who may have other characteristics, but one who is still an animal of realities. This moment of reality is essential; without it there would be no human diversity in an express and formal way. The human being is in its own right a diverse animal in the sense that belonging to the same species constitutes, by this moment of reality, another "reality" within the same species of reality.

This dimension I call the *individual dimension*. But that merely dimensional notion of the individual must not be confused with the general metaphysical notion of individuality. "Individual" can have several meanings. In the first place, individual is a characteristic proper to every reality as such. All reality is by itself something individual: to my way of thinking no {64} principle exists by which the real is individualized.[14] This individuality may have the characteristic of mere numerical singularity, or perhaps the character of a qualified individuality, a qualification according to which each reality is individual but in its own mode. In the second place, there is an individuality proper only to personal realities *qua* realities; this is the individuality of "its ownness" or "self-possession." The person has his own mode of individuality which consists of being a reality formally his own and only his own. In these two senses individuality is a characteristic of reality as such, and hence, is a characteristic which concerns realities independently of the fact that there may be or may not be other realities. But there is a third sense, that according to which individuality is a characteristic concerning existent realities that are precisely and formally "others", by virtue of an individual's specific respectivity to these others. It is "this individual" not only as individual reality, but as diverse from other individuals. Since this individuality is the flowing back of other realities over each one of those of the same species, I call it the *interpersonal individual dimension*. We must make this more precise.

Every human being is its own and its being is to be *I*. But this *I* is determined as a proper mode with respect to the *I*'s of other persons. And this mode has a very precise character: it is that dimension according to which the "*I*" is an "I" with respect to a "you", to a "him or them", etc. The *I* as worldly actuality of my substantive reality has this dimension with respect to other persons, which we call "each-being-thus":[15] the *I* has the dimensional character of being "I"; this is the "each-quality" of the "*I*". The its-ownness or self-possession of the *I* is beyond any "each-quality". While the *I* is the {65} worldly actuality of my personal reality, the I is the actuality of the human person with respect to other persons. This is the *I* as co-determined with respect to a you and to a him. In this fashion "I" am absolute but diversely. This is the individual dimension of the human person.

b) *Second dimension*. The re-flowing of the phyletic schema over each of the members of the *phylum* does not end here. The schema which I possess in myself—a moment not added to my reality but a constitutive moment of it—is a schema in virtue of which my reality extends from itself towards others of the *phylum* who are alive. This is not a moment of interpersonal diversity, but a moment of the turning according to which my reality has extended from itself towards the various living beings of the *phylum*.

This is a structural turning towards *living in society*. Indeed it is a structure which is rooted and emerges from the psycho-organic structures that I possess as a substantivity.

Above all, I repeat, this living in society is the result of a turning towards another reality of the same *phylum*: there is no turning from a man towards a horse, for example. At best, the human may freely incorporate into its own life other non-human animals, but no more than this. Living in society constituted genetically is a living in society with other animals of reality: that is, the moment of reality formally belongs to living in society. I do not share living in society with others because they are bipeds, or have a certain face, etc.; I share living in society because they are biped "realities", or "realities" with such a face, etc. There is living in society with other things insofar as they are realities. That is from the case with tame or domesticated animals: these animals do not {66} share living in society with humans insofar as *humans* are a reality, but rather humans incorporate them into their ownlife inasmuch as *the animals are real*. And so, the living in society of a human with other humans *qua* realities is what formally constitutes human *society* in the widest sense of the term, and also in its most radical meaning. The moment of reality is the essential character of all human social living. Animals certainly share living in society among themselves and form groups which are more or less coherent, ranging up to what has been improperly termed "animal societies". However, these are not societies but mere groupings founded in the signing character of certain animal stimuli. But this stimulo-signing character way of turning towards others is not social living in society, and is not society because it lacks the formality of reality. Social living in society is the result of psycho-organic structure, which is open to reality both in its suchness and in its formality of reality. This genetic turning toward living in society by some humans insofar as they are "real", towards others, also as "real", is the transition from animal grouping to human society. Because of this, not only the "natural" notes belong to societies, but also the notes which are "appropriated" as options when facing the real as real.

Since any animal of realities is a personal animal, it follows that this turning towards other humans *qua* real is a turning of my person toward the persons of all others. This turning may assume two forms. One is the turning towards the person of the other, but *qua* other. This is living in society of an "impersonal" character. The impersonal, actually, is a personal character: the animal is not and cannot be impersonal; it simply is a-personal. Human persons are living in society impersonally when each functions {67} only as "another". And this is what strictly constitutes society. But a person can turn towards another, not just as another, but as a person. This living in society is not society: it is a different form of living in society, which I have termed "personal communion".

Each animal of realities *turned* towards the reality of the other realizes this turning as *community*. And in this community, each human being who forms part of it is affected by the rest: this is the moment of the *héxis*, of the habitude of personal otherness. These three moments (turning, community, habitude) are grounded one upon the other. Their radical unity is the total reality of the social, of human sociality.

The human being has this character in his own right, that is to say, the sociality is a moment of human reality as such. The human being is, then, a *social animal*. This therefore is a character which belongs to the human being due to its psycho-organic reality. Indeed, this structure of my psycho-organic *reality* determines a dimension of my *substantive reality*. The *I*, the *you*, etc., not only diversify themselves, but they co-determine themselves. *I*, insofar as it encompasses the determination of a *you*, is now no longer an individual *you*, but just the opposite, it is a common being. My being, my *I*, is not only individual but congenerically communal: this is the *communality* of the human being, of the *I*.

What is this "common being"? Here "common" does not mean "communicated" or "participated", because communication or participation is grounded in something prior: in a character of human reality as "being"; here it means its communality. It is the "being" itself which by its own disposition is intrinsically and formally common, prior to any participation. The possibility {68} of communication is the communality of the human being, of the *I*. The *I* is common as an *I*. My substantive reality is, as we said earlier, absolutely relative. We have seen that *I* am diversely absolute, I am an *I*. Now we must add that *I* am communally absolute. The human being is communally absolute precisely in the measure in which schematically and phyletically it is living in society with other humans *qua* realities.

But this is not all.

c) *Third dimension*. The *phylum*, the species, is genetically forward-looking or *prospective*. A species could not be a species without being prospective. And it could also not be a species if this prospectiveness were not determined by a genetic factor. The prospectiveness is others, not insofar as I am diverse from them, nor insofar as I am living in society with them, but insofar as I am going to determine the continuation of the species. This continuity has two aspects. One merely bio-genetic: a father engenders children, etc. And this bio-genetic moment is not the simple affirmation that each human being may in fact have descendants, but a moment according to which the formally prospective is the *phylum* itself. However, this prospectiveness has yet another and different aspect, namely, that what is genetically determined is a person; that is to say, it has a *formal* moment of reality. Therefore, the otherness of real prospectiveness, *qua* real, is its unity with the bio-genetic moment, and constitutes a third human dimension: History.

This is a radically and constitutively genetic dimension. If the human being did not have a biological genesis, one could not talk about history. However, this *genetic transmission*, {69} absolutely necessary in order to have history, is utterly insufficient by itself. There is only history in the human being. The so-called "Natural History" is something merely extrinsic. The "historic" is not heredity. Neither is it evolution, because evolution proceeds *by mutation*, while history proceeds by *invention*, by an option of the being in reality. The human being is an open essence and because of this, its forms of being in reality necessarily have to be elaborated. Therefore, history is not—as has been claimed so often—a prolongation of evolution; rather, both heredity and evolution are just moments of history, aspects of the bio-genetic moment. On the other hand, history is *parádosis*, tradition, delivery. Of what? Of the forms of being here-and-now in reality. History does not exist except where the process of genetic transmission concerns the forms of being in reality as reality. Genetic transmission is but the vector moment of *tradition transmission*. From this it follows that the human being, this animal of realities who is in its own right a diverse animal, and also in its own right a social animal, is, finally, also in its own right an "historical animal".

What formally is this tradition? What is the formal character of the human being *qua* historical reality?

aa) Tradition is a "handing over" or a "delivery". And it has a character essentially *constituting* and constitutive of the human substantive reality. But tradition, in order to be constitutive, must be founded upon the form of reality received from the progenitors: it is a *continuing*. Without this, in each individual and in each society, history would begin at zero; that is, there would be no history. Finally, tradition delivers the {70} forms of reality to those who have been engendered: tradition is *progressive*. These three characters: constitutive, continuing and progressive are genetically linked. And in this sense a person himself is constituted by them: he is biographical. But with respect to our present problem, the biographic falls within the concept of history.

Therefore, what formally is history? History is not a succession of vicissitudes, nor is it narrative and still less testimonial or documental narrative. Furthermore, it is not "meaning". Tradition does not necessarily, and certainly not primarily, transmit the meaning of life. What it transmits, what it delivers, are the forms of being of the progenitors as possibilities of being in reality to and for the benefit of those who receive the history. The forms of being in reality, *qua* transmitted, are just possibilities. Because of this, any so-called "historical fact" is not a "fact" rigorously speaking. A "fact" always refers to the mere exercise of some acts; while possibilities are not an exercise but something which is appropriated or rejected or substituted in order to be able to be exercised. That which is now made possible as such is not an act. It is what formally constitutes the "event". An event is the realization of appropriated possibilities, not the mere execution of an act. The historical is a form of being in reality, a form received as a principle of possibilities. But history does not exist for itself; it is the history of human reality. How does the formally historical affect each person? History transmits, as I said, a principle of possibilities, and only of possibilities. What kind of possibilities are we dealing with?

First of all, it is not something usually referred to {71} as the possible in itself. In this sense, the possible is the non-contradictory. And this means "possible conceptually." But here I do not refer to the conceptually possible but to the really, physically possible. Physically, the possible is that which is "made possible" by something. And depending on how this "making possible" is constituted, we shall have different forms of possibility, which unfortunately have not been expressly and formally distinguished in philosophy. First, the possible is what is made possible by a potency, by a *dýnamis*. This is the idea which comes from Aristotle: the possible is that which is potential. But, as I have already pointed out, "possible" sometimes means not the potential, but what is made possible by a faculty. Not every potency is capable of producing its act. Therefore *potency* and *faculty* are not always the same. When they differ mere potency is not enough. For example, sentient intelligence is a faculty. Human intellection is possible; however, it is not made possible by mere intellective potency, but by sentient intelligence. Only this latter is a faculty. The same occurs with feeling (affecting feeling) and with the will (tending will).

Sometimes something is made possible not only by potencies and faculties, but by a set of possibilities that together make something possible. The Cro-Magnon man is, in potencies and faculties, as complete as the man of today. However, in contrast to us, he was unable to fly through the air because he lacked possibilities. This is what I have said is proper to history.

But formally there is a fourth sense of the possible. In order to carry out acts it is not enough to have potencies and faculties, nor is it always enough to have {72} possibilities of carrying out the acts. It is still necessary for certain objects and acts to be capable of being reached. For this it is necessary to have what we call "talents". And what talents make possible in human reality is what we call "capacity". Here are the four senses of the term and concept of "possible": by potency, by faculty, by possibility and by capacity.

Capacities may be acquired and lost, and they are sometimes transmitted through tradition. The history of each person is ultimately capacitation. History is a positive or negative process of capacitation. Transmission through tradition is a moment of the person as capacitated.

bb) In light of the foregoing, of what does human reality consist while "being" in an historical dimension?

History, by being prospective, by being transmission through tradition, has the character of a process. One might think therefore that the historical is formally the temporal (I am not going to enter into a study of time as such). In a certain way it is, but only in a certain way, because the temporal does not qualify the historical process without any other factors. There can be and in fact there have been histories temporally independent among themselves. Therefore, time as such is formally plural; there have been different times, that is, times independent of each other. Each historical process has its own time as a process. And in this "its" are two very precise characteristics.

First and foremost, time has a "form". There is a form of time, different according to different histories. Only when the historical has been unified does it constitute a "universal" History with a more ample form of its own. Consequently the form of time has been changed prospectively. Therefore, there is {73} a process of forming time. Each phase of the formation, as a phase, is what I will call a "zone of time". All substantive realities, by virtue of being actually, belong to a particular temporal zone. And this zone has a character and a very precise name: age. Age is not just a question of chronometry, but a question of belonging to a temporal zone. For this reason all humans who exist in the same age are not merely synchronic, but something more: they are contemporary.

Because of this, the temporal zone is not just a zone. To contemporaryness belongs another aspect: the temporal zone itself, as I have indicated, *qua* moment of the total temporal process. This is the "height" of the times, in the sense of "pinnacle" or "depths". The same action performed today and in the fifth century before Christ might not be identical because they have been performed at different heights of time. Prospectivity, then, gives two characters to time: form and height. The human realities of one integral historical process are not only contemporary among themselves, but are contemporary with respect to height.

Therefore it is now clear that what we may call its "temporalness" also belongs to the form of reality of the person and encompasses both form and height: this is the historic human reality of the *I*. The *I* is formally temporal.

The unity of reality and being, that is, the "being" a personal reality, the *I*, is at one and the same time a diverse animal, a communal animal and a temporal animal. By virtue of his phyletic specificity, the animal of realities is "being" in accordance with his individuality, in accordance with his communality and in accordance with his temporalness. These three moments constitute a unity, not conceptual but physical: they constitutively and physically envelop the moment of reality. {74}

With this we have finished the first chapter of the study of human reality, namely, what it is to be human. Now we must proceed to the second chapter: how can one be a human being.

---

1 ["In its own right" is the generally used English translation of Zubiri's technical term, *de suyo*, used by Zubiri to describe notes which pertain to a thing in an essential way.—trans.]

2 [Zubiri's Spanish term *respectividad* is translated here as *respectivity*; it also means *referentiality*. The reader should bear this in mind.—trans.]

3 [The word *actual* in Spanish means *present-day*. So *actualidad* means *present-day relevance*.—trans.]

4 [Spanish has two forms of the verb *to be*, which it is necessary to distinguish since Zubiri utilizes the distinction in his philosophy. One is *ser*, which has the implication of permanentness; the other is *estar*, which has the implication of *being here-and-now*. Whenever *estar* is used in any technical way, it will be translated as *being here-and-now*.—trans.]

5 [The Spanish word *ulterior* generally means *later* or *subsequent*, rather than *beyond* or *hidden*, which is the meaning of the English *ulterior*. For this reason *ulterioridad* is translated as *subsequentness*.—trans.]

6 [An idiomatic Spanish expression roughly equivalent to the English "out of necessity"—trans.]

7 [Spanish *forzosidad* is, in English, *necessariness or compulsoriness*. They will be used as appropriate.—trans.]

8 [*Intellective knowing* is the English phrase used to translate the Spanish *inteligir*, which refers to knowing by the mind.—trans.]

9 [i.e., in Latin and the Romance languages. Cf. *sapere* and *sapientia* — trans.]

10 [In Zubiri's terminology, works of fiction involve creation of content and postulation of reality. The whole process is referred to as "feigning" reality.—trans.

11 [Spanish *suidad* is here translated as "his own-ness", meaning basically "self-possession".—trans.]

12 [In Spanish these are *me, mí, Yo*—trans.]

13 [Zubiri is here using the word *phylum* in a generic sense, referring to common plan, rather than in the more specific biological taxonomic sense.—trans.]

14 [Zubiri is here referring to classical philosophy, according to which matter individuates things which share the identical form.—trans.]

15 [Translation of Spanish *ser-cada-cual.*—trans.]

CHAPTER 2

HOW CAN ONE BE A HUMAN BEING?

A human being is a personal reality, a reality formally "his own", a reality whose formal character is "mine-ness". It is a relatively absolute reality with respect to everything else and everyone else. And it is such, I repeat, formally. Therefore this mine-ness, this relatively absolute, is life. Actually, life is possession of oneself as reality, it is auto-possession. However, this auto-possession is an ongoing realization. To live is to be going on, taking possession of one's own reality as such. In summary, a person makes himself by "living". Life is personal realization. This realization is carried out by executing actions. The actions are not life but, on the contrary, life is molded through actions; and only because of this are such actions vital. They are vital because they are the possession of oneself. A person makes himself while executing actions; reciprocally, the actions are executed because life molds itself on them. Taken by themselves, the actions are not life but the argument of life. Therefore, two questions arise:

§1. What is a human being according to these actions?
§2. How does a human being make himself a person in his actions?

{76}

§1

WHAT IS A HUMAN BEING ACCORDING TO THESE ACTIONS?

As we have seen, each human being is a co-determined person individually, socially, and historically with respect to everything and everyone else. He always carries out his actions in accordance with these three interpersonal dimensions; that is to say, human actions are always configured in accordance with this triple dimension. So we ask ourselves, What is a human being with reference to his actions? Or put in another way, what is a human being as executor of his own actions with respect to reality itself and to other persons?

Above all, a human being who carries out his own actions is the *agent* of his actions. Such actions are primarily actuations of my potencies and faculties. It is necessary to emphasize that any action is proper to the entire substantive system comprising each human being. There are no actions of just sensing, intellectively knowing, willing, etc. Any action, I repeat, is carried out by the entire system with all its notes. What happens is that in this acting system, one or more of its notes may predominate in various ways over the others. The entire substantive system, when acting, exhibits this kind of predominating. To say that some note does not take part in a particular action does not mean that it does not form part of the action, but rather that it contributes something like a "futile" activity. Therefore, it does intervene in the action, because to be something futile *is* a real intervention. If we compare the entire system to the surface of a large pond, we may say that each action is like {77} an undulation of its entire surface. This undulation has its crests and valleys, both changing in the course of the action. Each action is first and foremost an actuation of the whole system of crests and valleys, i.e., of the totality of the notes of the system. It is always actuation of the notes as potencies and faculties that vary in predominance. Thus a human being is above all agent of his acts, or equivalently, is the agent of its own life: it possesses itself through actuation of its potencies and faculties.

Nevertheless, a human being does not carry out his actions only as their agent. The life of a human being is not just the life that it carries out, but at the same time is intrinsically the life which fortune delivers to him, so to speak. In accordance with the times, its social framework, and its peculiar mode of individuality, each human being lives within a context already partially traced out. This is the canvas of a life that has been given to each human before carrying out its actions as an agent and precisely to be able to do so. Life does not begin in a vacuum but in a determined vital context. We can also include in this context, at least partially, such phenomena as vocation, etc. Vocation is not perforce something merely natural, like the potencies and faculties, but is primarily a vital context. A human being certainly carries out actions as their agent but also at the same time as the *actor* of them. A human being, while agent of his life, is also actor of his own life. The person is in a certain sense the great character of his own life.

In sum, with its potencies and faculties, and within its given context, each human being carries out its actions. But with respect to certain limits, a human being is not just an agent {78} and actor of its own life. The fact is that within these limits a human being can execute very diverse actions. To do this it must *opt*. And to opt is more than to choose a particular action; to opt is to adopt a certain form of reality among others in that action. Each thing imposes on us the compulsion of a particular form of reality. Adopting that from from among the diverse forms of reality is just what opting is. Therefore, in this respect, a human being is not simply the agent and actor of its own actions. It is the *author* of them. As I said above, each action confers a form of reality. And when this form of reality is opting, I am the author of my own life, of my actions, author of my self-possession. But let it be understood, this is within very narrow limits, though in a very real area.

Carrying out actions as an agent, actor and author of them is how a human being makes its own personal life real. In this realization it realizes itself as a person, that is, it proceeds to acquire reality as relatively absolute. Now the essential question arises: why in its actions is the personal absolute reality only relatively so? And how does a human being make itself a person in its actions? This is what we must investigate next.

§2

HOW DOES A HUMAN BEING MAKE ITSELF A RELATIVE PERSON IN ITS ACTIONS?

As the one who carries out its own actions, a human being acquires its character of relatively absolute. What is this "acquiring"? It is a moment belonging intrinsically and formally to the person himself, because the absolute in the personal human reality consists in being absolute *when confronting* everything and everybody else. Without this "confronting" one cannot be a human person. Now, in order to be real "when confronting" it is intrinsically and formally necessary that there be something that one is "confronting". This necessity is imposed upon the human being by its own reality. In the measure in which it is imposed on each human, its reality, though absolute, is so only relatively. The relativity of my absolute reality formally consists in being so "when confronting", because this "confronting" is something respective, and is thus intrinsically and formally constitutive of my personal reality *qua* person. To acquire the character of relatively absolute is then to carry out actions "when confronting". When confronting what? When confronting all things, because all actions are carried out with them. I employ the word "thing" in the sense that it has when not contrasted with living beings, for example. In other words, "thing" is not taken to mean that which is understood by "thing-ism". In the present context "thing" has the broad and common meaning of "something", regardless of its kind. The things with which a human being carries out its actions as an agent, [80] actor and author are a-personal things, other persons, and even the very notes of his own personal substantivity.

Granting this, to be with things has an essential ambiguity that must be eliminated. Each human being builds its life with things. This "with" is not a moment added to human reality, a kind of extrinsic relation, but a moment belonging intrinsically and formally to the person precisely as absolute. A human does not begin by being absolute and *later* trying to configure itself among things; rather, a human is not effectively really absolute unless living with things in its actions. To live is to actually be interacting with things in one's actions. And here an ambiguity arises: there are two prepositions in the foregoing phrase, "with" and "in". This is not merely a syntactical construction, but the case of two essentially different moments in any human action. We may ask, where are we human beings, really and effectively, when we execute a personal action? Apparently the question is already resolved: I am in this country, in this house, with some friends, etc. But, is this formally true with respect to our problem? The truth is that we are among these things, that is, we are "with" them. But that is not all, nor even the primary matter. Certainly, we are never without things; that would be impossible. But what is essential is that where we are *with* things is *in* reality. Every human action, precisely because the terminus of its actions formally has a moment of reality, *is* precisely in this or that form of reality (which in extreme cases has been adopted). I repeat: we are *with* things but where we are with them is *in* reality. The mission of things is to make us to actually be in {81} reality. It is not the same to be *with* and to be *in*. That with which we are is what makes us actually be in reality. Consequently, to live is to possess oneself as a reality while being with things in reality. And this being is what configures our very form of reality. We cannot be in reality unless it is with real things, and in virtue of that real things have, with respect to our problem, the mission we might say of serving as the vehicle for reality itself. In each action, then, the human person has his place in reality. The human being grounds itself in reality as reality. Only in accordance with this moment of reality can each human be a person. The "when confronting" is but an aspect of the grounding aspect of reality. And now four issues arise:

I. What is this grounding of the human person in reality?
II. What is the structure of this grounding character?
III. How does this grounding character come about?
IV. What is problematical about the grounding character?

I

The person as grounded in reality

A human being is a person because it possesses a sentient intelligence, the formal act of which is the impression of reality. Since intellection is the mere actualization in the sentient intelligence of what the apprehended thing is in its own right, i.e., of what the apprehended thing really is, undeniably reality is that upon which each human being supports itself {82} in order to be what it really is, viz. a person, not only *de facto* but in an essential, constitutive manner. This should not seem strange because, as we have just seen, that *in* we actually are is reality, not just these or those real things. Therefore, the character of reality in one's actions is to support being a person. And this support has a very precise character: it consists in being the person's ground. In what sense?

1) In the first place, reality understood not as a real thing but as the formality of the "in its own right," is something ultimate in my actions. It is ultimate not only with respect to things themselves, but to the actions of my person. It is the ultimate support of all of them. Many things may fail for a man, perhaps even all of those with which he happens to find himself; but he thinks that as long as he is real and there is reality, not all is lost. This is an appeal to a kind of ultimate, supreme jurisdiction which the human being has. Reality supports a human as something ultimate: this is the ultimateness of the real. The very sad fact of suicide is proof of this ultimate character of the real. The one who commits suicide by removing himself from reality seeks to evade this ultimate support for being a person.

2) In the second place, reality has another moment, different than ultimateness. Indeed a human being, from the point of view of being the author of its acts, interposes a plan to adopt a specific form of reality between what it does and itself. In the most modest of his decisions each human opts for one possibility among others, e.g., the possibility of going for a walk, of talking, etc. All these are possibilities, but possibilities of what? I have already stated it: possibilities of a real and effective form of my reality, of my manner of being considered as absolute. And then, {83} the moment of reality has a special character: it is just what constitutes the possibilities. All the possibilities are possibilities inasmuch as they are possibilities of realizing myself in one form or another. Whence it follows that the moment of reality must have a characteristic of "making possible:" that which makes it possible for my reality to be human. All possibility is grounded in reality as "making possible."

3) Though ultimate and making possible, reality still has a subsequent character, that of being an *impellent* support. This is because when a human proceeds to act, not only can it carry out an action, it has no other recourse than to do so. The human being must do so inexorably. It has to realize itself and do so through an imposition of reality. But this does not comprise what might immediately come to mind, namely, an attachment to life. It

is not attachment to life, but something much more radical albeit more modest. It is the support of my own reality *qua* my own. If one wishes to talk about attachment, then it will have to be said that the attachment is to my character, relatively absolute. That is why, for example, the case of the suicide I mentioned above is possible. Reality is *impelling*. It impels us, *velis nolis*, to sketch a system of possibilities among which we must opt and which constitute the ultimate instantiation of our own reality. The realization of my person as relatively absolute is absolutely imposed on me by reality itself. Each human not only lives *in* reality and *from* reality, but lives also *by* reality. Reality is not only ultimate and possibilitating; it is also impelling.

The intrinsic and formal unity of these three characters of ultimateness (in), possibilitating (from) and impelling {84} (by), is what I call the "grounding character of the real". The real has this grounding character, where "grounding" means not only that it may be more important than others, but that it is foundational. In other words, reality grounds my personal being in accordance with the three characters that reality possesses: as ultimateness, as possibilitating and as impelling. These characters constitute the grounding character of the real.

As a person, i.e., as a relatively absolute reality, I am grounded in reality as such and the grounding moment has the character of ultimateness, of possibilitating and of impelling. In this grounding, reality is a great paradox. On the one hand, reality is what is most other than I, since it is what *makes* me to be. On the other hand, it is that which is most mine, because what makes me is just *my* reality-being, my "I being real". This strange unity is what constitutes the paradox of grounding. Then one may ask, in what does this grounding consist in itself? In what does the grounding character of the real strictly consist?

II

Structure of the grounding character of the real

The person, then, is gounded on the real. Clearly we are dealing with the grounding character of the real formally *qua* real, in other words, with the fundamentality of reality. And so, we ask ourselves, with respect to reality, in what does its fundamental character consist?

Let us say at the outset what this grounding is not. It is not a cause. This requires some {85} explanation. What is a cause? Modern Philosophy began its attack on metaphysics with a critique of the idea of cause. Everyone knows Hume's analysis: we apprehend that the pull of the rope precedes the sound of the bell, though we never apprehend that the pull produces the sound. The underlying idea was that causality is the production of reality. For Aristotle himself *aitía* is a production of varied nature, but always a production of reality. Of course, one may ask: can there be a unique, indisputable case of the production of reality? (I leave aside human actions in order to avoid the problem of freedom: is liberty a productive cause?). Here Hume's critique has a perfect application. Among the rope, the bell and the sound there is no perception of real production in our apprehension. Here, I repeat, is where Hume's critique is correct.

But Hume ignores another aspect of the question. In the first place, to my way of thinking, causality is not primarily and formally a *production of reality*, but something much more elemental though still undeniable: the *functionality*, the case of one reality *as a function* of another. That this functionality may have the character of a production is much more problematic; and whatever the solution to that problem, production is not the primary notion of causality. Causality is mere functionality. So in Hume's example, the *functionality* between the rope, the bell and the sound is undeniable.

Secondly, Hume has only thought about the *content* of what is apprehended (rope, bell and sound); he has overlooked the *formality of reality*, the impression of reality. And in the impression of reality real things, *qua* real, are *functionally* {86} united. They are not so just by virtue of what real things are with respect to their suchness, but are united in their very moment of reality. The functionality among things concerns not only their content but their character of reality. Therefore, to my way of thinking, causality is the functionality of the real *qua* real. And this is a fact of experience. How could I deny that even though I may not apprehend what happens between the pull of the rope and the sound of the bell, there is nevertheless in fact a functionality? The sounds of the bell do not appear unless there are pulls of the rope. Mere succession is, consequently, one form of functionality among many. The functionality of the real *qua* real is, I repeat, the strict notion of causality.

In the problem that here concerns us, namely, in what functionality consists with respect to my personal reality, we do not deal with the functionality of the real *qua* real. We are not dealing, then, with grounding in the sense of causality. To be sure, there is a functionality of mine with respect to the real *qua* real: I am born, and endowed with certain characteristics, etc. This is evident, but it is not what intervenes in the actions that I carry out for my personal reality. In my actions I do not find myself merely as a function of reality. I find myself with something quite different.

I find myself actually being in reality in such a way that it is this reality which, in a certain way, determines me to "confront" it. This determination is physical; it is not something merely intentional. Physical determination, without being a cause, is just what we call *domination*. To dominate is not to stand out, it is to exercise dominion. Dominion is actually a {87} real and physical character of the thing or person that dominates. Therefore, the reality which makes us be personal realities is dominating, that which exercises (let us say it this way) dominion over my "relative absolute". Indeed, reality is not a kind of sea in which real things may be submerged. That would be absurd. There is no reality outside real things. But in these real things their moment of reality is "more" than their moment of suchness. This real green is not only green (suchness) but it is real. And that is why to be real is more than merely to be green. The very fact that this suchness carries with it a form of reality (greenness reality) indubitably expresses that being real is more than being merely green. And precisely because of this, that moment of reality, even though "more" than greenness, is still in the greenness itself. Reality is "more" than real things, but is "more" in themselves. And to dominate is just this: to be "more" but in the thing itself; the reality as reality is dominating in this thing, in each real thing. It is not the case that being dominant consists in being more important than being green, but that the moment of reality physically determines, without being a cause, that the green is a form of reality.

Consequently, this dominion is what we may call *power*. To dominate is "more", it is to have power. Here "power" does not mean to be a cause. Power is what in German, for example, is called *Macht*. It is power in the sense, for example, of having power in a corporation, or having political power, etc. It is a valid concept which should have a place in philosophy. The moment of reality dominates over suchness, it has power. Because of this it is "more" than suchness. And this "more" is just an aspect of the constitutive respectivity of reality *qua* reality. {88} Now let us return to our problem. Reality as reality is what grounds; it is what is the ground or foundation of my personal reality. This means that reality as grounding my personal reality exercises a power over me. Reality is the *power of the real*. And this is not identical with causality. All causes dominate, but not all dominance is causal, nor is the causal moment in the cause itself identical to its dominating power. They are different and distinguishable. Causality is the *functionality of the real as real*. Power is the *dominance of the real as real*.

Power takes hold of that which it dominates. Dominance is "taking hold of." The power of the real takes hold of me. And thanks to this I make myself a person. Reality grounds personal reality through "taking hold of" in accordance with the power of the real.

How does grounding take place, that is, how does the power of the real take hold? This is the third issue with which we shall be dealing.

But before proceeding, let us direct our attention to an Appendix.

APPENDIX 1

THE POWER OF THE REAL

I commit to Appendices discussions that are a fuller development of points already covered in the text, or that comprise items falling outside the general context of the book but which may still clarify some of its ideas. The latter is what now occurs with the idea of the power of the real.

We have already seen that power is the dominance of the real, that is, the dominance of the powerful. But there is an important distinction to be made on this point. Power is, of course, a moment of the "in its own right"; to wit, it is *real power*. Some real things can dominate over others. This power can be dominant in two aspects. First is that of real things, the real things as real *sources of power*. Yet there is dominance in another respect: not that of real things but of the moment of reality itself *qua* reality. And then it is not the case of sources of power, but of what I have called the *power of the real* qua *real*. This power is the ground, the foundation of my personal reality. It is about this power of the real that we have been concerned. This power is that dominance according to which reality, the real as real, captures me. But in order to clarify these ideas, it may be useful to consider at greater length those sources of power as real powers, even though they may not be the power of the real.

These real sources of power are found, for example, in the more or less ancient religions in the form of gods. Disregarding the question of what these gods are and how they pertain to religions (points which both go beyond the present line of argument), let us concern ourselves only with the form in which these gods dominate over things. Those modes of dominance are precisely their sources of power, their real power. This power has many manifestations:

1) It is a power which appears to us principally as the power from on high, the "most high".
2) It is also a power of time as a living measure of reality.
3) It is a power of separation of forms.
4) It is a power of germination of reality.
5) It is a power of organization, primarily of life.

6) It is power of the future.
7) It is a power, not only of the material reality but also of the intellectual reality of man.
8) It is the power of the personal intimacy which binds man into families, tribes and nations.
9) It is the power which fills everything in space just as much as in time.
10) It is the power which hovers over life and over death.
11) It is the power which directs social life.
12) It is the power which is called "destiny". {91}
13) It is the power which rules the justice and the cosmic-moral structure of the universe.
14) It is the sacralizing power.
15) It is the enduring power.

The list could and should be extended greatly. But what has been said suffices to show how, independently of the underlying conception of the gods, the items in the list taken together disclose the complex physiognomy of the *real power* of the gods.

Now, when this power does not correspond to real things but simply to their reality, then *real power* becomes something more radical, the *power of the real*. It is with this power, and only with this power, that we are concerned as ground of our personal reality. We now pose the third question: How does grounding occur?

III

How does grounding occur?

Grounding is the power of the real, which grounds by taking hold of me. My being taking hold of by the power of the real is not a relation into which I, already constituted a reality, enter with respect to the power of the real; but it is an intrinsic and formally constitutive moment of my personal reality. It is a constitutive respectivity. Thanks to this taking hold of I am a personal reality in such a fashion that the power of the real is a kind of support *a tergo*, not in order for me to act as a living being but for me to be real. Not only is man nothing without things, he needs them because they compel him to make himself. Being able to and having to make himself is not sufficient; he needs an impulse to actually make himself. And this impulse is an intrinsic and formal turning towards the power of the real. Man is not a personal reality except when he actually depends upon the power of the real, so that in virtue of the aforementioned "taking hold of" we are not extrinsically subjected to anything. We do not "go to" reality as such, but on the contrary we "come from" it. The "taking hold of" implants us in reality. This paradoxical taking hold of, when it does take hold of me, makes me separate when confronting that very thing which has taken hold of me. Therefore, the taking hold of occurs by connecting us to the power of the real in order to be relatively absolute. This peculiar connection is just what I term *religation*. Religated to the power of the real is how we are sustained in it, so as to be relatively absolute. Put differently, {93} the formal subject of religation is not *nature* but the *person*, or rather nature "personized." In itself, religation does not affect man separately from things; rather, it affects everything in some form. However, only in man is it formally religation; only in man is it the formal occurrence of grounding. A person is not simply linked to things or dependent upon them, but is constitutively and formally religated to the power of the real.

This is not a mere theoretical conceptualization but an analysis of facts. Religation is above all else a fact that is perfectly verifiable. Moreover, religation is something which affects the totality of my human reality, from my most modest physical characteristics to my most elevated mental traits. And this is true because what is religated to the power of the real is not just one aspect or another of my reality, but my own personal reality in all its dimensions; indeed it is through all of them that I make myself a person. Religation, consequently, is not only a verifiable fact but a *complete, integral* fact. Finally, religation is something basic and radical. Religation is the very root of my personal reality. Not only is it verifiable and complete, but above all a *radical fact*. Therefore, religation is not one function among a thousand others of human life, but the root from which each life may become, physically and really, not only *an I*, but *my* I.

Religation is not *obligation*, because obligation presupposes religation. We are *obligated* to something because we are previously *religated* to the power that makes us be persons. In order to be obliged we have to be a personal reality already, and we are only a personal reality because we are religated. As I said in the preceding pages, {94} in obligation we are subjected to something through being personal realities. Hence in an obligation we "go to" something; in religation, on the contrary, we "come from" something. Therefore, "we go" inasmuch as "we have come from". In religation, more than the obligation to *do*, there is *yielding to the recognition of that which makes everything be.*

Nor is religation the feeling of unconditional dependency. In the first place, any feeling has an intrinsic and formal moment of reality. To be sure, in any feeling there is a moment of affection, e.g., in his feelings a man is affected. But this affection is a way of being in reality; otherwise it would not be a feeling. Any feeling is affectant, but this affection is a mode of being in reality. Any feeling is affectant just as any intellection is sentient. In the second place, in order for me to have a sense of dependency, the moment of reality must be actualized as something to which I am linked, as something prior to the feeling itself. Finally, the unconditionality is only possible when the one that is dependent is an "absolute". Any unconditional dependency presupposes a relatively absolute reality. That is, it presupposes religation.

Therefore, I find myself religated to reality in its power. Religation is religation to the power of the real. Man is relatively absolute precisely and formally because he is religated to reality as power. In relegation grounding occurs to the power of the real.

This unity of the power of the real and religation, as I said before, is precisely the "taking hold of.". It is not a unity that is real *de facto*, but rather a unity which formally transpires in the "taking hold of."

{95} And this unity has at least three characteristics. First, in religation to the power of the real the human being has an experience of what the power of the real is, and consequently an experience of what reality is as power. Religation has, therefore, an *experiential* character.

What is experience? Experience here does not mean *aisthesis*,[1] that is to say, it is not the sense datum. Neither is it what Aristotle called *empeiría*, the recognition (*mnéme*) of the same thing in different perceptions; experience here is not the empirical. Nor does it mean what we designate as *life experience*. Experience is something different. Above all, it is a kind of test to which something is subjected, a test which is not mere corroboration in a conceptual sense, for example. Rather, it is the operative exercise of the act of testing: it is *physical testing*. Of what? Of the reality of something. Experience is, then, physical testing of reality. Man addresses himself to reality in order to find a support in it, and in turn this reality has a great richness of notes, which are a "such-and-such-ification" of the moment of reality and, therefore, are determined by this moment as possibilities of realization. The insertion of these possibilities into the realization of my person is the physical testing of reality. The human being, through making his own person by means of religation, is doing the physical testing of what the power of the real is. It is the test of the insertion of ultimateness, of possibilitation and of impellence into my own reality. When I make myself a personal reality I am, therefore, an experience of the power of the real and thus, of reality itself. Such testing is carried out in all individual, social, and historical venues. From this point of view, all diversity of {96} individuals in the course of their lives, their social milieus, and the resulting historical unfolding at epochs is a fabulous, gigantic experience of the power of the real.

In the second place, religation to the power of the real is not only experiential, but a manifestation of the power of the real itself. So religation is not only experiential but also ostensive, something that *manifests* the power of the real. Here we are not dealing with a purely conceptual manifestation. Anything real has a list of notes that comprise its own richness. In one or several of these notes the reality of the entire thing actualizes itself. Those notes, in which the real actualizes itself, comprise its dimension of manifesting. And the actualization in each of its dimensions is precisely the manifestation. The manifesting character concerns the real *qua* real. Religation is, in this sense, a manifestation, a showing of the power of the real *qua* real. And what manifests this way is the power of the real as religating.

This manifestation is along the lines of realization of my person, of my mode of being relatively absolute. Still, the fact that it is a manifestation along these lines shows that what is manifested, namely, the power of the real, manifests that it has an *enigmatic* character. Religation to the power of the real is the experience that manifests what is enigmatic about this power of the real. Religation is, then, not only experiential and manifesting but also enigmatic. This is the third character of religation. We saw, indeed, that when we are with real things, that *in* which we are is reality itself. Any real thing imposes upon us that we adopt a determinate form of reality. And this is where the enigma lies.

An enigma is above all a mode of signifying the real, {97} not declaring what it is but only indicating it as a sign, just as does an oracle. Thus, Heraclitus says that the oracle at Delphos neither says nor hides anything, but that only shows it through signs. This mode of manifesting reality is what is called *aínigma*, enigma. The enigma is comprised by a certain ambivalence of characteristics not readily harmonized. However, the character of enigma concerns not only the saying, but also what is being said. What is said or manifested is an enigma because what is said, the real, is enigmatic.

Now reality, what is manifest, is indicated or is manifest *qua* reality; and this manifestation is enigmatic. This is so because reality, on the one hand, is a moment of the particular real thing with which we happen to be, i.e., the thing's own formality, its own reality. And the other hand, it compels us to adopt a form of reality. Which one? Not necessarily that of this real thing itself, but *a* form in reality as a whole. Now, this is a radical ambivalence, because that *with* which we actually are is this particular reality, and that *in* which we actually are is reality itself, reality as a whole. The two moments are inseparable to be sure, but they are very different. Anything humanly apprehended is real, but none is reality as a whole. And what is most important is the fact that it is each real thing compelling us to actually be in reality as a whole. This is what we expressed earlier by saying that real things transport the power of the real; they are its vectors. There are not two realities but only one, one unity enigmatically manifest in our experiential religation. We have to be in reality: it is demanded of us by real things in their reality; but none is that in which we are made to be. This is the power of the real as enigma: to be in reality itself, reality as a whole, with real things. It is an enigmatic power. {98}

We shall insist on this point in order to provide greater clarity. I said above that in real things their formal moment of reality is "more" than their moment of mere suchness. To be a *real* green thing is more than being something really *green*. And this is much weightier than one might think. By being "more", to be real manifests a real thing as a moment of reality itself. And therefore "this" real thing, this real green thing, is not reality itself. Nor is it the case that this reality, of this real thing, is like a concretion, as if it were a contraction of something superior: in such case "this" reality would be reality itself contracted into the real thing. But, what is reality itself as prior to or superior to these real things? This would be pure conceptualism, unless one turns reality itself into a sea wherein real things are submerged. And this is something even less tenable than pure conceptualism. Rather than contraction one should speak of an expansion of "this" particular reality towards reality itself. All the same, this will not take us any further. Reality itself is in "this" reality, but is so enigmatically. And this enigma is manifest to us in the very experience of religation. Reality itself is not "this" real thing, but neither is it something outside of it. Reality is a "more" but not a "more" on top of the thing, but a "more" *in the thing itself*. That is the reason why, when I am with "this" reality, I am in reality itself. For the same reason, "this" real thing can compel me to adopt a form in reality itself. This is not a question of concepts, but a physical character of the power of the real.

This is what religation is, i.e., to be taken hold of by the power of the real. It is not something merely intentional; rather, we are physically thrown "towards" reality itself by the very power of the real. And we are so, thus physically and really constituting personal reality, the relative absolute {99} in which each person consists. We are physically thrown towards something unspeakably enigmatic. By religation we are thrown physically towards the reality which has captured us, not in a blind way, but just the opposite, in an ostensive and experiential manner. Since the power of the real is enigmatic, this enigma impresses its character into the realization of our personal reality: this is the problematicism of grounding. We make ourselves problematically because we are gounded in an enigma, the enigma of the power of the real.

We have examined how a person is grounded in reality, what the structure of this grounding is, and how this grounding occurs. Now we must confront the last question: the problematical nature of grounding.

IV

Problematical nature of grounding

The foregoing problematical character is an undeniable fact.

1. At each moment the human being continues to unfold and develop with the passing of time, through the phenomena which fill this time. Such is, as I mentioned above, the *changeableness* of life as *it runs its course*. But human reality, *qua* personal, has something else besides changeableness: it is *restless*. This does not have the character of a running the course, but the impressing of an enigma: the enigma of being religated. This the enigma by which the power of the real has captured me. Restlessness is not restlessness in the sense, for example, of the {100} famous and splendid phrase of St. Augustine: *Irrequietum cor nostrum Domine donec requiescat in Te* ("Our heart is restless, Lord, until it rest in Thee"). Man is restless in Augustine's sense because he searches for happiness. In the problem of the ground this is certainly true, but it is a truth based on something more radical, i.e., it is not primary. What is primary is that, if man is restless vis-à-vis his happiness, he is so because he is restlessness in himself. And if he is restless in himself, it is for a reason much more radical than any aspirations and necessities he may have. Therefore, we are not dealing with the Augustinian type of restlessness, but with a more radical restlessness. Human reality has a life and this life is constitutively restless because the reality in which it is lived is enigmatic. That is why the life of man suffers from restlessness. This restlessness is expressed in two questions quite elementary, but which no one has been able to deny. First of all, there is the question, What is going to become of me? And since this reality that I am, is not given to me but I have to make it, the question acquires a more urgent sense: What am I going to make of myself? Each human action, as modest as it may be, encompasses this question and is an answer to it. The unity of this making, in view of my personal reality and of this reality as something made, is just what constitutes restlessness. Such is the restlessness of my own reality *qua* already taken hold of by that which is enigmatic in the power of the real. It is not, I repeat, the Augustinian restlessness, but the restlessness of the enigmatic.

This restlessness can be lived in different ways. Each human being can gloss over this question, but the *glossing* is just one way to live the restlessness. At the other extreme, the restlessness can be *anguish*. This anguish {101} would not be possible if human beings were not restlessness in their own reality. Only in the measure in which a human is restless can he or she be invaded by anguish. There is yet another way of living the restlessness: *preoccupation*. Of course, it is not necessary that a human be preoccupied with each action: if this were so, life would be impossible. But one cannot be preoccupied without being restless. That is why there is a more elemental but inexorable form of living the restlessness, not as preoccupation but as *occupation*. Each human being is occupied in making itself a person. And this, I repeat, is inexorable in each human action. Restlessness understood as such is something which emerges from myself, by the fact that in each action I acquire my relative absolute being. I am absolute in a relative way. And this relativity is the religation. Religation remits us experientially to the power of reality, and, therefore, my own reality is for me something enigmatic. And this enigmatic character is lived as a form of restlessness in each one of the moments of my personal life. This is the first moment of the problematic nature of grounding, determined by the enigma of the religation of the power of the real.

2. This restlessness emerging from myself has in a certain way its counterpart, so to speak, in another phenomenon that is also undeniable. In each instant of his life man possesses, in principle, that which is called the *voice of conscience*. It is the voice that in one form or another dictates to man what he has to do or not to do. It is not the same as restlessness, clearly, and besides it is not a voice that solves all problems; but it is a real phenomenon. Generally, this voice is referred to only when dealing with duties. But that is insufficient because, in reality, the voice is talking to us in every {102} act. In what does this voice consist?

Where does this voice come from? Clearly, it comes from the depths of myself. But, in what does this depth consist? It is not, of course, what could be understood by "depth" in the current "Depth Psychology". Because whatever this psychological depth may be, such a depth could not constitute the voice of conscience unless it came from a depth in a more radical sense. The psychological depth is at best a qualification of a more radical depth. Therefore, my radical depth is the absolute character of my reality. And the voice that arises from this depth is a voice primarily because the relative absolute is mine, I am myself and not another. Here, precisely, is where the voice of conscience arises.

This voice dictates something to me. What is this dictation and what does it dictate? The voice of conscience can be clear, obscure, even variable, because it will probably say to a European different things than those it might say to a Chinese or a Japanese (I do not know). And in all these dictations, what the voice of conscience dictates as something arising from the depth of my own reality is just a form of reality that I must adopt. Therein consists the dictation of the voice of conscience.

The voice of conscience dictates in an unappealable and unquestionable manner. Certainly this dictation is not always univocal and, so to speak, pleasant to hear. But it always tends to take on an unquestionable mantle. One might even think that this is what Kant called the "Categorical Imperative". But that interpretation is false, according to my point of view, for three reasons. In the first place, the voice is not an imperative in the Kantian sense. Kant conceives and enunciates his ideas in a propositional form, in the form of {103} a judgment, which greatly damaged his philosophy. In the second place, Kant always thought that this imperative was subjective, however transcendental one might wish, but still subjective. And this because Kant always confused the *subjectual* with the *subjective*. Everything subjective can be subjectual, but not everything subjectual is subjective. "Subjectual" means that the thing one is talking about is a *subjectum*, but not that it is subjective. (We leave aside now the fact that human reality, as I have detailed, is not even subjectual but is a substantive system). Finally, it is not the case of a categorical dictation considered objectively, but of a voice *qua* voice.

And thus, we must state that the voice of conscience is first and foremost a voice. And it is a form of sentient intelligence. Reality is what is "in its own right" that which is apprehended. And this "in its own right" is quite rich. Each sense has its mode of apprehending the real. The eleven senses distinguish themselves radically, not just by the *content* of the sensed quality, but by the *mode* of apprehending this content as something in its own right. There are, if I may be permitted the expression, eleven ways of apprehending something in its own right. Sight makes the thing present in its *eidos*, tact as mere presence. This tactile mode is in the intellective sense proper, for example, to the presence of God in the mystic, etc. The kinesthetic sense, like that of orientation and equilibrium, gives us the reality as "towards". This does not mean a sensing "toward reality" but that reality itself is sensed in the form of "towards", it is reality as "towards". We are frankly accustomed to think that to in order to apprehend something, we must have it *in front of* ourselves; that is the tyranny of sight. There are, as I have said, multiple ways of apprehending the real and one of them is apprehending it as "towards". Therefore, {104} in hearing, the sound is certainly apprehended as something in its own right, as much in its own right as color is in sight. But a thing itself is not apprehended as present to hearing in the same way as it is in sight. Reality is something of which we are "announced" only. Hearing refers to what sounds; because of this it is announcement in the most rigorous sense of the term. The voice of conscience is just like an announcing referral to the form of reality. And that of which it is an announcement is reality. From this point of view the human being is the voice of reality. The voice of conscience is nothing but the clamor of reality as the root of the absolute.

And this voice, this clamor, this announcement, is not just a communiqué; it "clamors", that is, hurls us physically, not only intentionally, towards the power of the real as enigma. It is the voice of the problematic nature of the enigma of the real, towards which we are hurled. It is in this precise sense that we are physically hurled towards the real in its reality, by the voice of consciousness. It is yet another radical moment of the problematic nature of grounding.

Still, restlessness and the voice of conscience are not the only moments of that problematic nature.

3. Man finds himself, then, inexorably hurled in the direction of having to determine the form of reality that he must adopt. This determination is just what constitutes *volition* or *willing*. As an animal, man tends to adopt a variety of forms. But as animal of realities, this tendency is a tendency towards forms of reality. The intrinsic unity of tendency and real determination is thus a sentient will. To sentient intelligence there corresponds a sentient will which consists in a tending to a determinate form of reality. How does {105} reality present itself with respect to the act of willing? In what does this willing consist? In what does that which is wanted consist? These are three questions which demand our attention.

a) For radical willing, its terminus does not present itself as an object or thing; rather, its mode of actually being present is by grounding our relatively absolute reality. It is not as if a thing "is" present; rather its mode of being present is "to ground". We are dealing, in fact, with reality as an enigma. And as such, the presence of reality means to ground, not only materially, so to speak, but formally as well. It is not a *reality-object* but a *reality-ground*. Therefore, it is not a thing that begins by being a real thing, to which it is added that it is also grounding; rather, its own mode of reality, its mode of being in its own right, is to ground, to be grounding. With respect to a reality-object (I beg forgiveness for the use of the term "object" in order to provide clarity to the phrase), this reality is already understood in and by itself as a reality and nothing more, before serving as a ground. The reality-ground is a reality (if it were not it would not be a ground) but its mode of actualization is pure grounding. Then we understand that we may be physically, not only turned, but "hurled" towards it. Therefore, there are not two moments, one of reality and another of grounding, but only one "reality-ground".

b) On account of this, I am inexorably hurled by grounding itself to adopt a form of reality. As this form has to be determined through choosing as a possibility, the determination is the adoption or appropriation of a possibility. And this is what formally constitutes willing: the adoption or appropriation of {106} a possible form of reality. All willing is the willing of a possible form of reality.

c) Ultimately, in what does this willing of a form of reality consist? It is clearly an adoption, though not arbitrary, and it consists of having the grounding reality actualized. This radical will is not the *will to live*, but *will to personal reality*. It encompasses my whole personal reality. Therefore it is not primarily about *living* but about *being real*. It is the *will to reality*. This reality is actualized in my intellection and *qua* actualized in it, is just what we call "truth". The will to reality is the *will to truth*. What is this will to truth? Truth has various moments. One is the most classic: an act of intellection which manifests reality. And since we are dealing here with my form of reality, one might think that "truth" means "authenticity." The will to truth would be will to authenticity. This is what Nietzsche canonized: *Wille zur Wahrheit*. But this is insufficient because there is a moment of the will to truth which is prior to the will to authenticity itself, and that is so because authenticity is authenticity as expression of a reality. With this we descend to a deeper stratum: to the will to be a reality merely actualized in my intellection. This is what I have called *real truth*. It is *truth* because it is an intellective actualization of reality, and it is *real* because what is actualized is the real itself as something in its own right. Truth is not identical to reality, but if I pay attention in the actualization of the real to the actualization itself, as differing from that which is actualized, I shall have truth: this is the *real truth*. This real truth has different moments.

One we encountered earlier {107} when I mentioned that religation is showing, manifesting, or revealing. Real truth is, above all, a *manifestation* of reality. This is the aspect to which the West has devoted most of its attention since the time of the Greeks.

Real truth has a second aspect to which Greece paid no attention. This is the aspect according to which something is real if it corresponds to what it promises: such is *truth as fidelity*. That was the sense of truth for the Semites. While for a Greek truth is "to be thus," for a Semite truth is "so be it" (*amen*, from *emeth*, truth). Concerning man, truth is security.

Yet, there is in real truth a third aspect that is in a certain way gerundial: real truth is what "is really effectively and actually being": this is the moment of *effectivity*.

Any real truth has three aspects, but sometimes one is more noticeable than the others. The unity of these aspects is what constitutes real truth. The will to truth is intrinsically and at one and the same time manifestation, fidelity and effectivity.

The reality-ground as such is real truth to these three moments. Man today is in a greater need than ever of attending to real truth. It is a will to truth which desires to discover more real truth each time, that is, more manifestation, more security, more effectivity of the real. And this real truth is real in all the modes of reality, among them that according to the "towards". We are, then, hurled "towards" in and by real truth, towards the real itself. Precisely because of this each human must adopt some form of reality among all of those possible. And this is not only an *obligation* but a *fact*; not only the fact that each human is in need, but the constitutive fact of the personal reality of each human. In {108} each of his acts man carries out a will to real truth. In it he has to adopt a form of reality. Consequently, this form is a choosing. Hence the will to real truth takes the form of a search. A search for what? A search for how real things fit into reality itself in order to opt for a form of reality. We need to investigate the way each thing articulates "its" reality with respect to reality itself. And this is the grounding in which my personal reality grounds itself in reality, in the reality-ground. To employ Bergson's expression, this experience can be called a "metaphysical experience", an experience of a search for a ground, for a grounding of the power of the real; an experience that with greater precision I will call a *theological experience*. It is not *theologic experience*. I shall deal with theologic experience in the Third Part of the book. Let us not confuse the theological with the theologic. The theological is what concerns the turning towards the problem of God. The theologic is what concerns God himself.

* * *

Let us summarize. We sought to learn in this Chapter how one becomes a human being. One becomes a human being by making oneself, in one's own actions, as agent, actor and author of them. By his or her actions a human being is *with* real things, but where he or she is with them is in reality. Real things are not reality itself; they are only vectors of reality. Being in reality is how a human being makes itself a personal reality, a reality relatively absolute. Reality is, from this point of view, the ultimate ground, both enabling {109} and impelling, of my personal reality. This grounding capability of the real is what constitutes the power of the real, the dominance of the real *qua* real. And this dominance dominates my personal reality, not through causality but through "taking hold of." This taking hold of is what formally constitutes what I have called "religation". Religation is reality capturing me. And this religation is not a material bond, but the mere dominance of the "taking hold of," of a power of the real actualized in my sentient intellect. Therefore, religation actualizes in my mind the shape of the power of the real which has taken hold of me. Religation, in fact, is primarily something not *conceptual* but *physical*, something experiential; secondly, it is something that manifests the power of the real; but it remains enigmatic because it does not make us see what comprises the difference as well as the unity of any particular reality (i.e., that of each individual thing) with reality itself (reality as a whole). To make oneself a person is the manifesting experience of an enigmatic power. The power of the real is actualized as something enigmatic. And since this power is a ground of my personal reality, it follows that the making of myself as a person in my actions is something problematic. This problematic nature shows itself as *restlessness*, as the voice of conscience, and as will to real truth. This truth has the three moments of manifestation, faithfulness and effectiveness. Therefore, the restlessness which the voice of conscience dictates to me is the will to real truth enigmatically apprehended. Consequently, we must proceed by searching. To make oneself a person is a *search*. It is definitely a search for the ground of my relative absolute being. Every search is problematic when that which is searched for is enigmatic.

As we make ourselves persons, in religation we search to clarify, not conceptually but physically {110} and experientially, the ground of the enigmatic radical unity of the reality of each individual thing, and reality itself, reality as a whole. This is something problematic in grounding, and its articulation concerns religation itself. And this is so because, depending upon the mode in which reality itself is articulated in each real thing, the human attitude likewise will be different, as will the horizon of possibilities which opens up to intellection and by which a person may acquire his own figure of reality. This articulation is a moment of any real thing; it is a moment of grounding which thus constitutes the ground of my personal reality. It is a moment of grounding because it is not a reality-object but a reality-ground. This is what we search for. The reality-ground is the solution of the enigma of reality and of my personal reality.

This problematic nature of the reality-ground is not something which takes us to the problem of God, but *is* actually the *problem of God*. What religation manifests experientially and enigmatically is God as a problem. The problem of God belongs therefore to the constitution of my own person insofar as it has to make its own reality, that is, its own *figure of being* absolute "with" things while actually being "in" reality. It is a problem which belongs to the dimension of my person as religated intrinsically and formally to the power of the real. This power happens in my life as an experience of reality *qua* manifested, faithful and effective. Therefore, God constitutes an intrinsically and formally constitutive problem of the structure of my own personal reality. It is not an arbitrary problem.

Because of this, the problem of God is not {111} formally a problem of the "beyond." That is a separate question with which we are not dealing; just the opposite: because the will to real truth and the problem of God inscribed in it are a dimension constituting the possibility of my very existence in reality, and support my being in this world. The problem of God is a problem that radically and formally affects the constitution of the human person and, therefore, is not a problem that formally concerns any "beyond". The problem of God, I repeat, concerns—precisely and above all—the reality of this world and our personal reality in it. Consequently, the problem of God is not the investigation of something which is "outside" the world but something which is *in* the reality surrounding us, in my own personal reality. To this something we are all problematically but inexorably hurled in order to be able to select the absolute figure of our being.

In what, radically, does this reality-ground consist, towards which I am hurled and for which I must search?

That is the Second Part of this investigation. In the First I have tried to clarify some concepts that refer to what man is as a reality. Now we find ourselves thrust from man to God: this is the problem of Divine reality.

In order to pose it adequately we need a nominal definition of that which is sought for; otherwise we would not be able to search for it. What is understood by God, regardless of whether one accepts His reality or not? At the beginning of this investigation we shall call "God" the possibilitating and impelling ultimate ground of the articulation—let us call it that—of real things in reality itself, reality as a whole. But this is not sufficient. I will also need to see that {112} what I have found in my search is not only something real that I call "God," but that this which is real is precisely God *qua* God. That is what we shall try to show in the Second Part of our investigation.

---

[1] [Greek for *perception.—trans.*]

PART II

DIVINE REALITY

CHAPTER 3

THE UNFOLDING OF THE PROBLEM: I. THE REALITY OF GOD

The problem of God is not a theoretical problem. We have studied this closely, but a review at this point is nonetheless appropriate. A human being is a personal reality whose life consists of self-possession in the realization of its own personality, in the configuration of its *I* as actualization in the world of its relatively absolute reality. This life is realized by virtue of the person, *qua* person, being religated to the power of the real as a ground that makes the person to be a person. Religation is a dimension not of nature *qua* nature, but nature *qua* "personized". This religation, therefore, is not just one more function among thousands of others in human life, but its radical dimension in the strictest sense of the term: it is truly the root from which each one person becomes, physically and really, not just *an I* but *his or her own I*. Thus, religated to the power of the real, a human being in each of its most modest acts not only elaborates the figure of its own *I*, but does so by taking a position, in one form or another, when confronting the ground that makes him to be. Now, {116} this taking of a position is constitutively and essentially problematic. *I* live and am always aware that I live the power of the real problematically, by living my own relatively absolute reality in a problematic way. What is problematic is the power of the real in my religation; it is precisely the problem of God. Whence it follows that by simply being a position with respect to the problem of the real, life is *eo ipso* the very unfolding of the problem of God. A human being does not *have* the problem of God, but rather the constitution of its *I* is formally the problem of God. The problem of God is not, therefore, a theoretical problem, but a personal one.

It follows that this problem has two co-essential aspects that we must study in succession. First of all, in the power of the real as constitutive of my religation, is there that which we call God? The issue is to make us see that His reality is manifested, in some way, in religation, that is, in the constitution of my *I* as its ground. Therefore—and this is the second aspect—humans have access to that ground in some form. These are, I repeat, two co-essential aspects of what we call "God"; but they have to be examined successively. Consequently, we must first show that there is something in reality that we designate with the name "God". And second, the mode of access of humans to this God has to be detailed precisely. In this chapter we shall limit ourselves to the first aspect of the question: the reality of God.

The reality of God is a problem embracing several questions. In the first place, What is the base upon which we shall inquire and reflect? In the second place, Is the reality of God intellectively justified? Third and finally, it will be necessary to classify some of the {117} characteristics of this presumed reality. Therefore, we must examine three points:

§1. The point of departure for the problem.
§2. Justification of the reality of God.
§3. Characteristics of the reality of God.

{118}

§1

THE POINT OF DEPARTURE FOR THE PROBLEM

In order to study the problem of the power of the real it is necessary to establish a firm basis for discussion. This basis is essential not only for its effect on the dialectics of the discussion, but above all because upon it depends the character of what, for us, is the ground of the power of the real. And this is not obvious at all, despite the fact that the question appeared definitely solved centuries ago. But it has not been.

I. Philosophy and above all classical Theology have traditionally started from reality, considered as that which we call "nature". Human beings are themselves reality because they form part of it. In this respect there would be no difference between humans and any other cosmic reality: they all are *res naturalis*. This is the reason why philosophers and theologians have taken the structure of the cosmos as the basis for discussion; and proposed to ground the existence of God with arguments based on cosmic facts. Their attempt, with all its variants, reached its culminating point in the famous "five ways" of St. Thomas. However, this does not appear to me to be the best road for our endeavor, because these celebrated five ways do not seem satisfactory, either in their point of departure or in their terminus. Let us put it briefly.

1. Above all, the starting point. In each one of his "ways" St. Thomas starts from what are for him {119} incontrovertible and therefore basic cosmic facts relevant to our problem. But are they? That is the question.

The *first way*, which St. Thomas calls the most evident (*manifestior via*), starts from "movement", that is, from cosmic change. Naturally, just stated in this way without further elaboration, change is an aspect of the cosmos. But this is not the "fact" to which St. Thomas refers. For St. Thomas motion is, as it was for Aristotle, a state of a movable being which consists in passing from potency to act. This is the "fact" upon which the *prima via* of St. Thomas is based. However, this is not and cannot be a fact; it is an interpretation of the reality of motion. And insofar as the naked fact of motion is controversial, the Aristotelian interpretation of it is problematic. That interpretation is indeed only one possible conception of motion among others; the pure fact of motion, actually, is not simply a "state" of the movable, nor formally a passing from potency to act. I am not saying that the argument is not valid, but that its starting point is neither firm nor manifest.

The *second way* begins by saying that in sensible things we encounter an order of efficient causality (*invenimus enim in istis sensibilibus esse ordinem causarum efficientium*). But, is this a factual truth? Because if we ignore human actions, can one provide just a single example of efficient causality in the cosmic experience? Successions, including regular ones, as many as you may wish. But, efficient causation? Efficient causation is but an interpretation of experience. When all is said and done, cosmic occasionalism is another possible interpretation, since it is by no means a metaphysical impossibility. {120}

The *third way* is based upon consideration of the possible and the necessary. For St. Thomas, as he tells us explicitly, the fact that there are things that are produced and destroyed is *eo ipso* the fact of the non-necessity of their reality. But is it? It would be so only if generation and corruption were not themselves something necessary in nature. Experience gives us neither necessity nor contingency. Experience only shows, formally, "what is"; it shows that things "are thus" and nothing else. The possible and the necessary are not facts given in experience.

The *fourth way* refers to the "degrees" of being of things: there are things that have more being or "entity" than others. But this is questionable. If, once again, we ignore human reality, is it true that experience actually gives us different degrees of being? Moreover, the assertion that inferior degrees are grounded on superior ones and therefore presuppose them is something quite problematic. One must address the possibility of evolution, which makes the superior flourish out of the inferior. So in view of all this, the idea of the degree of being turns out to be quite problematic. Under these conditions, one cannot speak of the degree of being as a fact which may serve as a point of departure to prove the existence of God.

Lastly, there is the *fifth way*: the fact that in nature there is an order of finality. But, is this a fact? Human actions have, at least partially, a finality. But the physical cosmos? There is in it a certain convergence among its processes. But is the "convergence" of cosmic processes a formal {121} ordering? This is not an immediate fact but a theory, perhaps true, but still a theory.

With all this I am not maintaining that the five arguments are invalid. Rather, I am saying that contrary to what is expressly affirmed in them, they do not start from facts but from something quite different, namely, from a metaphysical interpretation of sensible reality. And this is true even to the point that an essential difference in the order of facts as facts—the difference between human actions and the rest of the cosmic facts—has no role whatsoever in the conception of the cosmos which St. Thomas uses here. In the five ways we always had to make an exception for human actions. The vision of a human being as a mere *res naturalis*, i.e., not questioning the position of humans in the cosmos as a simple *res* (even without entering into other aspects of human beings) is a debatable metaphysical vision. And it is so because the basis of St. Thomas' discussion is not the *facts* but the *metaphysics* of Aristotle, which for St. Thomas is reason itself. By dint of considering it as the metaphysics of common sense, one ends by identifying it with the facts, with the given. But this identification fails, as I have just pointed out, even by omission. The metaphysics of Aristotle is neither plain common sense nor a datum of experience. This indicates a radical insufficiency at the very point of departure of the question.

2. But it is not the only problem. Because even if we were to acknowledge these ways, the point to which they lead us is not God as God.

Above all, the first way leads to a first unmoved mover; the second, to a first efficient cause; the third, to the first necessary being; the fourth, to a being in {122} the plenitude of being; the fifth, to a supreme intelligence. But do these five refer to one and the same being? That must be proved.

Moreover, even supposing that it could be proved, does this mean that what has been proved is that the supreme being is formally God, what we understand by God? We would still have to prove that this being is, precisely, God. Duns Scotus saw this clearly. That is why his proof of the existence of God has two parts. In the first, what is proved is the existence of a being that is first as efficient cause (*primum effectivum*), as end (*primum finitivum*), and as exemplar of being (we could call him *primum perfectivum*). Afterwards Scotus—in a second part—needs to prove that this first being is infinite and, therefore, according to him, God. But despite everything, the Scotus' proof is inadequate in both of its two parts. I will not now go into the first. Suffice it to say that the starting point of Scotus is quite different from that of St. Thomas: while St. Thomas starts from *cosmic facts*, Scotus starts with finite sensible *beings*. But, despite this, there is a common note anchoring both ways of thinking, one which is quite important from my point of view. I shall return to this later. What now concerns me most is the second part of the proof, namely, the identification at the end of the argument of the infinite being with God, because this leaves outstanding the very question that was supposed to be resolved. It would be necessary to prove, indeed, that when we refer to God we are referring *primarily* to an infinite being. Nothing could be further from reality. The fact is that Scotus searches for what the Scholastics called "metaphysical essence", or the first metaphysical concept of Divine Being; Scotus believes he has found it {123} in infinitude. But what we all understand by God, when we search for Him, is not a metaphysical essence, but something simpler: an ultimate reality, fountain of all the possibilities which the human being has, and from Whom the human being receives, through supplication, the aid and strength to be. Therefore the infinite being of Scotus is not *formally* (only with that are we dealing) this God *qua* God. First, even with respect to a metaphysical idea of God, it is not metaphysically evident that the metaphysical essence of God should be infinite. Second (and this is what concerns us most), because infinitude must concern God by reason of lastness or finality, and not *viceversa*, formally God *qua* God is what is "final". He would only be infinite because He is God, He would not be God because He is infinite. Third and finally, in order for this "ultimate" to be God it is necessary that He be *at one and the same time* and *formally* "possibilitating" and "impelling". Mere infinitude is not. Once again, at the end of these arguments we find ourselves in Scotus, as well as in St. Thomas, with a supreme being. But is this being God? That is the unresolved question.

Neither by virtue of its point of departure nor of its ending point does the cosmic structure (understood in the manner of St. Thomas or Scotus) appear to be the adequate way to ground the existence of God.

II. It might be thought that the point of departure for which we are searching would have to be found in the human being itself as something different from the cosmos. This would not be a cosmic way, but an *anthropological way*. However, the human being is a reality of quite varied aspects. Hence the anthropological way has assumed diverse forms throughout history. Let us look at some of the most important only. St. Augustine {124} reaches God starting with the fact that the human being possesses truths; and any truth, he tells us, bases itself upon a subsisting truth, upon "the" truth. Kant focuses on the will. The human not only wants things, but has to want duty for the sake of duty in a categorical sense. And this is possible only if there exists *in re* a good in itself. Schleiermacher centers his attention on the feelings. Among them there is one in which the human being is overcome by the feeling of unconditional dependence on the infinite: this is the feeling of an infinite irrational reality. Intelligence, will and sentiment are the three characteristics that the human being in fact possesses and which *as facts* may lead to a subsistent truth, to an optimum good, to an infinite reality. It is not my desire to discuss the progress of the mind along this anthropological path until it reaches God. The only thing in which I am interested is the point of departure itself, namely, that which conditions the character of the God at which we seek to arrive.

1. The starting point: Is the alleged point of departure really "facts", or "data" (the term is indifferent)? That is the first question, and it is more obscure than might appear at first sight.

A) Above all, when following this anthropological path, one starts with aspects of the human being which are undeniably real: intelligence, will, feeling. But what happens is that these aspects are just that: aspects. Whence the human reality from which one starts is only partial: it is not the human being, but only a part thereof. Under these conditions, those aspects taken as real notes of the human being are not strictly speaking *facts*, but more or less fragmentary *aspects* of a unique human reality. Now, {125} this human reality is one that never appears in St. Augustine, Kant, or Schleiermacher. Is it the case that a human being needs God as its ground only because it is intelligent, only because it is something that wills, or only because it feels one way or another? It would seem rather that we should take the human being as a whole. But this approach is opposed to the conception which these philosophers have of intelligence, of the will, and of feeling.

B) In fact, even taking each of these aspects in itself and by itself, that in them comprising the point of departure for our problem is anything but an unimpeachable revelation. St. Augustine starts from truth itself as something which resides in the interior of man, though in contrast to "the" truths which, in their plurality, would only be "veri-similitudes" (in the etymological sense of the term). The "fact" from which St. Augustine really starts is not exactly intelligence, but the radical dualism therein between truth itself and "the" truths. This presumed "fact" is nothing but the philosophy of Plato and Plotinus. Kant starts from the will as seat of the moral imperative. And as such it is, for Kant, a categorical will; something *toto cælo* different from—and even opposite to—the volitions which integrate the process of my mental life. There is thus a radical dualism between an intelligible will and an empirical will. But, is this a "fact"? The case of Schleiermacher's feeling of unconditional dependency is the same. It is not a feeling of the kind that a human being experiences when facing things, facing the other humans, or even when facing itself; but a sentiment of a radically different kind. And this is true not only by virtue of its object, the {126} infinite (which is not something given), but as happened with Kant's volition, by virtue of the mode of feeling being itself different, namely, unconditional. The intellection of St. Augustine, the volition of Kant, and the feeling of Schleiermacher are all shot through with an internal dualism. Because of this, not only are they partial aspects of human beings, they are also partial aspects of intelligence, will and feeling. This is the intrinsic dualism of those human aspects according to these philosophies. And that is no accident.

C) The fact is that at the root of each of these philosophies, one starts with a very fixed concept of the human being. Not only is the human being not considered as a mere *res naturalis*, it is in fact considered precisely and formally as something *contradistinguished* from any *res naturalis*: this is the human being in and of itself independent of cosmic reality. But since each human being, whether liking it or not, is in the cosmos, it follows that human reality is cut into two zones: one, more or less integrated with the cosmos, and a zone which goes against it or at least without it. The dualism internal to each of the aforementioned aspects of humans is thus the inexorable consequence of this impossible antithesis human being-cosmos.

The partial nature of the aspects, the dualism internal to them, and the contradistinction with respect to the cosmos are three characteristics of intelligence, will and feeling that are sought as the basis for our march towards God. But ultimately, they are a *segregation* of humans with respect to cosmic reality. But this segregation is not a fact; indeed, it is not even something viable.

2. And precisely because it is not, this anthropological way leads to a radically inadequate idea of God. The {127} segregation of human beings *vis-à-vis* the real world leads to a God more or less segregated from humans. It is true that St. Augustine, Kant and Schleiermacher integrate the God at which they arrive with the real world. But this is not the issue. What is decisive is that they *need* to so integrate Him because the God to which this anthropological way leads does not formally refer to the reality of the world. Subsistent reality, the highest good, and the infinite may be real in themselves; but their reality does not formally involve a reference to the rest of the real world, only to the human being. After having reached God, one returns from God towards the

world; and each of the three thinkers, in a different way, seems to lodge the world in God. But in itself, the God to which this anthropological way leads is, formally, a reality segregated from the world and therefore juxtaposed to and only afterwards convergent with it. Now, the God to which we all refer is not just possibilitating and impelling (be it in an intellectual, willing or sentimental way) but is also formally and at one and the same time the *supremum* of the real, of this reality which is cosmos and with which we all make our being out of the substantive. If the cosmic way does not reach a possibilitating and impelling God, this anthropological way does not reach a God as *supremum* of the real. In neither case is the point of arrival is God *qua* God.

So neither by virtue of its point of departure nor by its final point of arrival are these classical cosmic and anthropological ways the adequate road to reach God. From this stems the necessity to undertake a different road.

III. To do this let us remember once more what we said in previous chapters and which I restated at the beginning of this one. {128}

1. The human being is a personal reality whose life consists in making its *I* physically and really. The human person realizes himself or herself as a person based on the power of the real. Only in and by this support can a person live and be: that is the phenomenon of *religation*. A person is not simply linked to things or dependent upon them, but is constitutively and formally religated to the power of the real, which *eo ipso* constitutes the very ground of personal life. Religation is not mere *linking* or *sentiment of dependence*, but the constitutive and formal turning towards the power of the real as ground of my personal life.

a) Because of this, religation is above all a *fact*, the very fact in which my living consists.

b) Not only that, but religation is something precisely and fundamentally affecting the whole of my human reality, from my most modest physical characteristic to the most elevated "spiritual" traits. What is religated to the power of the real is not one aspect or another of my reality, but my own personal reality in all its dimensions, because it is in accordance with all of them that I construct my *I*. Therefore religation is a fact, indeed an integral *total fact*, because it is a fact which concerns my reality and my personal being. That is why the way of religation is formally neither cosmic nor anthropological, but is both things eminently.

c) Finally, religation is something basic and radical. By religating myself to the power of the real as ground of the construction of the *I*, religation is the very root of this *I* of mine, of this personal life of mine. It is not only a fact and a total fact, but above all, a *radical fact*; it is the root of my being. {129}

The path that we must now follow in our problem starts from this fact.

2. It might seem that this is an anthropological way, perhaps more complex than the usual ones, but when all is said and done just another anthropological way. Nothing could be further from the truth.

a) In religation, indeed, we are religated to the power of the real. But religation would only be something anthropological if it were a "relation" between human beings and things. However, it is not. We are not dealing with a "relation" between humans and things, but with the fact that religation is the "respective structure" in which the power of the real occurs. I make my *I* among real things and with real things, and this turning to them is not a *relation consequent* upon my "needs" (or anything like it) but the *constitutive respective structure* of my action itself. The power of the real is the power of each thing *qua* reality, be it cosmic or human. My own substantive reality is enclosed by the power of the real. From this it follows that religation is not something human in contradistinction to the cosmic, but the very occurrence of all reality in human beings and of human beings in reality. Religation is at one and the same time and in a radical sense, something human and cosmic. Here "at one and the same time" means that it is not a causal relation, but something *toto cælo* different: the dominance of a power. *Whether causally dependent or not* on things, a person is *formally dominated* by the power of the *real*. Because of this, to say that religation is the occurrence of the power of the real is the same as saying that religation is formally and "at one and the same time" something human and something cosmic. The way that starts from religation, *therefore*, is neither cosmic nor anthropological.

b) In what does this occurrence consist? The power of the real is the power of reality as something supreme, possibilitating,{130} and impelling. This occurrence is a "manifesting experience", and therefore, manifestation of the power of the real in its three moments. Whence the constitution of my *I*, the realization of my person, may be a problematic experience of the power of the real as something supreme, possibilitating and impelling.

In all its dimensions, notes and forms, to live and to possess oneself as an *I* is always but to move oneself, to make oneself in the power of the real. That is why religation to the power of the real is the base of our whole problem and the point of departure of the discussion.

3. In this experience, the outline of that which is sought is inevitably sketched, regardless of whether its reality is admitted or not. Put another way: without some idea of God, all talk about Him would be vacuous; God would be nothing but a verbal vagueness, more or less solemn. Whether to affirm, deny, or even ignore him, you need some idea of God. Where to obtain it? We are not dealing with a merely nominal idea chosen arbitrarily, but with an idea which in one form or another is at the very base of the discussion. This base is the religating experience to the power of the real. And so, this experience is the one tracing the outline of the very idea of God. That is the reason we all agree with it, not *qua* reality, but *qua* idea. What is this idea? To my way of thinking it can be reduced to three points.

a) God has to be the ground of the power of the real. Therefore, he is *eo ipso* an ultimate ground, possibilitating and impelling. If, by way of religation, we reach God, we shall have then reached a God *qua* God. God is not only a first cause, a first {131} unmoved mover, etc. To such a God no one would address a prayer or a supplication. The celebrated exclamation *tu causa causarum miserere mei* (Oh you, cause of the causes, have mercy on me) makes no formal theological sense. But the way we have taken avoids *a limine* the dissociation between supremeness on one side and possibilitation and impellence on the other, precisely because the power of the real has, at one and the same time and formally, all three of these aspects; it is the idea of a God *qua* God.

b) This God has to be a supreme *reality*, but not a supreme *being*. The identification of what is real with being is an important consequence of the acceptance of Greek philosophy. It is what I have termed the *entification of reality*: things are not entities unless they have being. Now, to be is always but a subsequent act of the real. Whatsoever a being may be, it is always and only being "of" the real. Subsequentness is the precise meaning of this "of". Therefore, reality and entity are not formally identical. Prior to being entities, and precisely in order *to be able to be so*, things begin by being real. The ground of being is reality. And this is still more true when we are dealing with the reality of God. God is not the subsistent being, is not the supreme being, not even when festooned with the attribute of infinitude. God is not a divine *entity*, He is supreme *reality*. The important assumption common to St. Thomas and Duns Scotus, to which I referred above, is just the entification of reality and, therefore, the identification of God with the supreme entity. No. God is beyond being. God has no being; only worldly things have being, which by virtue of "already" being real, "are" in the world. As ground of the power of the real God would be formally a supreme reality that is highest, possibilitating and impelling. {132}

c) In what does the "supreme" character of this reality consist? The power of the real is the ground of the constitution of my *I*. And my *I*, according to what we have seen, is something absolute. That my *I* should be absolute means that it is *I* "confronting" the whole of reality, that is, confronting reality as such. But this *I* is only relatively absolute because it is an *I* acquired by "confronting" reality as such, i.e., because it is an absolute that needs this reality as such in order to be absolute. In other words: the *I* is absolute, but *in its own manner*, relatively. If there is a God, He will be a reality that is the ground of my relative absolute being. Therefore, He will be an absolute reality, not in His own mode, but *simpliciter*; a reality which is fully real and absolute, not "confronting" reality as such, but "in and by itself" *qua* real. This is what I shall call "absolutely absolute reality". In this problem "supreme" means "absolutely absolute". And this would be, if it exists, divine reality.

The way of religation to the power of the real is then an experience that sketches the figure of a God before my eyes as absolutely absolute reality, highest reality, possibilitating and impelling, which is the ground of the power of the real. Such would be the point of arrival of our way: not only God, but God *qua* God. This experience is not just individual. There is also an historical and social experience of religation to the power of the real, and in it the idea of God progressively acquires a still more precise nature. But all historical experience of religation essentially presupposes its personal aspect: *to be able to move oneself in relegated fashion in the power of the real as formal structure of life itself, that is, of the constitution of my I*. This moving of oneself is problematic, {133} because the power of the real is constitutively enigmatic. And the enigma consists in this fact: The human person, *qua* religated to the power of the real, when making its relatively absolute *I*, does not know if it is being compelled by the power of the real itself to have to reach an absolutely absolute reality as ground of that power, and therefore of the *I*. From the foregoing we realize the completely necessary and indispensable character that fixing the base for discussion has. Above all, without it any discussion is lost in a vacuum. But with it we have achieved not only the basis for a dialectical discussion, but the basis for a real discussion. Religation to the power of the real actually sketches an idea of God perfectly determinate, common to all, and in its enigmatic character, already taking us to a live discussion, that is, to a live testing, not just a speculative one, of the reality of that absolutely absolute reality. Does this reality exist? That is the question we must now address.

§2

JUSTIFICATION OF THE REALITY OF GOD

As I indicated at the beginning of this chapter, the problem of the reality of God is not merely a theoretical problem, but a personal one as well. This is why the point of departure and the basis of the discussion is religation as completely factual and as the root of the construction of my I. This religation is an experience, that is, a physical enterprise, some characteristics of which may profitably be reviewed at this point, even at the risk of being repetitious. Above all, religation is something that compels us to make our own I. In religation *we are forcibly led* to build our own I. In the second place, we are led *physically*; that is, we are not dealing merely with some conceptual progression, but a real and physical progression of our person. In the third place, we are led physically but in a *problematic way*. Religation is the experience of the problematic nature of our own being; it is a problem which is physically problematic. And so, this physical problem is what we must now explain. It is the problem of God.

Justification of the reality of God is not a piling of speculative arguments on top of speculative arguments, but rather the intellective explanation of the progress of religation. It is an intellective explanation; as such it cannot but involve a moment of grounding. It is the explanation of an experience we *here-and-now experience physically*; and therefor it always has that resonance of a problem so characteristic of personal life. {135} This explanation will be carried out in several steps.

I

The human being is a substantive reality one of whose essential notes is intelligence. Formally intelligence is the capacity to apprehend things as realities. Therefore, reality is the formality proper to everything a human apprehends intellectively. Also, real things are given primarily through impression. Hence in each impression there are two distinct moments: one, which we may call (without questioning the finer points of the term) "content" or "quality" of what is apprehended, and another which is the moment of its formality as real, what I have called the "impression of reality". This is not a second impression added to quality, but rather both are moments of a single impression, the single impression of a real thing. I refer to this as "impression of reality" only for ease of communication. This impression, let us emphasize, is a physical moment of the thing: the thing is not only red, heavy, etc., but also real. Since to apprehend reality is intelligence, and to have impressions is sensing, it follows that the intellective apprehension of the human being is sentient: its intelligence is a *sentient intelligence*. From this we draw important conclusions.

1. It certainly follows that the human being is *among* the things it apprehends, but is in them *in* reality. The human being is a substantive reality which, thanks to its type of intelligence, lives in reality sentiently. Each new thing that reaches it not only follows the previous one or joins with it, but is {136} a new thing in reality: each human spends the entire course of its life in reality. The human being lives in the field of reality and in the real world. And among the "things" of its life its own substantive reality is inscribed. To put it briefly, a human being, by virtue of its sentient intelligence, constitutes and *moves himself in the "medium" of reality.*

2. Since my own substantive reality belongs to this medium, it follows that a human performs its activities, not only in view of their content but precisely and formally in terms of my own reality *qua* reality. Therefore the acts of a human are not only acts belonging to him in his own right, but are formally and in a double sense "his or her own", they are acts of *his or her* reality. Hence, a human being is a reality that is "its own": it is a person. "Personhood" is "its-ownness" (*suidad*). This is not a psychological character but a metaphysical structure.

3. What does a person do when performing acts? Certainly that in which its reality consists: talking, running, sleeping, etc. But the person does something else, because not only do I "talk", "run", "sleep", etc., but while acting, "I am" a speaker, "I am" a runner, "I am" a sleeper, etc. That is, in its acts, a human being acquires the figure of that which we call *I*. To live is to acquire an *I* which exhibits a figure of this or that type. And the whole of life is but the progressive configuration of my *I*: it is not "I eat", but rather "*I* am the one that eats", etc.

4. What is this *I*? It is the figure of the being which I acquire through my acts. A human being is a substantive reality, and the *I* formally consists in the worldly actualization of this reality. It is

the figure of my being in reality, of which I am a real part: it is *I* eating, *I* talking, etc. {137}

But that is not all. Not only am *I* who talks but "it is *I* who is". My *I*, my being, is something that configures itself with respect to the reality *in* which I am and *in* which I move. My being configures itself not only with respect of things qualitatively determined, but with respect to these things *qua* real. In other words, the *I* "is" confronting the whole of reality regardless of type: stone, neighbor, God himself. Confronting any reality *qua* reality, *I* am who I am. By virtue of this, the being of a human, his or her *I*, is an "ab-solute" being. It is absolute because it is mine, and because it is determined in function of reality itself *simpliciter*.

5. However, though the *I* is an absolute being, this is something acquired. By virtue of this we shall say that the *I* is the "relatively ab-solute" being. Relatively, because it is an acquired being; but absolute in the sense we have just explained. And since the acquired is absolute it follows that a human being is radically *restless* in life. And since this restlessness is constitutively inscribed in my reality *qua* reality, it follows that it is this reality that clamors in that restlessness. This clamor is the *voice of conscience*. The voice of conscience is the clamor of reality on its way to absolute being. Reality becomes present to me as an announcement in the voice of conscience.

Here we have the first step of our explanation: the personal life of a human being consists in possessing itself by making its own *I*, its own being, which is a relatively absolute being, an acquired absolute.

II

How does a person acquire it? A person makes its *I* with things, with other persons and with itself as reality. {138} This "with" is not a "relational" addition to the reality of the person but is a constitutive moment of it, a constituting respectivity. It is constitutive not only "naturally," that is, not only because the "with" stems from what a human being is in its own right, but because it is *formally* constitutive of the person: to be a person consists in being it "with." What is the nature of this "with"?

1. A person makes his or her life, realizes his or her *I*, his relatively absolute being, with that in he or she is. A human being is *among* and *with* "things" (in the widest sense of the term) but, as we pointed out, that aspect of them *in* which he is, for the effects of his absolute being, is reality itself. The "with" refers formally to

reality. A person, therefore, makes his absolute being with very reality of real things, that is, with reality *simpliciter*, as we mentioned. And so, in effect, the character of reality is that in which each human ultimately is. The *ultimateness* (completion or fulfillment) of the character of reality not only concerns real things (as is obvious), but is *eo ipso* the fulfillment of the absolute being of the person: the latter configures itself on the former. In addition, any personal activity is the realization of possibilities. But every possibility is grounded on the fact that it is reality that makes it possible for a human being to be an *I*. And thus, reality is the ultimate possibility of life, of the being of each human. That is to say, a human being not only is "in" reality but makes its absolute being "from" reality: reality is not only ultimate but *that which makes possible*. And not only this, but each human inexorably has to make his or her own absolute being. To be absolutely is not only a possibility, but a something compulsory that comes from reality itself. A human being not only lives "in" reality and "from" reality, but also "by" {139} reality. Reality is not only ultimate and possibilitating, is also *impelling*. Reality is, as I said, that "with" which a human being makes its own *I*, its absolute being. And it does so, indeed, because the structure of this "with" consists in being "in, from and by", i.e., because reality is ultimate, possibilitating and impelling.

2. Whence reality is not a kind of "object" to which my person is referred, but rather the very ground of my absolute being: reality is a power, the *power of the real*. The power of the real is not causality. Causality is the functionality of the real *qua* real. But power is the dominance of the real *qua* real. Reality is dominating, is power, purely and simply because it is real. And the dominance of this power is, in our case, the power to make us be absolute. Dominance is dominance of fundamentality of my absolute *I*.

3. How does it dominate? To be sure, it is not a type of physical force because it is a power and not a cause. Nevertheless, reality is a determining formal principle. Determination is not the same as causality. Although not a force, reality is physically determining. And it is so, not only because a determinate act, my act, is physical, but also and *above all* because reality in itself is a physical character of things. We have seen this already: the impression of reality gives us impressively the physical moment of the reality of a thing. From this it follows that reality *simpliciter* is something formally physical. By virtue of this, reality itself is in itself and formally a physical determinant of my absolute being. This singular characteristic of being something "physical" without

being a "force" is just what takes place in the essence of religation. That is why religation {140} is something physical, but is not mere connection.

Religated to the power of the real as ultimate, possibilitating and impelling, I find myself physically determined by it in my absolute being. Therefore, what determines us physically is reality itself, reality as a whole. Reality as a whole is what *"makes me be I"*. Absolute being is acquired through the physical determination of the power of the real as something ultimate, possibilitating and impelling. Here is the second step of our explanation.

III

What is this power of the real in things? The power of the real is a power that things have *qua* real; and *qua* real they constitute a part or moment (the term is unimportant) of that which we call "reality itself." Therefore, we ask ourselves, what is that reality in real things that, as a power, physically determines our *I*, and makes us acquire our absolute being?

1. Above all, reality itself is not a mere general concept. This we have pointed out before: it is a physical moment of things and also determines us physically. Whatever its concept may be, that which we call "reality itself" is a physical moment of things.

2. However, it is not like a kind of sea in which things would be floating or submerged. Reality itself is neither a mere concept nor something separate from things, as if it were an envelope surrounding them. Reality is always and only a characteristic of things, the formality itself of each thing *qua* real. Reality and its power are in real things themselves. {141}

To be sure, what determines a person is reality itself, but reality itself is a moment of things themselves. A human being is not in reality except by being among and with things.

3. Nonetheless, in each real thing, by the mere fact of being real, its moment of reality in a certain way exceeds that which it is concretely. The impression of reality is physically transcendent to each thing. Because of this, real things have the power of determining my relatively absolute being. What does this mean?

A) First, in things themselves, their moment of reality exceeds the specific concretion of each thing. To be real is "more" than being this or that. Reality is not like an ocean, but rather a character of things and in things; and yet this character has the peculiarity of not exhausting itself in that which each thing is. This is what I express by saying that to be real is "more" than to be this glass of water, this pair of glasses, etc. In a certain way, each concrete real thing is more than what it is concretely. What is this "more"?

At first sight one might think that it is a case of "composition" of the real thing and its character of reality. But this is not so. This idea of composition, at best, would be a special conceptualization of the "more", but it could never be the naked fact of the "more". Personally, I am far from admitting such a special conceptualization.

From another point of view it might be thought that reality is a mere transcendental concept, and because of this its content would be found as if "contracted" to each thing. In this case, what would be intellectively known *primo et per se* would just be {142} the being "and nothing more"; and it is *in being* (rather than reality) where we would intellectively know each thing as a contraction of being. In other words, it would not be the case that in the thing we intellectively know "more" than what the thing is concretely; rather, knowing a thing would be to intellectively know "less" of what being is. Confronting this conceptualization, let us put aside the fact that it identifies reality and being, and that it considers transcendentality as a mere concept. I do not share either of these ideas; I have insisted, actually, upon the difference between reality and being as a sequential act of reality, and also upon the physical character of the moment of reality. But what is decisive is something different: that truth resides in just the opposite of what we have been told. And this because what I intellectively know *in the thing* is that being real is "more" than being this particular thing. Where I intellectively know the "more" is *in the thing itself*, not in some being prior to it. Therefore, there is no contraction of reality itself to this real thing but, on the contrary, there is something like an "expansion" of the real character of each thing beyond what it concretely is. Therefore, when I intellectively know each real thing, I intellectively know in the thing itself that to be real is "more" than being this or that.

Composition and transcendentality (in the classical sense), are two conceptualizations of something prior and radical: of the sheer "more". They are grounded on the "more" but do not constitute it primarily or formally—as if the "more" were grounded in composition or transcendentality. Metaphysics has accustomed us to take the received concepts as if they were the primary characteristics of things. But this is not the case. With respect to our problem, it is necessary to consider the "more" in its preconceptual primacy. To say that to be real is "more" than being this or that particular thing means first that the moment of reality of this pair of glasses, {143} for example, is not to be identified "simply" with just being this pair of glasses, and second, that the moment of reality of this pair of glasses is a characteristic which exceeds in a certain way the reality of the glasses, because in this reality I am somehow given reality *simpliciter*. It is not the case that in this pair of glasses what I apprehend is "this real pair of glasses" plus reality, but that in this real pair of glasses its reality is not reduced to just being this real pair of glasses. The "more" is quite imprecise. And because of this the intelligence must determine it accurately. This "more" is given to me in the impression of reality. The proof resides in the fact that it is this character of reality *simpliciter* (and not the reality of the pair of glasses) that is what, in the pair of glasses, determines my absolute personal being. It is as reality *simpliciter* that we encounter the power of the real in the real pair of glasses. Reality itself *simpliciter* has a physical power.

B) And this is the second point. The character of reality is not only "more" than that which each real thing is in particular, but it is that *in each real thing* that determines my relatively absolute being *qua* absolute. The power of the real, although it is not a power outside or above concrete real things, nevertheless is a power of reality itself *qua* reality; it is something "more" than the power of concrete realities, since in each concrete thing, however modest, I am determining myself before reality itself as such; this is precisely the *root* of my absolute being. Reality itself has a physical power, which means that each real thing transports a character and a power which is not exhausted in the reality of concrete things which, as real, have power over me. The "more" is a *constitutive moment* of the power of the real: the power of the real is the power of the real in its total "more".{144} As a moment of things and a determinant of the *I*, the power of the real is "more" than the reality and the power of each concrete real thing. Each real thing carries *physically* in its reality the character and the power of reality itself *simpliciter*; this is the third step of our explanation.

IV

What is this character of reality according to which it has the power to determine my relative absolute being? To ask this question is to ask about the foundation of that unity between what something really is in its concretion and the moment in accordance with which being real is "more" than being this or that. It is also to ask in what this strange unity consists. Because it is in this unity wherein ultimately resides the reality of the thing, as well as the power of this reality.

1. Above all, we must recognize that when each aspect is taken by itself, something undeniable can be inferred. The difficulty starts when one thinks about something else equally undeniable, namely, that we are dealing with aspects of one and the same reality, with the reality of each thing. And this is because what now jumps out at us is that what we said in the previous step is not clear at all. What is the origin of the difficulty? At first one might think that the difficulty stems from a lack of precision and rigor in the ideas. But even allowing for this, the truth is that the difficulty has deeper roots. It is not a difficulty residing in our ideas, but in the constitution of the real thing. The thing itself, in a certain way, is ambivalent: on one hand there is its "immersion" in itself, and on the other there is its "expansion" to more {145} than itself; it is at one and the same time and formally "its own" irreducible reality and presence of reality itself. This ambivalence is real; any real thing, *qua* real, is this way. Consequently, the first thing to be done is to recognize this fact. The difficulty is not in the bluntness of the ideas, but in the structure of the thing itself. A real thing, *qua* real, is this strange ambivalent overlapping of being "this" reality, and being the presence of reality itself. This structural overlapping is what we formally designate as the "enigma" of reality. To say that any real thing is an enigma means that reality possesses that structural ambivalence. And conversely, to say that reality possesses this ambivalent structure, affirms that reality is structurally enigmatic.

2. The enigmatic character of reality is not something extraneous to the power of the real. Just the opposite. Precisely because reality is enigmatic we are religated to the power of the real in a problematic way. The power of the real is an enigmatic power, and because of this, religation religates me to it in a problematic way. What is problematic in religion is the living presence of what is enigmatic about reality. That is the meaning of the affirmation we have repeated many times: we are physically religated to the power of the real in a problematic way. Now we can see why. First, reality itself is enigma, ambivalence. Second, as a consequence, the determination of my relative absolute being is *eo ipso* enigmatic; this is what formally constitutes the enigma of life. Life is constitutively enigmatic because to live is to construct my relative absolute being, and this is enigmatic because the power of the real that serves as its foundation is enigmatic. From this several important consequences follow. {146}

A) The determination of my relative absolute being is the physical living presence of the enigma of reality. This living presence is restlessness. Restlessness, I have pointed out, is not agitation amidst the turmoil of life, nor is it necessarily a constant change of one's situation. On the contrary, restlessness is something much closer to a type of quiescence, that strange mixture of rest and motion, that species of dynamic repose. Such restlessness is always just restlessness for the absolute of being. It is not the restlessness that takes us from one thing to another, as for example the restlessness which St. Augustine mentions; rather it is an intrinsic and formal restlessness belonging to each act, because in the least of his acts, a human being, when making its absolute being, always senses in an express or muted way this double question: What is going to *become of me*, of my absolute being? And, what am I going to *make of myself*, given that I myself am the one making? The unity of these two questions is radical restlessness: the restlessness of being relatively absolute.

B) Since the power of the real is enigmatic, the intelligence confronts the reality given to it as something that is present, but is propelled by reality itself "towards" its radical enigma. The intelligence is not only intentionally "*directed*" towards, but physically "*propelled*" towards. The "towards" is not a going "towards" but rather is a moment of the apprehended reality itself: it is not the case of "towards reality" but of "reality as towards". The impression of reality is not the exclusive monopoly of any type of sensing—of the visual, for example—but covers all sensing, including orientation and equilibrium. That is why reality is not only something present as in the case of sight, but has other ways of being present. One of them is {147} the "towards". And these diverse ways are not simply juxtaposed but are intrinsically articulated (I cannot enter into this problem here) into a unitary apprehension of reality. All the ways, insofar as penetrated by the "towards", take us from themselves "towards" something beyond what is immediately apprehended in different ways, sound towards the sonorous thing, etc. The essential point is that it is not our reflections, but reality itself that is taking us towards this beyond. We are being taken by reality through reality. Hence, in our case, the enigma of reality is the intellection of reality in a very precise "towards", namely, towards the radical ground of each real thing. The power of the real not only determines us physically in a problematic way; this determination *is* the very problem of the ground of the structure of reality *qua* reality. Religation is religation to reality in its enigma.

3. Propelled by reality itself towards its enigma, our intelligence can discover what the knot of the difficulty is. The power of the real, like any power, is grounded on the properties (let us put it this way) that the thing having that power possesses; if did not possess them, it could not have the power. And here is the knot of the difficulty. The power of the real is grounded on the constitution of reality *qua* reality. The power of the real, as a determinant of my relative absolute being, is a power which is grounded on reality itself. However, that reality is not the one belonging to *this particular pair of glasses*, because to be real is "more" than being this pair of glasses. But neither is the power of the real simply the power of that reality which this pair of glasses is. Because together *with* the pair of glasses, that *in* which I now am is in reality itself *simpliciter*; for it is there that I determine {148} myself in my relative absolute being, as we already pointed out. From this there are two decisive consequences.

A) The reality on which this power is grounded is not concrete real things. In other words, all things are real, but none is reality itself (reality as a whole). But reality itself is real because it determines me physically, making me be relatively absolute. Therefore, there is another reality on which reality itself is grounded. And this reality is not one more concrete thing, because it is not "*a*" reality but the ground of reality itself. And as ground of a power determining my relatively absolute being, it must be an absolutely absolute reality. This is just what the reality of God is. Only because this reality exists can there be a power of the real determining me in my relative absolute being.

B) But I find this power of the real in the concrete reality of each thing. This means that the absolutely absolute reality, that is, God, is present *formally* in things constituting them as real. The presence of God in real things is primarily that of a formal character. God is not primarily present in real things as the cause is in its effect, but is present as constituting them formally as real. The possible effective causation of God with respect to things is a later interpretation required by something prior: by the formal presence of God in things. And this presence consists in the fact that the reality of each thing is constituted "*in* God." God is not a reality which is there *in addition* to real things and hidden behind them, but is in real things themselves in a formal way. Therefore, absolutely absolute reality is certainly different than each real thing, but is constitutively {149} present in each in a formal way. That is why each real thing is intrinsically ambivalent. Each thing, on one hand, is its own irreducible reality; but, on the other, is formally constituted in the absolutely absolute reality, in God. Without God "in" the thing, it would not be real, it would not be its own reality. And this unity is precisely the resolution of the enigma of reality. The ambivalence of reality simply consists in this double moment of not being God, yet being now, formally, constituted in God. That is why a thing is "its own" reality and a presence of reality itself; that is why the power of the real is in it. I shall return to this character of the real later.

Consequently, God exists, and is formally and wonderfully constituting the reality of each thing. Because of this He is the ground of the reality of each thing and of the power of the real in it. Here we have the fourth step of our explanation.

Reviewing the previous steps, we shall put it simply: the personal life of a human being consists in possessing itself, and through religation making its own *I*, its own being. This being is an acquired absolute being and therefore is relatively absolute (first step). It is acquired by means of the physical determination of the power of the real as something ultimate, possibilitating and impelling (second step). As a moment of things and determinant of the *I*, the power of the real is "more" than reality, and therefore, "more" than the power of each real concrete thing (third step). But the power of the real is grounded essentially in the nature of reality itself. Hence, this power is grounded on an absolutely absolute reality, distinct from real things, formally constituting them as real things by virtue of that absolutely absolute reality. This reality, then, is God (fourth step). {150}

It is by this constituting presence of God in things and of these in God that the power of the real in things becomes possible, that power through which *I* live, i.e., through which I make my absolute *I* with them. I make my life with things, and without them I would not be able to live. But what I do with them, I do thanks to the fact that they are constituted as real in God. Without God as a *formally* constitutive moment of the reality of things they would lack their primary and radical condition of being determinants of my being, simply because they would not be "reality". And conversely, only by being real do they have that power, and they are real only be being so in God. Thanks to this, my being is grounded in God insofar as He is constitutively present *in a formal way* in what things have of reality. Real things, through their power of the real, give me God *in their very reality* when they give me their reality To justify the existence of God is simply to explain the truth of this phrase. This justification is certainly a grounding, though not a speculative reasoning process; rather it is intellective knowing of the true progress of our religation. That is why this "proof" is not a demonstration of the mathematical variety. It always has the resonance of the progress of personal life. And therefore it only becomes complete through the development of the entire book. The whole book is what gives this proof the demonstrative power of a physical experience.

V

What now remains is to clarify the point at which we have arrived, in order to recognize that we have reached God *qua* God. It is not {151} a question of inference, but an examination of where we are in the intellectual understanding of the path of religation.

By that path we have reached the determination of my relatively absolute being, of my *I*, thanks to the power of the real. This power is grounded on the constitution of reality itself. hence this way is not anthropological or cosmic, but a higher one, the way of reality. Through it we discover an absolutely absolute reality which, as we have just seen, is the ground as much of the power of the real as of the reality of the things in which that power is grounded. This ground is a ground formally constitutive of reality, and therefore of my *I*. Thus, being formally present in real things, the absolutely absolute reality, i.e., God, has two aspects. First, the aspect according to which by its own nature it is what *grounds* of the power of the real; and second, that aspect which concerns the power of the real as *grounded* in God.

1. The absolutely absolute reality is the ground of the power of the real. Now, the power of the real is reality as dominant and as ultimate, possibilitating and impelling. Therefore, absolutely absolute reality has at one and the same time and by elevation these three aspects. In other words, it is God *qua* God. Having reached this point, we can well perceive how different it is from the terminus of the cosmic and anthropological ways. It is only God *qua* God that is the reality which is absolutely ultimate, the fountain of all the possibilities which a human being has to be able to live, and on which it supports itself in order to be. None of these moments considered in isolation comprises what we all understand by "God," nor what {152} this term means throughout the history of religions. That is why the *Theós* of Aristotle is not God properly speaking. One might think then about the famous distinction of Pascal between the God of the philosophers and the God of the religions. He is correct but only partly correct. First, because we need to be told in what the God of religions consists; and Pascal does not tell us. Second, because the God of religions is the God that one always reaches philosophically as long as philosophy

does not buttress itself with Greek notions. The way of religation has philosophically reached an absolutely absolute reality which is an ultimate, possibilitating and impelling reality, that is to say, the God of religions *qua* God. This requires more detailed examination.

When we say that God is the ground of the power of the real, "ground" certainly designates some form of causality, but not one of the four causes of classical metaphysics. By repeated study of the distinctions between these four different types of causes, we tend to think that they exhaust all the possible types of causality. But much more importantly, we loose sight of causality as such. From my point of view, causality is the functionality of the real *qua* real. Taken in its fullness, this concept of functionality is liberated from the idea of "influence", and most importantly, leaves open the type of causality which may intervene in each case. The reality of the real, as its own physical moment, is grounded on the absolutely absolute reality; therefore, a functionality of reality itself with respect to God exists. But this does not prejudge, even remotely, the type of this functionality. Let us consider it.

A) To say that God is the ground of the reality of {153} things does not formally imply that God "makes" all things, that He is their efficient cause, or even that He is their creator. Not all the gods of the various religions have that character of creator, but they do not thereby stop being ultimate realities. Yes, the Christian God is creator. But on this point I share the thinking of Duns Scotus, that creation is a truth of *faith* but not of *reason*. The foundational ultimateness of God simply means the following: in real things reality itself is a physical moment of them. And this moment would not exist unless grounded on the presence of God in them, as a formal constituent of their reality. Without God, things would not be real. God is, then, the ground of the ultimateness of reality and of its power. What kind of grounding this may be is a question that remains open for the time being.

B) God is the ground that allows reality to be possibilitating to humans. All human possibilities are inscribed in reality. Consequently, as ground of the character of reality, God is not just one more possibility, but the possibility of possibilities. He is the absolute possibility, another kind of grounding. That is why human beings, by the power of the real, find themselves turned towards God as absolute possibilitator: this is God as donor of possibilities. To be sure, just as in the case of fulfillment, this possibilitating character of God remains open to subsequent determinations. Primarily and formally it does not mean omnipotence, providence, or mercy. These are truths of faith, but not of reason. They are truths grounded in what formally refers to God in a primary way. In this respect the only thing which primarily fits God *qua* God is to be absolute possibility. Only by being this, can He be what faith {154} says about Him: merciful, etc. It is the possibility of making the *I* from God, or to put it better, the possibility of being from God.

C) Finally, God is ground of reality as the impelling power in the construction of my *I*; He is the ground of the compulsion to be my *I*. The question remains open as to the type of this compulsion. Of course, it is not mere physical "force": God is not the prime mover of my life. Nor is He an obligation; any obligation presupposes the compulsion to be *I*. The character of compulsion is given by the nature of that to which we are compelled, viz. to be my *I*. My *I* is to be relatively absolute and God is absolutely absolute reality. For this reason the human being, it has usually been said, is a "little God". But it is necessary to say in what his "smallness" consists; and this is not generally forthcoming. To my way of thinking, it consists in that a human's absolute being is acquired and therefore is relative. "Little" means "relative": the human being is a relative God. And so, to say that reality is an impelling power means, on the one hand, that the absolute is "in reality" absolutely inexorable, by being now intrinsically supported and grounded on the absolutely absolute reality in which God consists. God, in this sense, is the firm support of my being, of my *I*. The Semites called God a "firm rock." This subtle and inexorable unity of the relative and the absolute, present in the absolute of my being, is, in a certain way, a dynamic unity since it is that which impels humans to make their own absolute being.

As an absolutely absolute reality, God is the ground of reality as radical ultimateness, possibility of possibilities, and compulsoriness of my realization as absolute being. These are three different ways of {155} grounding, and therefore of the functionality of the real with respect to God. They cannot be reduced to any of the four classical causes, and still less be juxtaposed among themselves. On the contrary: by being an absolutely absolute reality, God is, at one and the same time and formally the ultimate, possibilitating and impelling reality. Because of this He is God *qua* God.

Here we have the foundational character of divine reality. What is the nature of this power of the real insofar as it is grounded in God?

2. The power of the real, as we have seen, is grounded in God as formally and constitutively present in real things. This means that in some way the power of the real intrinsically and formally

incorporates, as a moment of its own, the power of the absolutely absolute reality, that is, the power of God, or better yet, God as power. How does it do so? Certainly, the power of the real is not formally the power of God, just as a real thing is not formally God. But the power of the real "transports" the power of God, transports God as power: real things are, on that account, the "seat" of God as power. Insofar as it is grounded in God, the power of the real is "vehicle" and "seat". What is this double character?

God, I reiterate, is present in things formally constituting them in their reality; only because of this is there in things a power of the real as determinant of my absolute *I*. Therefore, the mode of presence of God in the power of the real consists in this power being a "manifestation" of the absolutely absolute reality. Furthermore, to be a "vehicle" formally consists in being "manifestation". The power of the real manifests {156} God as power in things precisely when determining my absolute being. Also, since the power of the real is grounded, as I say, in the reality of God present formally and constitutively in real things, it turns out that what this manifestation manifests is just this constituting presence. And this presence, as manifested in the power of the real, is what makes things be the "seat" of God as power. Real things and the power of the real are not God, but they are more than mere "effects" of God. Formally they are what I shall call *deity*. To be a seat is to be deity. Deity is not, indeed, a pseudo-divine vaporous character but the very reality of things, a reality that as power manifests their formal constitution in God. The Greeks used to say that Nature, *Phýsis*, is divine, is *theíon*, because according to them it is immortal and inexhaustible; in other words, it is always young. This is not admissible today from any point of view. Nonetheless, with this notion the Greeks touched something essential that has not found its proper place in philosophy: the character of things which are neither gods nor divine, but still have something of this character, viz. they are formally deity. Real things *qua* real are the deity manifesting God, who is in them formally, constituting them. And because of this character of deity they are the manifestation, the vehicle of God.

Religation is the radical dimension of my substantive reality *qua* personal, that is, insofar as that reality makes its *I*, its being. From this it follows that with the experience of this making one is experiencing the power of the real, and consequently the power of deity (here experience is physical demonstration of reality). Therefore, it is an experience which profiles not only the idea of God, but {157} His absolutely absolute reality insofar as it is manifested under the form of deity. And this experience is the radical experience of the human person insofar as it makes the figure of its own *I*.

This experience, as I indicated a few pages earlier, is not only individual but historical. History is, in this respect, a vast historical experience of deity, indeed, of real things as the seat and vehicle of God as power. We must not understand this experience as the primary radical form of experience; without personal experience historical experience would not be possible. But historical experience is the one that gives the experience of the deity its ultimate concrete profile. Of course, that experience has continued to adopt concrete forms throughout the history of the world's religions. This theme will be reserved for other studies. (An allusion was made to it in Appendix 1 dedicated to the power of the real.) And thus, slowly but surely, history continues to sketch out the figure of deity. We must add that this figure is not exhausted in the life and the history which has transpired until now.

Let us summarize: God *qua* God is the absolutely absolute reality as ultimateness, possibilitation and impellence, formally present in real things and constituting their reality. That reality is *eo ipso* deity and manifestation of God, not in a general and abstract way, but in all the concretion history reveals to us. Such is the reality of God, justified by the way of religation.

As a sort of conclusion to this point, let us emphasize some aspects of what we might call the role of God in life as construction of my *I*, of my relatively absolute being. {158}

VI

What I understand by the role of God in the construction of my *I* is the way the fundamentality of this construction is exercised *on the part of God*. Strictly speaking, the subject was discussed throughout the earlier part of the book, but once again, it may be useful to explicitly disengage this aspect of the question for detailed examination.

1. Let us return to the conclusion we have reached. Religation religates us to the power of the real, or rather, the power of the real keeps us religated. This is a power that, in one of its aspects, is grounded in God, who is formally present in real things, which are, therefore, deity. By virtue of this, that which in religation religates us is God, through the deity of the power of the real. Now, among these real things my own substantive reality is present. In it, consequently, God is also constitutively present. And it is this

presence which, in a religating way, determines the construction of my relatively absolute being, of my *I*. Therefore, the presence of God in my substantive reality is not merely a real presence in itself. If it were just this, God would be but a mere *object* among others, perhaps the most sublime of all objects, but nothing more; and therefore the most that I could do would be to direct myself to Him. This is not the case. God is not an object but precisely and formally the terminus of religation. I am not *directed* but *religated* to Him. Therefore, God is not an *object*; prior to being an object and in order to be able to be one, He is *ground*. He is foundational in my destination to be absolute. Here I consider fundamentality only with respect to human life; in subsequent paragraphs I shall refer to the fundamentality of everything real as such. To be ground is {159} more than to be an object. The object *qua* object is mere *objectum*, something which is "in front" of me as that which it is, in and by itself, and therein exhausts its mode of presence. On the other hand, a ground is a reality which certainly manifests itself to me, not "in front" of me but "in" my intelligence, not only insofar as what it is in and by itself, but as far as it is grounding my entire life. We shall anchor this difference terminologically with the expressions *reality-object* and *reality-ground*. To be ground is not a relation extrinsically added to the reality-object. That is to say, it is not the case that something is present as an object in and by itself, and that "later", in addition, it may be something with which I act in my life. No. In the reality-ground its very way of presence in me is a grounding presence; so that fundamentality is an intrinsic moment to the way by which that particular reality is present to me. Therefore, there are not two moments, one of reality-object and another of fundamentality, but only one single type of presence: reality-ground. This in no way prevents that presence from being a presence of reality in and by itself: in reality-ground we have present "at one and the same time" *reality*-ground and reality-*ground*. Indeed, this is the case of the reality of God. God is present to me as reality-ground. Therefore, my "relation" with Him is not a theoretical "consideration" but a vital "intimation". Only the ground is the terminus of religation. The distinction between reality-object and reality-ground is absolutely essential. Consequently, God is ground and only by being so can He become an object for me at any moment. By being ground, His presence in me is in a certain way dynamic; this is the religating dynamism. It is not a mere real presence, {160} but an unfolding of the self-same religating fundamentality in the constitution of my *I* itself, i.e., of my life. And this unfolding is precisely what I understand by the function of God in my life.

2. God is formally and constitutionally present in my reality. And since this reality is the one that makes my absolute being, it follows that the presence of God in life, in my *I*, concerns my whole being in a radical and total way. Because of this, God is not primarily a resource that a human being needs to carry out its life or fix its problems. On the contrary, He is the constituent of my being and, therefore, is the ground of the *plenitude* of life in all its being. And I am not talking about the God of Christianity, but of God *qua* God. The God of Christianity is but the definitive revelation of God *qua* God. As a consequence of this, Christianity addresses the plenitude of life, primarily and formally, not by the "Christian" (so to speak) nature of its God, but because in Him the nature of God *qua* God is expressed. And conversely, this idea of the Christian God would be impossible if God as such were not a formal constituent of the plenitude of life. Likewise, God is not primarily that to which a human directs itself as to "another" world and "another" life, but is just what constitutes this life and this world. The ""other" world is a matter of faith and not of pure reason. That is why, if one wishes to speak about a return to God (we shall deal with atheism in the next Chapter) it is unnecessary to be a prophet in order to say that each human will return to God, not to escape from this world and from this life, from others and from itself, but on the contrary to be able to maintain itself in being, to be able to continue being what it will inexorably never cease to be {161} and must be: a relatively absolute *I*. Therefore, the function of God in life is, above all, a function that addresses itself to the plenitude of life and not to its indigence. God is not primarily a "help" for acting but a "ground" for being. In this manner, God is ground of life in a triple way: as Author, God makes me make myself, be *myself*; as Actor, God is the *route or plan* of my life and of my history; as Agent, God makes me act. Consequently, God is the ground of my freedom, of the plan of my life, and of the carrying out of my own acts.

3. This formal constituting presence of God in the life of each human, as plenitude, may seem to diminish the distinction between God and humans, because on the one hand, I am real while being so in God, and on the other hand, I am not God but my *I*. The same occurs in the case of any real thing, as we shall see in the next paragraph; but here I limit myself to humans. In actuality, the matter does not have anything to do with tracing out boundaries between God and humans, as if here were my *I* and God were in front of me and outside of me. The "distinction" between humans and God does not mean the drawing of a "boundary" which circumscribes two precincts. To distinguish in

this context is not to reduce things to two juxtaposed and confronted areas, the terrain of God and the terrain of humans. Nor is it "frontier building". On the contrary, precisely because human beings are not God, it is God who is makes humans not be God, and that this "not-being-God" be a way of being "in" God. With all due metaphysical rigor, this structure is not a limitation, but on the contrary, an implication with a special character: a constituting tension, a tension which I would call *theological tension*. I have repeatedly pointed out that in humans there is always the radical restlessness about their own relatively absolute being. Now we understand why: {162} because human life is a constitutive and constituting theological tension. That my *I* may be absolute does not mean that in itself it has nothing to do with the real world and with God; on the contrary, it means that it has to do with everything, including God himself, but in an absolute way, i.e., *divinely*. That is, I have to deal with God divinely. Therefore, the function of God in life is not only to be its plenitude, but also to be the dynamic tension in the march towards the absolute of my being. This is the reason why, when it is said that a human being has a spark of the divine, a truth is expressed; but it was necessary to rigorously conceptualize what this "spark" is. It is not some vague similarity of properties, but the constituting tension of my relatively absolute being in the absolutely absolute reality: the constituting tension of my *I* as something absolute in God. It is an aspect of that which is theological in each human being.

There are two important consequences:

a) We are dealing with a theological tension constituent of my *I*. Hence, as I indicated above, it is not God who makes my *I*; *I* build my own *I*. But God is the one who "makes me make" my *I*, my being. That is the properly dynamic aspect of this tension. God is not mere *natura me naturans*, but *realitas me reificans*. Because to make my *I* is to constitute my reality in the form of my being, i.e., to make my reality be *realitas in essendo*. This making that I be my *I*, that I be my relatively absolute being, is essential to the function of God in my life. God is formally *quoad nos* the absolutely absolute reality which "makes things be" relatively absolute. God makes my human reality build its *I* in its own life.

b) Since any act, however minuscule and lacking in transcendence it may be by virtue of its content, contributes to the building of my *I* and my {163} relative absolute being, it becomes clear that any act is formally a *taking of a position* with respect to God. Because of this, insofar as I am the constructor of my *I*, no act, however modest in content, lacks transcendence: everything has

UNFOLDING OF THE PROBLEM: THE REALITY OF GOD   123

the transcendence of constituting me in God. The human being is *implanted* in divinity, metaphysically immersed in it, precisely because any action of his is the configuration of his absolute substantive being.

This is the functional structure of God in life: it is *ground* (and not object); it is ground of life's *plenitude* (and not of its indigence); and it is so in the form of a *dynamic tension* (but not of juxtaposition). This functional structure constitutes life, not in a hidden but in a rather open and evident way. Nothing of what has been said, granted the reality of God, goes beyond analysis and intellectual interpretation which if not immediate, is at least evident. What happens is that humans may ignore it, or may give different names to what we have called "God" and "function of God". But what those names designate is the same reality we have tried to justify. Hence, even though someone may ignore it, he or she will never be able to turn his or her back on this structure of the construction of his *I*.

And yet, someone may distance him- or herself from it and even submerge it in darkness. Because what humans support only with difficulty is not precisely God, but the absolute character in which their *I* consists. In the tension towards their absolute being they find themselves invaded by an internal and radical relaxation, by something like a *fatigue of the absolute*, a kind of theological fatigue. He would like to rest, to disentangle himself, even if episodically, from the necessity of always having to take a position on the absolute. Then {164} it is easy to reduce God to the category of a mere object one deals with. *Eo ipso* humans have delineated the way to believe they are living without God. But this is merely a distancing of oneself from Him. The *fatigue of the absolute*, the *objectifying* of God and the *distancing* of one's life from God are three essentially connected phenomena, each grounded on the previous one. They do not comprise the only source of atheism, by any strech of the imagination, but are a very general occurrence. Only the revitalizing power of religation can inject new vigor to the asthenia of the absolute; only this vigor can disclose the constituting tension of life; and only this tension is able to discover again a God present in the depths of the human spirit and of every reality. This is the culminating point of the way of religation.

So far we have seen first the point of departure and the basis for the discussion of the problem of the reality of God. Afterwards, we have attempted an intellectual justification of this reality. To conclude, let us say something concerning the characteristics of the reality of God. That will contribute to a final touch of clarity and rigor for this problem.

§3

SOME CHARACTERISTICS OF THE REALITY OF GOD

I. First we discuss some characteristics that concern God considered in Himself.

1. Above all, God is, as we have repeatedly seen, an absolutely absolute reality. If we wish to refer to the metaphysical essence of God as is done in classical theology, that is, to that concept which (according to our new way of thinking) would be the first and radical one by which we conceive God, I think that the metaphysical essence of God is to be an absolutely absolute reality. Indeed, this is something we have already seen: an absolutely absolute reality is the reality which is "in and by itself" full and absolute reality *qua* reality. At first glance this might seem to be another way of expressing what some classical theologians thought when saying that the metaphysical essence of God consisted in the identity of his essence with his existence, i.e., God would be that entity to whose essence pertains existing. But to my way of thinking, this is not correct either with respect to the two terms (*essence* and *existence*) or to their alleged identity. One might think it would be enough to conceive that existence belongs to the divine essence, i.e., that its essence is existential. But the fact is that we would have to add that in God his existence is pure essentiality (essential existence). God is distinct from existing things not only by virtue of that in which He consists, i.e., because existing pertains to that in which God consists; but He also differs from existing things by {165} reason of His very existence; what we call "to exist" is in God something *toto cælo* different than what we call "to exist" when referring to real things. From this follows that God is not a formal identity of essence and existence in the classical sense, but a reality that, through elevation, is not only above and beyond the difference of essence and existence, but also above and beyond its alleged identity. This is so because reality always consists in being "in its own right". And absolutely absolute reality is the absolute in its own right, something that by elevation is above and beyond the difference and identity men-

tioned. In God essence and existence are identical because He is the fullness of the "in its own right" in and by Himself, and not the other way around, as if He were the absolutely absolute reality because in Him essence and existence were formally identical. Therefore, we must not confuse the "in and by himself" with this identity. The metaphysical essence of God is to be absolutely absolute reality.

2. This reality is one and unique. We have actually come to this reality because it is the ground of the reality of real things *qua* real. Now, the reality of things is intrinsically and formally respective. In virtue of this, all things constitute a world. World is, for me, the respectivity of the real *qua* real. The world is, therefore, one and unique. By being its ground, God is essentially one and unique also. Aristotle thought that the *Theós* as supreme substance was the unmoved mover of the cosmos. But if there were different *kósmoi*, one would have to say that there would also be different unmoved movers, that is, different gods. And he admitted this with respect to the astronomy of Eudoxus, which counts 47 or 55 independent celestial spheres. But in my conceptualization one must distinguish carefully between *cosmos* and *world*. Cosmos is the {167} unity of real things by reason of their own nature, of what I have usually called their "suchness". From this point of view there would be no problem in admitting the possibility of different *kósmoi* independent from each other, that is, without any type of interaction. They would not constitute a *universe* but a *pluriverse*. Nevertheless, this is not the point of view we must take on the question at hand. All these *kósmoi*, though "cosmically" independent, are indeed "really" respective as realities. Hence, even though it might be possible to have different *kósmoi*, it is metaphysically impossible to have different worlds. The world is not, and cannot be anything but one and unique. Thus, God as ground of the world cannot be anything else but one and unique also. Not having distinguished cosmos and world constitutes a serious failure by Aristotle in this problem. Polytheism is metaphysically impossible: *uniqueness* is a characteristic of God. Here uniqueness does not mean a numerical characteristic, but something *transnumerical*. Uniqueness is an internal and formal characteristic of the divine reality. It is not the case that the absolutely absolute reality is unique because there are no others but rather, on the contrary, there can be no others because the absolutely absolute reality is, in and by itself, absolutely one.

3. The absolutely absolute reality is a reality of absolute concretion. God is not a vaporous absolute, because He is not "the"

absolute but "the reality" that is absolutely absolute. And this reality is concrete. It is not a case of taking the concrete as opposed to the abstract, but of taking it as primary *absolute concretion*. It is not a concretized reality but a reality absolutely concrete. Its absolutely absolute character carries with it the absolute {168} concretion; a concretion which does not constitute its reality, but on the contrary, is an absolute that, as absolute, "brings forth" (this is an inevitable anthropomorphic language) in itself the concretion of the absolute. This absolute concretion incorporates different aspects.

a) The absolutely absolute reality is *eo ipso* a reality absolutely "its-own". It consists, then, in absolute "its-ownness". Therefore, it is essentially personal, because personhood formally consists in its-ownness. If God were not absolutely His-own, He would not be absolutely absolute. In His absolute concretion, God is essentially personal.

b) Because He is absolutely absolute reality, He is absolute "dynamism". Every reality *qua* reality is in fact dynamic, not only in itself (which is obvious) but, as I see it, *by itself*. Dynamism is neither action nor operation; to my way of thinking, it is what I have called "outward self-expressing."[1] Every reality is real by being the plenitude of that which it is; and this plenitude is a moment of the "outward self expressing", a *formal moment* as such. Dynamism is not consequent upon reality as action or operation might be, but is a constitutive moment of it, of its formal constitution *qua* reality. And so, God, as absolutely absolute reality, is absolute dynamism, an absolute "self-giving". Since by virtue of being absolutely absolute reality He is absolutely "His-own", it follows that this self-giving cannot be transitive, either in the sense of making another out of Himself, or in the sense of making Himself out of Himself. It is a giving to Himself, that which He already is as His-own. It is, then, purely and simply auto-possession in His-ownness. Now, auto-possession is that in which life formally consists. Because of this, auto-possession in absolute its-ownness is *Absolute Life*. In it God does not make himself as a reality, that is, {169} the divine life is not a becoming; the only thing that in this life "occurs" (if I may be permitted such expression) is the plenary actuality of the absolutely absolute reality for itself: absolute auto-possession is but "auto-actuality". Therefore, God is absolute life because He is absolutely His-own, i.e., because He is a person. Contrary to what is usually said, I consider that God is not a person because He is living, but is living because He is a person. His life, his auto-possession, is grounded in his His-ownness. That God has absolute auto-possession means that His possession is a consequence of the fact that the *autos* is absolute dynamism; and this is so because He is an absolutely absolute reality, i.e., absolutely His own, indeed, because He is a person. We can then affirm that the absolute concretion of the divine His-ownness is to be life.

c) What comprises this auto-possession? Auto-possession is, as we have indicated, absolute actuality for itself. This actuality is, above all, actuality in the sense of presence of reality to itself. Also, this actuality is what formally constitutes what we call "intelligence". In virtue of this, the divine life is first and foremost life in intelligence. And since the actuality of the real in intelligence is what I have called "real truth," it follows that divine life consists in being its own real truth. But this is not enough, because auto-possession is essentially possession, that kind of active repose in itself, in its own reality, i.e., fruition. *Fruition is repose in the plenitude of one's own reality.* And so this actuality in the sense of fruition is what formally constitutes that which we call "volition". Therein, if we may put it this way, the plenary its-ownness of the absolutely absolute reality is consummated. By virtue of this, the divine life as {170} absolute is auto-fruition in auto-presence; it is fruition in its own real truth. In God, the absolute actuality of His reality as His-ownness is intelligent and volitional life. God not only has intelligence and volition, but is necessarily intelligent and volitional because He is absolute His-ownness, because He is a person. As seen from the perspective of men, in God intelligence and volition are the two aspects according to which the absolutely absolute reality possesses itself, the two aspects according to which God is His-own. The concretion of the absolutely absolute reality, of reality absolutely His-own, is absolute life; and the concretion of absolute life is intelligence and volition. In men, the his-ownness is consequent upon the nature of that which constitutes our substantive reality: we are persons *because* we are intelligent and volitional. Intelligence and volition are the mere *factum* of our substantive reality; and only by presupposing this *factum* are we persons necessarily. We are persons as a "result of" or by "implantation in" reality: human personhood is our mode of implantation in reality. Because of this, the being of a human is relatively absolute. But in God His substantive reality is absolute; therefore, it is absolutely His-own; He possesses Himself absolutely, and consequently is intelligent and volitional. In God, to my way of thinking, personhood is not consequent upon substantive reality nor upon His life, but is the very principle of it. Intelligence and volition are the way of being absolutely His-own, the way of realizing Himself with respect to what He already is as person. This clearly shows that, in God, intelligence and volition are necessary intrinsic moments of His substantive reality. The His-ownness is the ground of life, and life is the ground of intelligence and volition. {171}

Recapitulating, God is a reality absolutely personal, in a dynamism of absolute life, auto-actual in intelligence and volition. Here we find the absolute concretion of the absolutely absolute reality. We have developed the point without reference to feeling, but the same can be said of feeling as affection of His own reality.

Even at the risk of tiresome repetitions I beg indulgence to insist particularly on two points. In the first place, classical philosophy and theology have grounded the characteristics we have expressed in just the reverse order. They began by stating that human beings and God are two "analogous" realities because of intelligence and volition. By virtue of this and in an eminent way, God would have life and be a person. But to my way of thinking, the order of grounding has to be the reverse. That upon which the analogy has to be based primarily and formally is upon the character of "absolute": a human being in its relatively absolute being, God in his absolutely absolute reality. This is the primary and radical analogy: the analogy of the absolute. Therefore, it is not the case of a vague formal likeness of our intelligence and volition to the divine intelligence and volition, but that this "likeness" is grounded on the "analogical" character of the absolute. From this it follows that while in each human being its intelligent and volitional life is the reason for its personhood, in God His absolute personhood is the reason that He is alive and his life is intelligent and volitional. This is the first observation.

The second refers to the characteristics of God themselves. When we say that God is personal, living, intelligent, volitional, etc., we must avoid the serious error of taking these {172} terms in an anthropomorphical sense, as if God were a kind of gigantic human spirit, although purified of all the human limitations. This is absurd. How the reality of God may be in itself, it is impossible for us to know. Consequently, the aforementioned characteristics have to be taken in the strict sense according to which we have proceeded to conceive them. When we say that God is personal, the only thing we say is that He is a reality absolutely His-own. When we say that He is living, we understand that God is a reality that fully possesses itself. When we say that He is intelligent and volitional, we wish to express purely and simply that He is absolute actuality of His own transparent reality and sufficient to itself, etc. Neither should feeling be conceived anthropomorphically. That these characteristics may also be found in human beings in some measure cannot be denied. But we should observe, first, that we have not arrived at them through humans, but through what the absolutely absolute reality is. And second, that if a human being possesses them it is precisely because its being is relatively absolute, i.e., because God possesses them in an absolutely absolute way. God is not a kind of immense spirit or soul but rather absolutely absolute reality. From this stem the characteristics that concern God insofar as He is formally and constitutively present in things.

II. God is, with respect to real things, the foundational or grounding reality: I would call it *realitas fundamentalis*. Grounding is a character of the absolutely absolute reality. It is not a constitutive moment of absolutely absolute reality, but rather consequent upon it, because the absolutely absolute reality, precisely by being such, is real in and by itself, {173} and not because it is the foundation of real things. Real things are grounded upon the absolutely absolute reality, though the latter is independent of the former. Therefore, the foundational characteristic of God is not constitutive of their reality but merely consequent upon it. Fundamentality is not their *ratio essendi*. At most it would be their *ratio cognoscendi*; actually we cannot know God by ourselves except as ground of real things. This is essential for the problem of God. For the time being the question remains open about the type of that "consequentness".

This grounding is a characteristic of God by virtue of being absolutely absolute reality and in His whole concretion, i.e., as personal, living, intelligent, volitional, etc. But here it is necessary to reflect a bit in order to eliminate some ideas which may readily be propounded, viz. that the grounding of God may consist primarily and formally in His intelligence, in His volition, and in His feelings as such. To my way of thinking this is not correct. The human being needs an intelligence to open itself to the power of the real, because its being is relatively absolute. But God, as an absolutely absolute reality, does not need to open himself to reality; rather, He constitutes it from Himself directly, in a manner of speaking. God is certainly grounding in His whole absolute concretion, which means that His grounding is intelligent and volitional; formally, however, He is not so, insofar as He is intelligent and volitional, but insofar as this intelligence and this volition are absolutely absolute. God is not grounding things as a kind of spirit underlying them; this would be an absurd animism. God is grounding things as an absolute outward self-expression. To ground is to express oneself outwardly. {174}

Hence, that God is fundamental or foundational or grounding means that He outwardly gives reality, the reality of things. As I indicated above, the precise nature of this giving remains an open question because the giving is in multiple ways.

Three characteristics pin down the nature of this grounding.

1. Above all, grounding is the presence of God in things. As we saw, it has the character of a formal presence. It is not a presence derived from its eventual effector character but, on the contrary, God is effector in order to be present in things in a formal way, as their grounding formality. And as this formal presence concerns the character of reality of each thing, it turns out that this formal presence is intrinsic to real things. Not every intrinsic presence is formal, but every formal presence is intrinsic. That is, the presence of God is formal to things, and only because it is formal is it also intrinsic. Furthermore, it is what is most radically intrinsic in them because, as I just pointed out, it concerns reality precisely as reality. However, that God is present in real things as intrinsic grounding formality does not mean that between God and things there is no real distinction. It only means that there is no "separation", either physical or metaphysical. Distinction is not separation. This characteristic, according to which God is present in things with a formal and intrinsic presence, yet things are not God, is precisely what I call the *transcendence* of God "in" reality. A formal and intrinsic presence is a transcendent presence. Here is the first characteristic of the God's grounding: transcendence.

But it remains to fix the exact meaning of {175} this transcendence. To my way of thinking, to transcend does not mean to be "beyond" things, because on the contrary, God is formally and intrinsically *in* them. The transcendence of God does not consist in being beyond things but the other way around. Transcendence is precisely a mode of being in them, that mode in accordance with which they could not be real in any sense, unless they formally included in their reality the reality of God, without this in any sense making God identical to the reality of things. The way God is in things is to be transcendent in them. And this is, to my way of thinking, what is essential about the divine transcendence: not to be "transcendent *to*" things, but to be "transcendent *in*" things themselves. For this reason I shall constantly use the expression "God transcendent in things", the precise meaning of which we have once and for all explained. Each thing, in what it is, in and by itself, has in itself its own transcendent formal foundation or ground. From this it follows that each thing leads us, not to go out of the thing itself but to enter into it deeper and deeper, into its own transcendent foundation. To be in the thing is to be transcending it, not outside, but inside the thing itself. To be in the full reality of a thing is *eo ipso* to be in God in it. As we shall see, to march towards God is to penetrate further and further into a thing. Each thing itself makes me transcend in it.

The preceeding allows us to forcefully eliminate two serious errors between which it has been common to oscillate. The first is the error of thinking that the formal presence of God in things turns them into moments of the unique reality of God: this is pantheism. It is impossible. God is formally in things, but "making" that they be in God realities different from Him. Here "making" {176} simply means "grounding". The "in" is an "other-ifying" (if I may be permitted the expression) "in". Things are different from God precisely and formally because God is "in" them, but transcendent. The second error is the opposite. It consists in thinking that because He is radically different from things, God is the great absence, the great foreign to the world: this is agnosticism in its varied forms. In all of them, this is the extreme way of conceiving God as "beyond" things. But it is equally impossible. The fact that God is not things does not consist in His being distanced from them. If this were so, things would not be real. That God is in things means that things are real only by formally "including" in their own reality that reality which is greater than themselves, God. *God is transcendent, but in them.* The transcendence of God is neither identity nor remoteness, but transcendence in things. The *realitas fundamentalis* is, above all, a transcendence in this sense. The transcendence "in" makes God to be, in some sense, intra-worldly.

2. God is transcendent in real things *qua* as real. Furthermore, any reality is, *qua* reality, constitutively respective. And this unity of respectivity is what I have called "world". Hence, the formal and transcendent presence of God in things is a presence in the whole world as such. God is transcendent in things, and because of this He is transcendent in the world. Indeed, for the same reason that the transcendence of God is not identity or remoteness, the presence of God in the world is neither remoteness nor identity. It is not remoteness because God is not the "other" world. God is not extra-worldly, He is absolutely intra-worldly. But He is not identity either: God is not the other world but is other than the {177} world in which He is, because His otherness is just the formal ground of the respectivity of the real *qua* real, i.e., the ground of the world. To the unity of the world corresponds not only the uniqueness of God, but also the very *worldliness* of God. God is not present in the world simply because He is

present in each and every thing, but rather He is present in the world precisely and formally because any real thing is essentially and constitutively worldly. God is simply transcendent "in" the world. The grounding activity of God is the worldly transcendence of God. The world formally carries God in itself.

3. This presence of God in things is not only formal and intrinsic but also constituting. The reality of God, in its whole grounding concretion, is an absolute outward self-expression, self-overflowing. On this point the absolute of the self-expression means that He is giving reality to things, constituting them as real. The presence of God in things is a constituting outward self-expression and self-overflowing. This means He is in things "making them be real", i.e., making them be in their own right, and to act from what they are in their own right. This is what I have usually called the *fontanality* of the absolutely absolute reality. God is *realitas fontanalis*. In the special case of human beings, this is what comprises what I have called "theological tension"; the sheer fontanality in everything real is the homolog of the theological tension in human beings. The transcendence of the reality of God is a fontanal transcendence.

This is the definitive essence of the grounding of God: to be fontanal transcendence. And He is such because He is an absolutely absolute reality. Precisely because this reality is absolutely concrete, His fontanality is {178} also personal, living, intelligent and volitional. We have seen before that God is a possibilitating and impelling ultimateness because He is the ground of the power of the real, of a power in its turn ultimate, possibilitating and impelling. Hence, we now understand why He is, and has to be what He is, since we are viewing God not only from the perspective of real things, but from Himself also. It is because He is personal, living, intelligent and volitional that God is in Himself, adequately, an ultimate, possibilitating, and impelling fontanal reality. That is why His manifestation in the power of the real is what makes of this power something likewise ultimate, possibilitating and impelling, which in turn constitutes the ground of religation. This is, to my way of thinking, the intellectual justification of the reality of God.

But the problem has a second aspect: the access of humans to this reality, the access of humans to God. There are, as I mentioned at the beginning of this chapter, two co-essential aspects here: the reality of God and the access of the human being to God. It will be useful to deal with them separately. This may generate some inevitable tedious repetitions; however, it may also provide us with greater clarity. Let us then tackle the problem of the access of human beings to God.

---

[1] [The Spanish expression *dar de sí* is not exactly translatable into English, but roughly means "outward self expression" rather than the literal "self-giving". The idea is a self-giving in the sense of an overflowing, of sharing—trans.]

CHAPTER 4

THE UNFOLDING OF THE PROBLEM: II. HUMAN ACCESS TO GOD

At first glance, it might appear that what was said in the previous chapter would suffice to solve the problem of human access to God. And to be sure, it is in the reality of God where the key to His access resides. However, this access presents certain peculiar problems of its own which we must consider:

§1. What do we understand by access of human beings to God?
§2. God as accessible reality.
§3. What are the characteristics of this access to God?
§4. What is the precise and formal root of this access?[1]

§1

WHAT DO WE UNDERSTAND BY "ACCESS?"

1. On the basis of everything said thus far we have discovered that the absolutely absolute reality, God, in His absolute concretion is formally and constitutively present in real things as their transcendent ground, in the sense of a font, and manifested in them as deity of the power of the real. But strictly speaking this is not formally the access of humans to God. It would rather be access of God to the world, because the fact that the world is accessible to God is not something immediately obvious. The *Theós* of Aristotle lives thinking and desiring nothing but his own reality; the *Theós* neither knows the world nor acts upon it. Classical theology insists on the presence of God in created things. For St. Thomas God is in things by means of three concepts: first, because all things are in His hands. God has power over all of them. Therefore, He is present in things through His *power*. In addition, all things are present to the intelligence of God, who is in them due to this *presence*. Finally, God is in things through *essence*, because all are a participation in the entity of God. Nevertheless, this leaves the question that concerns us here unanswered. Let us admit without question, for the time being, that God is in things according to that triple concept: through essence, presence and power. But what we ask is not how God is in things, but rather how one thing, the human being, has access to God. If it is not obvious that God has {181} access to the world, neither is it obvious that humans have access to God. A God absolutely ignored and unknown due to his own characteristics, would be real but not accessible to humans. The access in question is, above all, an access not in the sense that the reality of things is in God, and God in the reality of things, but in the sense that there are acts that a human being may perform through which he or she has access to God.

2. Still, this is not enough, because having justified the reality of God intellectually, it is certainly clear that God is known by humans in some way. But, to understand a reality does not mean that we have access to it simply on that account. The act or acts of access to God by humans are not those which are formally intellectual, but rather those acts which physically and really take us to Him, insofar as He is absolutely absolute reality.

3. Clearly, all these acts are moments or aspects of the unique act in which the life of a human being formally consists: the constitution and configuration of its relatively absolute being, of its *I*. The question then becomes, what would it be to have access to God in the radical act of the constitution of the *I*? It is an access in the order not of human *reality*, but of my being. This is a problem which is connected in an essential way with the one posed in the last chapter, when dealing with what I called the function of God in life. There, we were concerned primarily with what God does, in and with humans, in the constitution of his *I*. On the other hand, we now ask ourselves about what it is that a human being does to access God, when living as an *I*. Certainly, what we said there is not extraneous to what we may have to say here; indeed, just the opposite. This is why I warned that {182} some repetitions are inevitable and may become tedious.

Therefore, it is along these lines that we ask ourselves in what the access to God consists.

A) In the first place, because a human being is a substantive reality provided with intelligence, it is an essence constitutively open to its own characteristic reality. Human reality not only has certain properties according to which the human being acts, just like any other reality; but differently from all others, human beings act from and by their own character of reality. In other words, each human being is an essence open to itself as reality, and which acts openly. That to which this essence is open in the order of its activity is the constitution of the figure of its relatively absolute being, of its *I*.

B) The structure of that openness has, with respect to this radical act of the essence, a very precise structure: the open essence is formally religated. Its openness is therefore a religated openness. Open to what? To the ground of its life, to the power of the real as ultimate, possibilitating and impelling. In this dimension of religated openness, each human is hurled from the power of the real "towards" that upon which this power is grounded, towards God. It is not the case that God is going to be "in front" of us. The access to God is not an "encounter" in itself, but a "remission". Thus far the reality of God is a reality in the manner of "towards", in real things themselves, which are real precisely "in" God. Because of this, each human being, *velis nolis*, while making its own *I* with real things *qua* real, is making his *I in* God (finality), *with* God (possibilitating), and *by* God (impelling). This "towards" {183} takes place in a dynamic theological tension "between" a human being and God, a tension at the same time personal and historical.

C) But this is not yet formally the access to God. Because as we have just indicated, that to which a human being formally directs himself is towards real things; one might even say, towards reality itself, reality as a whole. It is true that God is formally and constitutively in the reality of real things; and this is why when things give me their own reality, they are giving me God in that very reality. However, if this were all, humans would be moving in God by the mere fact of being and moving in reality—which is true for any human, whether aware of it or not. In this sense we all have some access to God. But then, that to which a human being directs itself is towards real things. And therefore the access, strictly and formally put, would be an access to things but not to God, who, if one wishes to employ an expressive scholastic term, would be accessed *per accidens*, i.e., that to which humans have access in itself would be to real things, and would only reach God because it so happens that God is in things. Humans would reach God without intending to do it. However, this is not the case, because, as we have already seen, God is formally present in things, but without being identical to them: this is the transcendence of God. Hence in the access to real things humans are hurled "towards" their own transcendent font "in" them. And this transcendence is the one that strictly poses our question. Because then each human being, when accessing things, would be hurled in them towards his own transcendent ground. In that case, God would not be accessed *per accidens*, but *per se*, for Himself, since He has access to things, which are real "in" God. And thus, the system of acts that apprehend {184} God for Himself in things, transcendent but formally present in them, is what constitutes the access we are searching for. It is the case of having access to God not without knowing it or *per accidens*, but expressly and formally, i.e., directed towards God *qua* God.

This does not mean that we are searching for acts through which we may "find" God, because then the reality of God would always be a reality as "towards". We do not find God in things, but rather we find ourselves "sent" to Him. Our intelligence has discovered the reality of God in things, and humans exercise some acts formally and precisely directed "towards" that God. This only means that if we were able to reach the terminus of this "towards", then yes, we would find a God that would justify the road taken.

Finally, in the achievement and configuration of my relatively absolute being, the reality of God already justified would have to be the terminus of acts directed formally and expressly towards Him, not in a supererogatory fashion but as necessary terminus for the constitution of my *I*. This is what we understand by "access". Does this access really exist? The first thing that has to be investigated precisely is whether God is something accessible in this manner. That is the second question.

{185}

§2

GOD, ACCESSIBLE REALITY

Accessibility is a characteristic (let us put it this way) that concerns not human beings but God. If God were a reality beyond everything real, the great absent and alien, He would be a reality inaccessible in itself. That is not the case: God is constitutively accessible. It is necessary to demonstrate this on the basis of characteristics of His own reality. This accessibility is expressed in four concepts, which made their appearance before, but which must be repeated now. They are concepts referring to God Himself, in particular, that face of God which opens onto real things. I emphasize this to preclude the error of thinking that we speak about human beings. No, we are speaking about God. We shall speak about humans in the paragraphs following these.

1. God by His own characteristics is formally present in things without being identical to them; this is what we have called "God's transcendence as a font". Real things are real "in" God; and because of this His presence in them is formal. But this God is, as we have seen, a reality of absolute concretion: He is a personal reality (this is why He is alive, intelligent and volitional). And in this, His absolute formal concretion is how He is in things as their formal constituent. When we say, therefore, that real things give us God in themselves when they give us their own reality, we must add that they give us a personal reality absolutely absolute. What things give me is God as a person. God is not a personal reality {186} beyond things, but is personally present in them, formally constituting their reality. Because of this He is constitutively accessible in real things themselves. Never, not even in the most sublime access of the great mystics, is God accessed without things or outside of them. Real things are the personal presence of God. And precisely because of this, He is constitutively accessible. God is accessible in and through the world. The turning towards God is not extra- but inter-worldly. Things are not only real in God but in the person which God is. Real things are in themselves the concretion of the personal accessibility of God. God is accessible in Himself and the form of this accessibility is the constituting ground of things.

2. God does not have the same type of presence or constitutionality in all things. In all of them He is, certainly, their formal

personal constituent. But the manner of presence of God in something will be in accordance with the nature of its reality and the way He is constituting its reality at the moment. The types of reality are, to my way of thinking, two: closed essences and open essences. In closed essences, i.e., in those essences which are only in their own right what they are, God is constituting them, constituting their "in themselves". It is a personal presence only "in-themselving" so to speak.[2] The case is very different with the open essences. Open essences are not only in their own right, but are "their-own". Because of this they are persons having a relatively absolute being. Hence, God is in the open essences, if I may be permitted the expression, "making-them-their-own".[3] His presence is "own-making". Therefore, the fontanal presence of God in the reality of the human spirit is an *inter-personal transcendence.* God is {187} accessible to humans precisely and formally because each human being is a person. In order to avoid any anthropomorphism when speaking about the personal reality of God, I have emphasized that this does not mean that God is a kind of spirit subjacent to every real thing; it means only that God is absolutely His-own and is absolute "His-ownness". And by virtue of being such, He is intrinsically accessible to any relatively absolute person. Real things give us, in their own reality, the absolute His-ownness in which God consists. And thus, since this relatively absolute person is precisely the *I*, it is easy to think that the absolutely absolute person is a kind of exceptional "you"; i.e., one tends to think that the inter-personal accessibility is a relation from *I* to *Thou*. This is another form of anthropomorphism. That humans address God by calling Him *Thou* is inevitable in a human being who wishes to designate with the *Thou* a personal reality different from his or her own. But God is transcendent to any *Thou*. He is in the *I*, making it be *I*, and yet is not formally a *Thou*, because He is not an *I*: this is the inter-personal transcendence of God. Furthermore, the very possibility of addressing ourselves to God as a *Thou* is grounded squarely on something previous: on the inter-personal presence of God in human beings. God is not inter-personal because He is a *Thou*, but on the contrary (within the limits indicated) His possible "Thou-ness" is but the human expression of inter-personal presence. This presence is not inter-personal because it is the relation "*I-Thou*", but is "*I-Thou*" because it is an inter-personal presence.

As such, the presence of God in humans as a font acquires a very unique character. We have already seen that in the case of human beings the presence of God as a font in all of reality is converted into a dynamic tension. Therefore, {188} the concrete

142   UNFOLDING OF THE PROBLEM: HUMAN ACCESS TO GOD

form of this tension is to be *inter-personal tension*, that tension between two absolutes, through which the grounding is making the grounded to be absolute. By reason of this mode of presence of God in each human being, God is intrinsically accessible by Himself. Human persons are, *qua* persons, the concrete accessibility of the absolute person *qua* person. Only in and for human persons is God formally accessible *qua* person.

3. In this inter-personal tension, God is a *manifestative* personal reality. Let us be clear about this, I am here talking about what God is, not that humans are simply apprehending that manifestation as such; our problem at the moment is just the accessibility of God. Therefore, God is accessible because His inter-personal presence is not only real, but manifestative. What kind of manifestation is it?

Any manifestation is an unveiling of the thing manifested. But there are several ways of unveiling. Ordinarily we tend to think that when something is manifest it means that it is immediately present "in front of" our eyes. But human intelligence is sentient, and senses reality intellectively according to all the possible types of sensing and not just according to the sense of sight. If I perceive a sound, the sound as such is immediately present to hearing, but the sonorous thing is not. With sight, not only is the form or color of the thing present, but we believe that the thing itself is so as well. With hearing, on the other hand, the sonorous thing is not immediately included in the sound itself; rather the latter remits to the former. This remitting is not a relation consequent upon the sound, but belongs to its own formal characteristic: the formal characteristic of a sound {189} consists in remitting to the sonorous thing. If in sight the unveiling consists in a "formal presentation" of the thing, in hearing the unveiling consists in "remitting". By virtue of this, sound is what makes a thing be a *notum*; in this etymological sense, sound does not give us the thing but is an "announcement" of the thing. Sound unveils or manifests the thing in the form of an "announcing remission". Now, things are real "in" God, in God as a person, and God is in them constituting them formally. But God is "in" them as something transcendent. By virtue of this, He unveils or manifests Himself (in the things in which He is) in a "remitting" way; real things are, *qua* real, "announcements" of the personal reality of God. God is in things, but without being them: this is what I understand by transcendence of God. Correlatively, things *qua* real are "remitting" us to their own intrinsic and formal transcendent ground in which they are sustained as real. This is the reason why the proper way for the transcendent to manifest itself as transcendent is as an announcing remission, a manifestation of the "auditive" type.

In human beings, as we pointed out, transcendence has a special characteristic: it is an inter-personal tension. And there is, of course, announcing remission. But there is something else, because God is present more than personally: He is present inter-personally. Then the tension in which God unveils or manifests Himself has a unique characteristic. God is not "in front of" my eyes, but has a certain type of presence which we might call "immediate." In hearing God is announced by means of His announcement, the real thing. But in the inter-personal tension, God is announcing His presence in a type of manifestation more proper to touch than to hearing. In touch we have more than just {190} announcement, but less than the formal presentation of the thing: we have a "naked presence" in which reality itself is apprehended through "probing" without being seen. This is the apprehension of naked presence by probing. It is as if God in His dynamic tension were not letting us see Him, but making us feel immediately His naked presence through a kind of knocking with His knuckles at man's door. If the proper way to manifest simply personal transcendence in the sense of a font is "announcement", the proper mode of manifestation of the inter-personal transcendence in tension is "probing". A human being may be able to ignore the fact that these internal impulses belong to God present in him or her. But this is another question, because, I repeat, I am speaking not of humans but about God insofar as He is accessible. God is accessible because He manifests Himself in those kind of dynamic tension jolts.

Religation, I pointed out, is a manifestative experience of the power of the real. And this experience throws us experientially towards its ground in things themselves, towards God in them. And this God is manifestative in an audio-tactile way, i.e., at one and the same time as announcement and naked presence through probing.

4. But, what is manifest about this God *qua* manifest? *Qua* manifest, God is truth. That is, God is manifestative of His truth. This is the concept in which the accessibility of God culminates. What is this truth?

Truth does not mean here some presumed "conformity of thought with things", but is a characteristic of reality itself, that characteristic according to which we say of something real that it is a "true reality". What is truth in this sense? Clearly it is the actuality of the very reality of the thing in the intelligence; because of this, I have usually called it "real truth". {191} It is real because it is the actuality of *reality*; it is truth because it is the *actuality* of that reality. Now, the capacity (let us put it this way) of a real thing for this actualization has three dimensions. According to the first, we say of a real thing that it is a true reality when in each one of its notes the real thing itself is patent. Thus, a hard thing is truly hard when that which is actualized in the hardness is the very reality of the thing, i.e., when it is a "hard-thing". Real truth is then the *patency* of reality in all the richness of its notes. In the second place, we say of a real thing that it is true, if it corresponds to what it offers to me in its notes, i.e., when I can rely on the characteristics it presents. In the case of men, for example, someone is a true friend when he is faithful to the friendship he offers. According to this, truth is actuality in its dimension of *firmness*. Finally, we say of something that it is a true reality when it is "physically" real *in actu exercito*, so to speak. The actuality of reality according to this dimension is the *facticity* of being here-and-now in existence.[4] Patency of richness, firmness of its reality, and facticity of this reality are three congeneric and simultaneous dimensions of the real truth, and therefore belong to reality itself as a capacity to be actualized in the intelligence. It is in accordance with this capacity that we measure reality in its character as true.

Now, God, absolute person, as ground of reality and consequently of its capacity of intellective actualization, is absolutely true reality according to this triple dimension. Because God is absolutely absolute reality, it follows that all of Him is actualized in the {192} unfathomable constitutive richness of His reality. By virtue of being absolutely real reality, He is essentially the firmness itself of that which His richness offers. By virtue of being essentially real reality, He is essential facticity. God, then, is the absolute real truth. Indeed, it is in accordance with this triple dimension that He manifests Himself in things, because it is due to this triple characteristic that He is their ground. And to ground, to be the foundation, is to outwardly self-express or self-give What God outwardly self-gives (in the aspect we are studying) is reality. Due to this, reality is *donation*.[5] Here, this does not mean a free or gratuitous donation, but rather that "donation" is only the noun form of the self-giving. And since the donating "self" is absolute His-ownness and therefore personal, His donation is essentially an absolutely personal donation. Whence it follows that real things, insofar as they make their richness patent, are maintained with firmness and have facticity, i.e., insofar as they are true reality, they are the very concretion of the truth of God as donor, and therefore, are *eo ipso* the accessibility of the true real-

UNFOLDING OF THE PROBLEM: HUMAN ACCESS TO GOD

ity in which God consists. God is supremely and formally accessible because He is a personal donor in accordance with His true reality.

In the case of human beings, the accessibility of God as true reality necessarily has its own unique characteristic, just as the presence of God in the depths of a human being has its own unique characteristic. It is not just a mere personal presence, as in other things, but an inter-personal presence. This presence is realized in a dynamic tension. In that tension is how God outwardly self-gives the being of the human person, his *I*; i.e., it is through the dynamic tension that a human being makes from itself its own relative absolute being. God gives me that I may be *I* and make my own *I* with all its richness, with all its firmness, with all its facticity, {193} i.e., in its whole real truth. This is God as donation of the real truth of my *I*. The donation of God in inter-personal tension is a thrust towards perfection, towards security, and towards facticity. Because of this God is constitutively accessible in His true reality: the true reality of human beings (and of all things) is the concrete form of the accessibility of God in His truth.

In conclusion, God is essentially accessible through His personal presence in all real things, through His inter-personal presence in human beings, and through His manifestation by notification and naked presence, all of which constitute the ground of the richness, the firmness and the facticity of things and especially of human beings. This grounding is a personal self-giving. And in this characteristic, the four concepts we have studied are fused. In addition, since in this donation God is transcendent in things, it is evident that in them He is accessible as Himself, precisely and formally by being the donor of reality. If God did nothing else but simply be in things, His accessibility would merely be *per accidens*. But since the personal presence of God is donating transcendence, it follows that God is accessible *in things* but *through Himself*, although in the form of announcement and naked presence. Therefore, God is accessible in Himself and through Himself, not in an unrecognizable type of mystical action, extra-worldly or trans-worldly, but purely and simply because by His being in things He is outwardly self-giving them their reality. The personal transcendence of God in things is His accessibility itself.

This accessibility is a characteristic incumbent upon God but not human beings. Therefore, it leaves outstanding the question of whether and how humans can have access to this God, and how they can have access to this God who is accessible in Himself.

{194}

§3

THE ACCESS OF HUMAN BEINGS TO GOD

The accessibility of God, we said, is not the same as the access of humans to God. However, this does not mean that the access is an extrinsic relation between humans and God—as if God were an object that humans may or may not propose to reach. Just the opposite: the access is an intrinsic moment to humans, precisely and formally because the inter-personal presence of God in them is the presence of a God in and by Himself accessible. Consequently, the *accessibility of God* is already an *inchoate access of human beings*. God is found "in" things and only in them. From this it follows that the transcendence of God in things is already an access to God. But, let us add, it is only an inchoate access. Then we ask ourselves, in the first place, what is this access insofar as it is *inchoate*, and in the second place, what is the *fullness* of its nature.

I. The presence of God in human beings is inter-personal and occurs, as we have seen, in a dynamic tension. This tension, like every tension and especially inter-personal tension, is a unity encompassing its two termini with the tension. We have seen in the preceding pages what this tension is from the point of view of God: it is a manifestative tension in the form of notification and naked presence as "towards". But in this tension human beings themselves are included. They reaches towards things determined by the power of the real; and it is this power which carries us through religation to the constitution of our {195} I. This power is grounded on the reality of God in things. And that involves three essential consequences.

1. In religation we are borne along by the power of the real. Now, the ground of this in things, their power of the real, is the formal and constitutive presence of God in them. It follows that, in the final analysis, to be borne along by the power of the real is to be borne along by God. It is God who has, so to speak, the first word in this being borne along by Him. That tension which is grounded on God encompasses humans in a tense manner: God is the "pre-tension" which carries us towards Him.

2. In this "pre-tension" we proceed towards things dragged by the power of the real in them, that is, by God himself. With respect to us, the inter-personal tension acquires the character of a

"dragging". Dragging is the specifically human moment of the tension in which we are formally constituted. Because of this the accessibility of God is at one and the same time the dragging with which we proceed to God in the "pre-tension".

3. This power of the real that makes us be through religation is the power of reality itself in all real things. And this power is grounded on the fact that God is present formally in them without being identical to them, i.e., is grounded on a God transcendent "in" things. It follows that since we are religated to the power of the real in things, in them God drags us toward Himself precisely when going to things and being actually in them. By being transcendent in things, God makes me transcend; He is, if I may be permitted the expression, "transcendentifying". We previously saw that to transcend is to have each thing take us to its own transcending depth. Now, this transcending is a movement which determines each thing in us precisely and formally {196} by the constituting presence of God in it. The movement of transcending is, therefore, a movement determined by the transcendence of God itself in each thing. God is, in this dimension, not only *transcendent* but *transcendentifying*.

By virtue of these three concepts taken together, i.e., by being pre-tension, dragging, and transcendentifying, the accessibility of God is *eo ipso* an inchoate access. Essentially, the three concepts comprise the theological essence of religation. In fact, religation is the incontrovertible fact that we are tied to the power of the real as ground of our *I*. But having known intellectively that this power is an intrinsic and formal seat and vehicle of God, it becomes clear that the essence of religation is this inchoate access, comprising the accessibility of God in things, and above all in ourselves. Every human being inchoatively has access to God through God. Saint Augustine wrote that God could say to human beings: "You would not have searched for me if I had not found you". That is true. But it is a partial truth, because it is not primarily the case of a search but of a true access, however inchoate, but still a true access. Whether they know it or not, all humans are inchoatively accessing God.

II. This access is, as I mentioned, only an inchoate access. But the grounding of God is, as we saw, personal outward expression or donation. By virtue of this, humans have access to God through religation in a tension that has a very precise characteristic: a tension that is the human correlate of the donating tension, i.e., the tension in surrender. Surrender corresponds to donation. The fullness in the form of access of humans to God is "surrender". God gives Himself to us in {197} things as a "towards" in the form of notification and naked presence. That is the reason why the fullness of the form of access to God is to give ourselves to Him in a "towards": this is the surrender we are discussing.

All humans, as I said, have an inchoate access to God. But this inchoate access does not unfold into a full access in each person. For this to occur, it is necessary to have formal knowledge that God exists as an absolutely absolute reality in His whole absolute concretion. This knowledge is precisely what was justified in the previous chapter. Grounded on this knowledge, i.e., on the situation of a human being that has intellectively known the reality of God, is how we bring about the surrender to Him. As I have just pointed out, this surrender is not identical to the inchoate access; but nor could it exist unless inscribed within that access and facilitated by it. The surrender, the fullness of the access, is nothing but the unfolding of the inchoate access. The surrender is not the primary access of humans to God but is its full unfolding. Paraphrasing St. Augustine, we might think that God could say to humans: "You would not surrender to me, if I had not brought you to me." We then ask ourselves, what is the unfolding of the inchoate access into its fullness of access?

In order to delve into this problem we must pay attention to three points: What is surrender?, What are its moments?, and What is the character of the union with God through tension in the surrender?

1. What is the surrender? Negatively put, we must erase the idea—nefarious for many reasons—that to surrender is to abandon oneself. To abandon oneself would be to escape from oneself; at best, it would be to trust that God accomplish things by Himself, without my intervention. This would constitute a gigantic act of laziness or desperation. Surrender is just the opposite. Above all, it is an {198} attitude, and a positive action, one that is active. To the action of God donating reality, human beings responds with a positive action in which the person is not taken to God; rather, the person by himself accepts his being taken in an active and positive way, i.e., the person "goes to God". While going to real things he surrenders to God who is in them, constituting them formally, i.e., giving reality from Himself. In things, a human being surrenders to what is transcendent in them. As I have just said, a human being "would not go" to things unless he or she were "brought". Because of this, the going is nothing but positive acceptance of being brought, i.e., its unfolding. Being brought by God, a human does not drift with the current, but by rowing in reality goes towards God. A human being makes its *I*,

its relatively absolute being, surrendering itself to the absolutely absolute reality, to God.

But let us not forget: God and His donation are personal. Therefore, the surrender is not just a positive action, but a strictly inter-personal action that is formally directed from the human person, who is an *I*, towards the person of God. To the personal donation which is the grounding presence of God in things and in humans, the human person responds with that special form of donation that is the surrender of the self. I said that going towards God is the unfolding of the being brought to Him. Now we can see why: the going towards God is donation; and since donation is grounded upon the inchoate donation, the surrender is the unfolding of the latter. How?

2. The surrender of the human person to God has different moments. Here we encounter once again the three dimensions of the power of the real, religation, and God himself, i.e., finality, possibilitation, {199} and impellence. But each time they acquire a clearer and more precise meaning.

We already saw that, as absolutely absolute reality, God is the *ground* of reality as radical finality, as possibility of possibilities, and as destination of my absolute being. These are three characteristics which pertain to God *qua* God. Hence, by virtue of this, the *surrender* of humans to God has three rigorously determined moments.

A) Surrender to God is, above all, a going towards God as absolutely ultimate reality. In this respect, the surrender acquires a concrete characteristic: veneration. To venerate does not primarily mean to obey–that is something derivative. What is primary in veneration is recognition of how relative I am, when facing the absolutely absolute person which God is. It is like a disappearance before God. This is what the verb *latreúo* expresses, "to adore". To adore is to venerate the unfathomable plenitude of this ultimate reality. Naturally, in this veneration all the moral moments are involved, which we need not recall now. But what is radical in each of them is veneration in the sense just explained. When going towards real things, each human bows before the reality of things and in them venerates God as personally transcendent. To the donation of reality humans respond with veneration for the donor: this is the essence of personal adoration.

B) Humans surrender to God not only as finality, but also as supreme possibilitator. In this respect surrender has a specific moment: to *supplicate*. Humans not only venerate God in adoration, but person-to-person, supplicates God for the possibilities of their lives. As I mentioned before, God is the donor of possibilities. This is {200} the essence of prayer. Prayer is not, in the formal sense, a formulary; it is a supplicating surrender of the mind to God. Adoration can also be called "prayer," but I prefer to reserve the term for acts of supplication. Humans supplicate God in things and with things. They does not leave things aside to proceed toward God; it is in things themselves, with all their richness and with all their difficulties, where human beings surrender to God in supplication so that God grounds in them possibilities favorable to him. Prayer is only possible by this transcendence of God in things.

C) Humans surrender to God as supreme impellence. Perhaps this is what most clearly reveals the positive character of the surrender. Humans rests on God as the strength of their lives. This is not the strength that I ask of God in order to do what I must do, but the very strength, the firm and strong support in which God consists. Indeed, humans deliver themselves to God in this respect as *refuge*, not to act but to be. To surrender is to accept refuge. Of course, from this refuge we inexorably derive the assistance to act. But that is something derivative: what is primary is the surrender to God as refuge of my being.

To the three characteristics of God with respect to religation, viz. as final, possibilitating, and impelling reality, there correspond three moments of the surrender of humans to God: veneration, supplication, and refuge. It is through this triple aspect that the unitary and simple act of surrender by the human person to the divine person proceeds. They are three moments in some way different but essentially inseparable. Any veneration, for example, is a supplication and a going to God as refuge, etc. What happens is that in each case one characteristic can predominate over the others. And {201} precisely because these moments of surrender are grounded on the acceptance of the reality of God as ultimate, possibilitating, and impelling, this surrender constitutes the unfolding of the inchoate access. Essentially, inchoate access is religation itself; the surrender is nothing but the unfolding of religation.

3. What is the nature of the unity between human beings and God in the dynamic tension of surrender? One might think that this unity is the result of the action of God and the reaction of the human being; in such case the unity would be a "correlation". But this is absurd. Not only is the unity not correlation, but on the contrary (if one still wishes to talk about correlation) the correlation is the result of the unity. And this is so because it is not the case of a unity between just any two realities, but between two very precise realities, between two persons. It is a unity from

person to person. And since we are dealing with a donation of God and of a surrender of the human being, in which God himself has the initiative (God is pre-tension), it follows that in one form or another, this unity of donation and surrender is the *unity of personal causality*.

The unity of divine donation and human surrender belongs to this type of personal causality. More than union, it is communion between the human person and God. The human being surrenders to God, accepting his or her own personal being from a donating God, who is also personal, and who donates my reality and my being. The unity between donating God and surrender is, therefore, a functionality of the real *qua* real, and for this reason, is strict causality. Furthermore, this causality is a functionality between God "by being who He is" and each human "by being who he is". Because of this, the dynamic tension is not just causality but inter-personal causality. And this is essential {202} for the correct understanding of the whole theme of the theological in human beings. Henceforth let this point be clearly noted.

A) The inter-personal causality of the theological tension is not a causality of two persons who are, in principle, strangers to each other. God and the human being are certainly different but they are not strangers. God, as we indicated, is intrinsically and formally present in each real thing, transcendent "in" it. Therefore, His presence in the reality of each human person is also intrinsic and formal to it. It follows that in the inter-personal dynamic tension, God and each human person are not extrinsic to each other, but just the opposite: God *qua* person is intrinsic to each human personal reality. The causality of the "donation-surrender", consequently, is not extrinsic but intrinsic; it is a functionality *from within* human reality, not from outside of it. Furthermore, it is functionality from what is most radically internal to the person, since it stems from what the person is *qua* reality. God, as I pointed out, is transcendent "*in*" things and therefore is a person transcendent "*in*" the human person. His action in humans concerns the very root of the vital act of the person, the act of the constitution of his *I*. The person of God is, if I may be permitted the expression, a formal moment of a human being making its own *I*. Precisely because of this, it might appear that a human being not only makes his or her whole being but does so completely. However, this is not true. Yes, a human makes his or her whole being, but does not make it totally *qua* person in contradistinction to the divine person. Each real thing includes in its reality the reality of God. Now, reality is dynamic by itself. It follows that by including the reality of God, any real thing (and especially the human person) formally includes {203} in its own dynamism the dynamicity of the divine person. Because of this, while it is indeed true that a human being makes his or her whole being (since each, by being its-own is its own reality), the human being nonetheless does not make it totally on his or her own because it is reality, and therefore it is dynamicity "in" reality, and "in" the dynamicity of God. The movement of God is not a second movement added to the one that starts from myself; rather the movement that starts from myself is already formally and in itself, a movement of God. Correlatively, from the point of view of humans, to ask help from God, for example, is not to ask help from someone who is outside and is asked to bring help, but rather to ask for something like an intensification of one who is already present in ourselves, and in which we are already radically dynamic; it is to ask help from a God who is transcendent *in* me. To resort to God is to resort to my own transcendent depth. When surrendering to God, a human being surrenders to what is most radically his- or her-own. To avoid false interpretations I direct attention to what I explained above concerning the reality of God as the transcendental depth proper to each real thing.

B) As with any personal causality, such inter-personal causality is rigorously metaphysical. And this acquires its greatest reality when referring to the inter-personal causality of God and each human being. The dynamic tension between God and humans is comprised of those phenomena we might tend to consider as puerile sentimentalities. But no: they are the very forms of God's causality in the life of the human person. Conversely, any form of human functionality with respect to the divine person inexorably occurs in accordance with these forms. And since this causality is, as we have just shown, radically intrinsic to {204} the human person, it follows that these functions are moments of the intrinsic and formal dynamism in which the life of the human person unfolds *from itself*. This is due to the fact that one of the two persons, the divine, is formally interior to the human, and therefore, the help that God provides stems from the very depths of the human person. To help, to console, to listen, etc., are not mere psychic phenomena, but are the metaphysical forms through which God is constituting me in my being. Because of this, each human being, whether he or she knows it or not, has the experience of God. This is not the empirical experience of an object, but a metaphysical experience of the ground of his or her personal being. This experience is *in itself* the experience of God. God is something experienced. Correlatively, humans, as we saw, surrender to God-donor in veneration, supplication and refuge. These are the forms of inter-personal causality between God and humans, from the human point of view.

Summing up, donation-surrender is the metaphysical structure of the inter-personal causality between God and each human being, in the theological tension of his or her life. In this causality, therefore, the access of humans to God *qua* God takes place. It is an access that, as we have seen, has three moments. Furthermore, this access, with all its moments, can and does have several forms: one can access to God through several directions and aspects. Then we ask, what is the radical dimension of surrender underlying all these forms and directions, i.e., What is the formal root of the surrender, of the access of humans to God?

APPENDIX 2

PERSONAL CAUSALITY AND MORALITY

Classical metaphysics and positive science instantly react against the idea of personal causality. Science, because it understands cause as an antecedent, linked to the presumed consecutive effect by a law. Does it make any sense then to apply causality to the personal unity of donation and surrender? Laplace said that in his science he had never felt any need to appeal to the God-hypothesis. But the fact is that Laplace's arena is physics and astronomy, sciences with which, apparently, it is obvious that God has nothing to do, in the sense that He does not intervene in the equations of the phenomena. But, is it equally obvious, at least with respect to appearances, that we never feel the necessity to appeal to God when it is a question concerning a human being and his or her life? This case is not as obvious precisely because the inter-personal texture, and that proper to each person, do not have the form of law of the type that physics calls "causal". But then one thing is clear: "cause" is not synonymous with "law". On the other hand, classical metaphysics is based on the four causes of Aristotle. That metaphysics will not deny (how could it?) that the action of God in pre-tension is causal; but it will strain to interpret this action as an efficient and final causality. And this appears inadequate to me, not because there is no causality, but because what is unclear is the idea of causality itself. By repeated subdivision of causality into four causes, causality as such has not been conceptualized {206} adequately. Now, to my way of thinking, as I have repeatedly stated, causality is functionality of the real *qua* real. And this opens the field to many other types of strict causation, types which can be fitted into Aristotle's four causes only with great difficulty, and in an inadequate manner.

The fact is that the causality of science and that of classical metaphysics is a causality among things, among "what" things are. But from person to person there is a functionality, and therefore a strict causality, among persons, among "who" the persons are. It is not a mere application of classical causality to persons, but a type of causation irreducible to those of classical Metaphysics, and still less reducible to the concept of scientific law. This is

UNFOLDING OF THE PROBLEM: HUMAN ACCESS TO GOD   155

what I call *personal causality*. However repugnant it may be to natural science, to my way of thinking there is a causality among persons that is not given in nature.

In life there are numerous inter-personal "relations" irreducible to classical causality. When I am with a friend or with a person I love, the influence of the friendship or love is not reducible to mere psycho-physical causation. I am influenced not only by *what* the friend is, but by the friend for being *who* he is. Likewise, the communion of persons is something *toto cælo* different from a social union or unity, etc. Above all, to this order of personal causality belongs everything moral. That human beings have a moral dimension is something that belongs to their "physical" reality. Virtue is certainly not something that humans have by nature, but it is something more than just a value; it is a real and physical appropriation of certain possibilities {207} for living. That is to say, it is a moment of my personal being, of my personality. And it is precisely this which, to my way of thinking, constitutes the moral dimension in humans, i.e., "the" moral in human beings. It is unnecessary for each human to have *any particular* moral virtue, but it is physically inexorable that he or she have *some* moral virtue, which means that "the" moral is a "physical" dimension of humans. The moral is physical in its own way. Morality, in the sense of values, rights, and duties, is only possible upon the foundation of "the" moral in humans. There is moral good only because human beings are are moral. Furthermore, each different morality is but an articulation of that inexorable human dimension: the various moralities are inscribed in *the* moral. Now, this means that the moral is not found in the naked substantive reality of humans, i.e., in *what* each human is individually and specifically, but rather in his or her personized nature. Humans are moral reality because they are nature, personal substantivity. Because of this, the so-called "moral causality" is strictly and formally personal causality. And the same must be said, to the greatest degree, of religation.

Science and classical metaphysics had a tendency to see a psychological phenomenon in friendship, for example. The metaphysical structure of human realities would thus be prior to such phenomena. However, to my way of thinking, this is not so. Continuing with the example mentioned, friendship is a metaphysical modality of inter-personal causality. Conversely, any person, in whatever measure he turns towards another person, is exercising a personal causality whose metaphysical modes are precisely and formally friendship, companionship, counseling, etc. In classical causality, collision, pressure, attraction, etc., are the modes of exercising physical causality. In personal causality {208} these modes are friendship, companionship, support, etc. To my way of thinking, there can never be enough emphasis on this theme of personal causality, and its metaphysical modes. It is a central theme in any metaphysics.

{209}

§4

THE FORMAL ROOT OF THE ACCESS OF HUMAN BEINGS TO GOD

Clearly all forms and directions of the surrender of humans to God are variations of a unique and unitary movement towards God, of that movement in which the human being goes to God *qua* God. This is the very root of the surrender, or better still, the radical surrender itself. All types of surrender presuppose this radical surrender: they are inscribed in it and are the directional modalities of it. This surrender is what we call, in a more or less vague and nominal manner, *faith*. Faith in itself is a surrender, and is the radical form of the access of humans to God.

Of course, this affirmation is just a mere postulate, because unless one details with full rigor what is understood by faith, the affirmation has little substance. On the other hand, such an affirmation may appear surprising in view of the fact that in the previous chapter we have attempted an intellectual justification of the reality of God. So, it might not seem that the access of humans to God is a matter of faith. Intellection and faith do not appear to be compatible. Nor is this the only problem. The fact is that, as we have said, the surrender of human beings to God has several forms and directions according to the type of persons involved and the situations in which they find themselves. And this is because each human being surrenders to God in all his or her individual, social, and historical concretion. The diversity of ways and types of surrender to God are the {210} inexorable consequence of that concretion. Hence, concretion is essential to surrender as such; in other words, it affects faith itself. Faith is essentially and constitutively concrete.

If we wish to penetrate into what the access to God is, it will be necessary to consider the three questions that have just come to our attention:

> I. What is faith formally considered, i.e., what is faith *qua* faith?
>
> II. What is the unity between intellection and faith?

158 UNFOLDING OF THE PROBLEM: HUMAN ACCESS TO GOD

III. How do we make faith concrete?

These are the three steps which must be covered in order to reach an understanding of what faith is.

I

What is faith formally?

We take faith here in all of its dimensions as a human phenomenon. But in order to avoid lengthier discussions, I shall aim almost immediately towards what is of primary interest to us, faith in God.

In general faith has usually been understood as an assent to a judgment grounded upon the testimony of another, and that consequently faith is an intellectual knowing. In this type of understanding two things are clear, the object of faith and the formal characteristic of the act of faith. The object of faith is the truth of a judgment. The character of the act of faith is an assent because of a testimony. In the problem concerning us here, faith would have as its object a series of affirmations about {211} God, and would consist in assenting to its truth based on a testimony, which ultimately would be the authority of God Himself.

That this exists in some form or another in any act of faith is more or less plausible. But only "in some form", because the important question is another: Is that the first and formal structure of any faith, and especially faith in God? Once we frame the question from this perspective, the inadequacy of the foregoing concept of faith becomes clear both with respect to what concerns the formal character of the act of believing and its own proper object.

In the first place, from the viewpoint of the believer, faith does not consist in the connection between testimony and what is contained in the testimony, but rather in admitting the testimony as testimony. But this implies that what is primary and decisive in faith is found not in the *assent* but in the *admission*. Now, admission is a phenomenon surpassing the limits of intellectual assent. So it then becomes necessary to ask what, precisely, admitting is. With that the problem of faith has emerged intact from this discussion. In the second place, it becomes clear that faith, as a type of admission, does not rest primarily and formally upon a judgment. It is certain that faith rests upon something true. But, is the truth of a judgment the radical and primary form of truth? Not at all. Therefore, the least that must be said is that faith does not consist in the assent to a judgment, but in the admission of what is true. This moves the problem along different paths, both when dealing with the faith as such and when dealing with faith in God in particular.

Above all, one thing is clear: admission is a mode of that we have been calling "surrender". Surrender, as we saw, is a going from ourselves towards another person, giving ourselves to that person. Each human surrenders to God accepting His {212} I, His own personal being, in terms of the personal reality of God. Therefore, faith is primarily and radically the surrender of my person to a personal reality, to another person. What there is in faith as assent to a testimony is but an aspect of something more primary, namely surrender. Faith is not *assent to a judgment*, but *surrender to a personal reality*. The act of faith is an act of surrender, which requires, on the one hand that we say in what faith consists as surrender to personal reality, and on the other that we clearly present the characteristics of this surrender *qua* surrender.

1. The nature of the surrender in which faith consists is specified by the nature of that upon which the faith rests, i.e., by that to which the faith surrenders. We have just mentioned it: faith is surrender to a person, to a personal reality. The question then reduces to inquiring about the aspect of this personal reality to which my person formally surrenders in the act of faith. Unless that is stated, we have done nothing but blow smoke with respect to the most general act of surrender, that which is proper to faith, namely the belief in truth. Faith is a surrender to a person, which encompasses a belief in truth. On the pretext that faith is not based formally upon the truth of a judgment, theology and the philosophy of religion have embraced this way of surrender to a person, without questioning the moment of truth; and with that, what properly belongs to faith as an act of surrender has been lost. This is, to my way of thinking, a serious defect of current theology and philosophy.

The surrender constituting faith is a surrender to a person inasmuch as that person entails truth. What is this truth? That is the issue. One might think that it is the {213} case of a truth communicated by the person to whom the surrender is made. In other words, faith would be the surrender to a person insofar as that person communicates a truth. In the case of divine faith, it would be to believe *that which* God communicates. The surrender of faith would consist, as St. Augustine said, in a *credere Deo*, in believing God.

Saint Augustine himself vociferously attacks this concept of faith as inadequate, because what is decisive is not to believe what a person says, but something deeper and more radical: to believe *in the person* himself. In the case of God faith is *credere in Deum*, to believe *in* God, and not simply *credere Deo*, believing God. However, what is it to believe in a person, and in particular, what is it to believe in God? For St. Augustine, the matter presents no doubts: *credere in Deum (est) credendo amare, credendo diligere*[6] (to believe in God is to love while believing). Taken from the point of view of our analysis, faith would be personal surrender through love.

An issue inevitably arises when we face this Augustinian concept of faith as personal surrender. According to it, faith would be an act of love, an act of surrender. But this is clearly inadequate: faith is not only an act of love but a surrender to a person *qua* bearer, so to speak, of truth. And St. Augustine would not deny it. What happens then is that the notion of believing in God, *credere in Deum*, involves a certain internal duality in St. Augustine. There would be, on one hand, an *amare*, a love which rests upon the person as such, and on the other, a belief, a *credere* which would rest upon the truth "borne" or communicated by the person in question. However, faith is a unitary phenomenon: it is a loving which must encompass believing intrinsically and formally, or put differently, it is a believing that is an intrinsic and constitutive moment of loving. Now, {214} this can only occur if the truth to which faith refers is not the truth borne by the person in which one believes, but rather is the truth in which the person consists in himself. We are not dealing, therefore, with the truth of what the person says or does, but with the truth which is that person himself *qua* reality. Hence, faith is, intrinsically and at one and the same time, loving and believing. This is, to my way of thinking, just what constitutes believing in God: faith is the surrender to a personal reality *qua* true. Here is what we have been searching for. Faith, as I said, is an act of surrender to a personal reality. Now, what is specific to this surrender and makes of it an act of faith is that the surrender rests upon a person *qua* true. It is necessary, therefore, to justify and explain this conceptualization.

Everything depends upon what is understood by "truth". We have said so repeatedly. Primary and radical truth is not the conformity of thought with things, i.e., truth is not primarily a property of thought, but a property of reality itself, that characteristic according to which reality itself is actualized in the intelligence. This is what I have called *real truth*. This truth has, as we indicated, three dimensions: patency of reality, firmness of reality, facticity of reality. Patency, firmness, and facticity are the three dimensions of the intellective actualization of reality. Now, with respect to a personal reality, this truth takes on particular characteristics which make of it a *personal truth*. In the first place, personal reality actualizes itself in the form of a *manifestation* of its own reality. But let us not confuse this manifestation with making a statement; personal reality can be manifested in a thousand other ways. In the second {215} place, personal reality has that type of firmness which is *fidelity* to what it offers to be. Finally, in the third place, personal reality actualizes itself in accordance with that characteristic making it something *indisputably a fact*. Personal reality is a reality which *qua* reality is a truth that intrinsically possesses these three dimensions at the same time.

Consequently, the surrender to a personal reality *qua* real personal truth, i.e., *qua* manifest, faithful, and indisputable fact, is precisely the formal essence of faith. We will only have penetrated into this phenomenon after we liberate ourselves from a narrow concept of truth, i.e., as if truth were only manifestation, and at that, an enunciative manifestation. For faith—we shall see this in a separate paragraph—a certain manifestation is necessary. But also co-essential for faith is that the person to which it surrenders—human or God—be a person with a fidelity upon which one can rely, and in addition constitute a reality as indisputably a fact as the sun or the mountains. To believe in a person, to have faith in him, is to surrender to him in this his real personal truth, and not in the truth of what is communicated. Faith in what a person communicates is only possible founded upon faith as a surrender to the person *qua* truthful.

This is, in its highest form, the case of faith in God. God is absolutely personal reality. Hence, His real personal truth is also absolute: it is, at one and the same time, as we indicated, absolute manifestation, absolute fidelity, absolute indisputability. Because of this, our surrender to Him *qua* real personal truth is faith. And because of it, faith is inscribed totally in the theological dynamic tension between God and humans. Faith, in fact, is a metaphysical form of inter-personal causality {216} between the divine person and the human person. God *qua* true is intrinsically and formally present to the human person *qua* real and true. Therefore, *surrendering oneself to God in faith is surrendering oneself to the transcendent ground of one's own person*. Conversely, faith is a motion towards my internal transcendence; it is faith in personal transcendence, faith in the real truth that, in a manifestative way, faithfully and indisputably effective, constitutes me by being a font. *Faith in personal transcendence* is already *faith in God*. The unity of these two italicized propositions is faith as dynamic tension of my real truth in the real truth of God.

This surrender to God in faith is the formal character of any surrender to God. Every surrender is, as we have seen, acquiescence, supplication, and refuge seeking. But these three moments are precisely and formally moments of faith; because it is faith that makes them possible and necessary at the same time. In faith, each human *de facto* surrenders to the personal reality of God as manifested, faithful, and indisputably effective. These three dimensions of the personal truth of God are unitarially included in the act of faith in the divine person, in the surrender of each human being to the personal reality of God *qua* true. Now, in its aspect of surrender to the personal reality of God *qua* manifest, faith is acquiescence. In its aspect of surrender to the personal reality of God *qua* faithful, faith is supplication. In its aspect of surrender to the personal reality of God *qua* indisputably effective, faith is refuge seeking. So, faith is acquiescence, supplication, and refuge seeking. If it were to lack any of these moments, it would cease to be faith. Therefore, faith, as surrender to the personal reality of God *qua* {217} true, is the very essence of acquiescence, supplication, and refuge seeking, i.e., it is the very essence of the surrender of humans to God, of the access of humans to God.

Such is faith as a surrender, specified by the nature of that upon which the faith rests. Now we must take a further step and ask ourselves, what are the characteristics of this surrender to the true personal reality of God *qua* act of surrender?

2. The characteristics of faith *qua* personal act derive in good measure from the very nature of its object:

A) Faith rests upon the true, but is not mere assent: it is surrender. Naturally, it is a surrender involving, according to what we have said, a moment of truth: it is a surrender to the personal truth of another, be it a human being or God. Now, in this dimension, the constitutive surrender of faith is what we call *personal adherence*. That is the first characteristic of faith.

In faith, one human person adheres to another person, *in casu* to the divine personal reality. Adherence is not the assent, but rather assent is the enunciation of the adherence, an enunciation generally only of the intellectual type. Furthermore, the adherence is prior to any assent not just because the latter is founded upon the former, but because strictly speaking the adherence is in a temporal sense prior to *any* expressed assent. Precisely because the adherence is extended to a person, we are admitting everything that this person may manifest to us beforehand, even if the manifestation is never complete. However, this does not establish it as *blind faith*, as it is usually called (we shall return to this theme), but as a *personal faith*, something entirely different. In a certain way, it is a faith which, even if it does not see everything, at least in principle it makes it possible to see. {218}

As a determinant of an adherence, we commonly express (not in a technical sense) that faith is "inspiration": that which moves one towards adherence is the faith which a person inspires. In this adherence, each human incorporates him- or herself into the person that is believed, and in a certain way links himself to that person's fate. And since the person to which one adheres is real truth, it follows that the person adhering, in some way, acquires the properties (let us use that expression) of the personal truth belonging to whom he adheres. By virtue of this, the one who adheres has strengthened his own real truth in and with the real truth of the person adhered to; he has become, so to speak, more true: more manifest, more faithful, more factual or real. This leads us to a second characteristic of faith:

B) Faith is not only personal adherence, but an adherence that has the characteristics of a *firm certitude*. What is this firmness? It is a *personal assurance*; not a psychological obstinacy. Of course, this assurance admits of degrees; there are adherences which are more and others which are less firm. What are these degrees? They are not, as the philosophy and theology of the beginning of the twentieth century imagined, degrees in the scale of assurances, from mere possibility passing through probability until certainty, which would then be nothing but the upper limit of the probabilities. No. Faith, adherence, ascribes itself fully to certainty and *is within it*. Assurance is not the limit of probabilities, i.e., of insecurities. Between certitude and probability there may not be discontinuity, but there is always a distinction of nature. Faith as certitude is always firm adherence. Negatively stated, faith excludes the fear of erring. And it is this fear which admits degrees from within the certitude itself. The degrees of certitude are not measured by insecurities, but by the positive energy, so to speak, with which {219} the adherence springs forth from the mind and installs itself in it. To have a greater faith than someone else does not mean to have more probability than this other one, but to believe with more energy. The firmness of an adherence is intrinsic and does not refer extrinsically to probabilities and possibilities. To lose a certitude does not mean reducing it to a mere probability or possibility or impossibility, but reducing it to something uncertain, to have lost the energy of the personal adherence, regardless of the causes and motives that produced the loss. Faith, in this aspect, is a personal assurance more or less strong, energetic and resistant.

This firmness discloses a double aspect in faith. Until now we have discussed faith *as act*. But this act, precisely because it is firm, leaves the one who executes it in a state: this is faith *as state*. The "I believe" of the act, is accompanied by the "I have believed" of the state. This state is not merely individual. All humans are born and live in a society. And every society has a world. Here "world" does not mean the respectivity of the real *qua* real, but the system of ideas, values, norms, customs, etc., which are current in that society; and therefore the individuals in that society consider them as "being there". By being there they are *tópos*, place, something which is at hand. These ideas, etc., are principles or powers which determine the life of the individuals who comprise the society in question. The system of these principles or topical powers of a society is what, to my way of thinking, constitutes their world. Their ideas about God form part of their world. As a moment of the world, faith is something upon which one is based firmly, with security. This is the faith in which each human is constitutively installed in a society. The individual may not share this faith for a variety of {220} reasons; as we shall see later, an installed mind is not a closed mind. But if the individual shares that faith, generally it is not a faith that has issued from the depths of his personal mind, but rather has been shaped by the form of his social world. At any rate, faith is not only an act but also the firmness of a state of surrender, of adherence, be it individual or social.

C) This surrender is always personal. As such, we already pointed out, it is not merely a being "carried", but an active and positive "going" from our own selves to God. If we were just "carried", we would be "dragged" by a power that does not depend upon us. This is what occurs with the inchoate access of humans to God. In that access, it is God Himself who, by reason of being "pre-tension", drags us from Himself towards Himself, regardless of whether humans are aware of it or wish it. But concerning the plenary access, i.e., of our surrender to God, we ourselves are the ones going; therefore we are, ourselves, the ones who provide the surrender. Surrender is donation. The person to whom we grant it is not extraneous, of course, to our donation. But his function is not a "dragging" motion, as in the inchoate access, but a motion of mere "attraction", including in this concept all the varied forms with which a person can request without forcing us: solicitation, insinuation, suggestion, etc. Each person accepts and makes this attraction his own, or he rejects it. Only by making it his own, is it converted into a personal surrender. To surrender oneself consists precisely in making this attraction ours. And to make an attraction ours is precisely to choose. Indeed, this is what is radical about faith: faith is choice. Here is the third characteristic of that surrender in which faith consists, *qua* surrender. What is always radical about human beings is choice: {221} love, vocation, religion, etc., are essentially choices. And faith is a choice to surrender to a person *qua* true. It is a choice of our whole reality and not merely of the intelligence, feelings, or will; it is a choice of our reality for the radical and ultimate figure of our relatively absolute being, of our *I*.

Choice is not an inclination or tendency of our soul, but an act of our person, if one wishes, an act of our reality *qua* personal. And because of this, by being a personal choice, faith is radically free. "Free" means here that we are not dragged to it without coercion, but simply attracted: freedom consists in our being the ones who determine whether to make this attraction our own. It follows that freedom is not arbitrariness. A free choice is not an arbitrary choice, but one that is not forced. Hence, precisely because that attraction exists, the choice is grounded squarely upon that which attracts us, i.e., upon that which it offers us in its personal truth.

In summary, faith is a surrender or personal adherence, firm and made by choice, to a personal reality *qua* true. Ultimately, faith is simply to make our own that attraction with which the personal truth of God moves us towards Him. It is in this faith that the radical access of humans to God consists.

But serious problem remains. Such surrender, indeed, is a faith. But the God we are now referring to is not the God of any particular religion (Christian, Brahmanic, Phoenician, or any other). It is purely and simply God *qua* God; a God, in this sense, which is personal but common to any religion: this is God as absolutely absolute {222} reality in His absolute concretion. Since that reality does not present itself to us immediately, but at most in a "towards", it was indispensable to justify His existence intellectually. But even though justified with a strict line of reasoning, it is unclear how this reality may be an object of faith, of a free choice to surrender my person; this is the problem of "intelligence-faith", the second of the three great questions that faith posed to us. The first was the formal characteristics of faith. Let us proceed now to the second: the unity of intelligence and faith.

II

Intelligence and faith

The problem of the "relationship" between intelligence and faith is usually presented in classical philosophy and theology in an apparently simple way: Is it possible for a truth to be true for reason and faith "at the same time"? Let us ignore for the present that in this formula intelligence and reason are not properly identified; to avoid lengthy discussions let us accept the terms of the formulation. It is commonly thought that the difficulty resides squarely with the "at the same time". Of course, it is understood that this is "at the same time" for me. A difficult theorem is always a truth of reason "in itself", but for a layman in mathematics it is a truth of simple belief. Then the above question means: how is it possible that the same truth can be for me a truth of reason and a truth of faith simultaneously? Because if reason has proved the reality of God, it makes no sense {223} that this reality should be for me an object of faith, and still less of a faith whose essential characteristic is to be a free choice.

Naturally, the force of this argumentation is based upon a certain notion of what reason and faith are. The point of departure is that faith consists in "believing what we have not seen", which presupposes that "knowing is seeing". In that case the "at the same time" of reason and faith would be the "at the same time" of not-seeing and seeing. But this is impossible. It is commonly added, that when dealing with "religious" truths, reason alone is not enough to admit them; some "moral dispositions" are also required. But what these dispositions are, and above all what their function might be with respect to the rational proofs in question, is left rather obscure. And since the sense of the "at the same time" of reason and faith depends on this, the problem has now been displaced: we had been told before that the problem consisted in something being seen and not seen "at the same time"; now we are told that the problem consists in the relationship between reason and moral dispositions. Certainly, this does not help to clarify the issue. In order to reach the root of the question it will therefore be necessary to confront the two problems mentioned:

1. What is the essential difference between intelligence and faith when we are dealing with the reality of God?

2. What is the radical characteristic of the "at the same time" of intelligence and faith?

1. *Difference between intelligence and faith.* Let us begin by reviewing and discussing the classical theses.

A) One usually begins by saying, or rather presupposing, that "knowing is seeing". Is this true? I refer, obviously, to intellectual knowing. Now, only a narrowly conceived notion of intelligence could have produced this type of concept and led to it being regarded as something obvious since the time of the {224} Greeks. To intellectively know, according to my way of thinking, is not formally to see, but to have in my intelligence the actuality of the real apprehended as real. It is true that it is not enough to have something actually in the intelligence, to say that we know what it is; but it is undeniable that whatever is missing to arrive at that knowledge has to move *formally* in that actuality, and will have to consist in making that actuality fuller. What is essential, therefore, is this primary actualization. Its primary form is impression. And yet, sight is not the exclusive form of knowing, precisely because it is not the exclusive form of the impression of reality, nor, consequently, of intellection. Each sense, as we indicated above, presents to us not only what is real, but reality itself, in its own form. Through sight (in the simplest way we think of it) a thing itself is formally present; through hearing a thing is present in the form of "announcement", etc. In all the senses and especially those of orientation and equilibrium, we have reality apprehended in the form of "towards". This propels intelligence along the road of searching, and is the commencement of reason. But to be sure, once we are propelled along the road of this "towards", there is no guarantee that what we will find will be "seeing" the thing searched for. It is quite possible that the best of our intellection may not have this visual character. When the physics of elementary particles formulated its equations, it became manifest that particles are not classical particles or waves. Particles and waves share characteristics, and in this consists our true knowledge of them; but these particles not only have never been seen, they are not even visualizable as the physicists once thought. We knows about elementary particles by moving in reality "as towards," not by having it {225} before us as in the case of sight. And the reality found this way is present in a law, but it is not visual. The knowledge of elementary particles is not seeing. I have emphasized this example, so fundamental to modern science, to preclude the comment that denial of the identity between knowing and seeing refers primarily to theological issues. To know is not necessarily to see.

B) But neither is it the case that faith is "believing what is not seen." If one thinks that knowing is seeing, it follows that whatever is not-seen is excluded from intellective knowing and is placed in the category of the irrational: such is blind faith. However, this is not true. Is it true that in faith nothing is seen? Here it is usual to take "seeing" for the presence of what is made known in the intelligence. Then we will have to affirm that in faith something *is* seen, in the sense that something pertaining to what is believed is actually present in the intelligence. And this is because reality can be present in many ways, as many as the senses that each human possesses. Let us reiterate: by hearing, a thing itself is not formally present as we usually think it is by sight. But, how can we possibly say that in the sound that is heard there is nothing present belonging to the thing that sounds? The thing itself is not formally present; but it is a fact that sound is formally and intrinsically remitting to the thing itself, because it is "its" announcement. The announcement is always "of" a thing. This "of" is not an extraneous relation between what is heard and the thing, but a formal moment of sound itself. Therefore, this "of" is the "announced" presence of the thing. The remitting presence, as poor it may seem, is a true presence. The presumed poverty of hearing is fed by our apprehension of the physical world. And yet, as soon as we enter the domain of personal realities, hearing suddenly acquires an enormous volume, to {226} the point where one could very well think that this volume is greater than the one from sight. The same could be said about the sense of touch: merely being touched by something real is already a presence. Certainly, it is not present to us in the same manner as is the real; but it is the presence of what I usually call "naked reality". And this moment of "nakedness" formally belongs to the tactile; it is presence and "nothing else" but presence. This "nothing else" is precisely the nakedness, as an intrinsic and formal moment of the tactile. In addition, the real, as we have said repeatedly, can be present to us in the form of "towards". Please allow me to insist: it is not a question of a presence "towards the real", but rather "reality as towards". In the "towards" resides the directional presence of reality. And we would have to say something similarly appropriate for the remaining senses. But that is not the point. The only thing relevant here is that the real is present to us not only in a visual form, but also in forms that are not visual, and perhaps not even visualizable. However, in all of them the real is categorically present for us. Furthermore, these diverse forms of presence are not simply juxtaposed, but possess a *primary* unity. They constitute unitarially and *a radice* that which we call "the presence of reality for us". And this is true above all with respect to pure sensing. The many forms of sensing do not exist, each in and by itself, in order to later constitute a synthesis; on the contrary, their diversity is the analytical differentiation of sensing: "the many" senses are the analyzers of "the one" sensing. And since it is always the case of intellective sensings, it follows that the structure of the presence of the real in sensing is *eo ipso* the structure of intellection in its diverse aspects or types. Intellection as such is "at one and the same time" the apprehension of the real *in all its forms*. In their primary unity, {227} these modalities carry sentient intelligence over different roads. The "towards" of the notification carries intelligence "towards" the sonorous thing, towards the announced. The "towards" of "nakedness" carries intelligence to probing the type of thing it is, etc. This is true even with respect to sight: the "towards" takes us from the *eidos* to the intellection of the thing's internal structure.

This is why we must distinguish and refer to the *different types of intellection*: there is an auditive intellection, a tactile intellection, a directional intellection, etc. These are not metaphorical expressions; or rather, not more metaphorical than those terms having their origin in vision and with which it has been common to express and conceptualize intellection: intuition, evidence, etc. This has been taken as the structure of human intelligence, though it is nothing more than the structure of visual intellection. For this reason I have elaborated of a theory of sentient intelligence as such in all its aspects and modes. In this task, the only essential thing was to reach this full concept of intelligence.

With this concept we now have the instrument, so to speak, that forces us to better conceptualize the presence of the real in humans. It is not necessarily a presence either visual or visualizable; but it is always a real presence, and therefore a mode of intellection, however poor in many of its aspects, but still a true intellection. What is not visual is not necessarily irrational. This is the case with faith in God. God is not present to us like a thing that might be visual or visualizable; but this does not mean that He cannot be intellectively present to us in any form whatsoever. And in this sense, faith is never absolutely blind. It always involves some presence of the real in notification, nakedness, and direction. {228} Therefore, it always involves an intellective moment.

Let us conclude by saying that knowing is not seeing, and believing does not consist in being blind. From this discussion we recognize not only the inadequacy of the classical formula of faith with respect to intelligence and faith, but something positive and much more important, to wit, that it is necessary to begin by attending to the manner in which God is present to us. And this manner is what becomes decisive in our problem, because upon it depends the difference between intelligence and faith, as human attitudes concerning reality.

C) In the course of this study we have already discussed the manner in which God is present to us; but it is convenient to review it now, even if briefly. God is not a reality present to us as a thing is present to our sight, nor is intellection of Him of the type belonging to any reality we find in our life, i.e., in the construction of my being out of the substantive, of my *I*. And yet, there is a certain presence of God in reality, and with it there is a certain type of intellection of Him in human life.

a) Human beings are essences open to things as real in the construction of their own *I*. In this construction, the real is a power, the power of the real. And this power holds us and sustains us as constitutively religated. This power of the real, therefore, is immediately present to us in religation.

b) But this power of the real presents to us the constitutive enigma of everything real. Every real thing is, actually, ambivalent. On the one hand it is its "own" reality, but on the other, its reality manifests to us that it is in some way "more than what it is" itself. This is the constitutive enigma of every real thing. And this enigma is also immediately present. In religation to the power of the real, the formally enigmatic {229} character of the real *qua* real is immediately present to us.

c) Whence we obtain the particular type of intellection due to this presence. In the enigma we are not "in front of" that in which the enigma is rooted, as we would be if we were in front of a thing we can see. Rather, in the immediate presence of the enigma we are thrown "towards" its root in things themselves. This is reality "in the sense of towards", and therefore, an intellection "in the sense of towards". Indeed, there is an authentic presence of this root, but only "in the sense of towards". Conversely, though only "in the sense of towards", it is still a concise presence and therefore strictly speaking an intellection. It is a directional intellection because it is reality as directionally present. Reality is not presenting to us the merely intellectual problem of "resolving" an enigma, but is taking us to it. In the enigma we are not simply "directed" towards its root, but we are physically "hurled" after it.

d) In this intellection each human, I say, is hurled "towards". And the terminal point of a "towards" is always a somewhat difficult problem. Actually, the "towards" throws us towards a terminus which is not determined by the "towards" itself. Furthermore, it is a terminus which is not of itself univocally determinable. Indeed the "towards" is an intellection which is not only undetermined, but with a wide range open to many possibilities. Moreover, a human being does not determine the terminus of the "towards" arbitrarily, but with respect to a particular ground. To pin down the terminus, the intelligence needs to perform several acts; they can be encompassed under the general category of "proof", "demonstration", etc. The terminology is indifferent to us. And the case is the same whether we are dealing with the enigma of reality, a problem in theoretical physics, in biology or in history. The only thing that will vary is the grounding as a function of the nature of that which forces us to it. In the case of the enigma of reality, the {230} immediate presence of this enigma has hurled us towards its ground "in" things themselves. This grounding is, therefore, a "proof" of the terminus of the "towards" as the root of the enigma, and therefore, in a certain way, of its "solution": God. The immediate presence of the enigma of reality in religation to the power of the real is a directional presence of the reality of "something", which intelligence proves to be God. It is not a visual intellection of God because God is not only not "seen" but is not even "visualizable". But yet, it is a strict directional intellection of Him. God is present in the real only directionally; but directionally He is indeed really present in the real. Humans do not immediately know that what is directionally present is God. That is why they have to prove it; and by the same token, the proof is not so much that there is a God, but that something among what is, is really God.

But, let us reiterate, we are dealing with a directional presence in the power of the real, to which we are constitutively and undeniably religated. Because of this, what the intelligence proves is the reality of God as ground of our religation in the construction of the *I* belonging to each of us. And this is what is essential in the question we have been debating: the difference between intelligence and faith. Everything we have just mentioned in the foregoing two pages is a succinct repetition of ideas previously developed; it is a repetition intended only to orient and provide the exact outline of this problem. Therefore, let us say that the problem of the difference between intelligence and faith is a problem situated entirely within the nature of the terminus to which our proof has led us: God as ground of our relatively absolute being.

D) Indeed, the terminus to which the proof leads is {231} God. But to God, not as a reality that is the object of investigation, but a reality as ground of the power of the real in religation. As we earlier pointed out, *reality-object* is not the same as *reality-*

ground. The reality-object "is in front" of me and its presence exhausts itself in its own affirmation, so to speak, as being what it is in and by itself. On the other hand, a reality-ground is certainly a reality in and by itself (if not, it would not be a ground), though its presence is not one of affirming itself through what it is, but in *being my* ground, it is *in me* grounding myself. As a ground, a reality-ground is happening in me, something quite different than the presence of a merely being in and by itself. It "is not in front" of me, but "happens in" me, is happening in me. It is present and religating me in the power of the real. The formal terminus of the proof of God's existence is God as ground of the power of the real in religation, i.e., as reality which is happening in me. But then, the proof has two facets. On one hand, it is a proof of God as *reality*-ground. But on the other, it is a proof that He is reality-*ground*, i.e., that this reality, by being a ground, is happening in my own life's happening, as an ultimate reality, possibilitating, and impelling. This produces a twofold attitude in human beings. On one side it is the attitude of *knowing* about the reality of God; on the other, it is an attitude that can be the *acceptance* of that divine occurrence, an acceptance which is the essence of surrender. And since all surrender is radically faith, i.e., surrender to the personal reality of God *qua* true, it follows that the proof of the reality of God as reality-ground places the problem of "intelligence and faith" not *outside* intelligence, i.e., as if it were a {232} problem "intelligence vs. no-intelligence", but *inside* intelligence itself; it becomes the problem of "knowledge and surrender". Once the question is posed in this manner, it becomes clear that, on one hand, knowledge and faith are essentially different even though we may have demonstrative knowledge, but on the other, they are essentially connected to each other even without any demonstrations. Let us explain this.

a) Knowledge and faith are essentially different. The matter is clear in cases where the truth in question is the result of great faith and limited knowledge. This is the case of the mysteries of Christianity, which cannot be demonstrated. It is not necessary to insist on this point. But what concerns me is that there are truths, like the existence of God, of which we can have great knowledge, yet, this knowledge by itself is not faith. In such cases knowledge and faith are not only different but perfectly separable. This is so because knowledge of some reality, even when rigorously conclusive and evident as a mathematical theorem, does not entail a surrender, a faith. And this is not because (as usually claimed), if we know something well it is not necessary to have faith in it, i.e., because such knowledge leaves no place for doubt;

rather, it is because knowing and surrendering are two irreducibly different attitudes. The matter is clear when dealing with a reality-object. The reality-object can only allow for knowing, not because faith is not needed in this case, but because of the characteristics of that which is known, i.e., to be a reality-object formally excludes being the object of surrender. Theology and classical philosophy have considered God as a reality-object; from this stems the impossibility of having faith in a God whose existence has been demonstrated. But that entire approach is mistaken: God is a reality-ground. {233}

When dealing with this type of reality, to know that it is happening in me does not automatically entail a surrender to God, regardless how conclusive, evident, and convincing the proof. And this is because the fact that God may be happening in me is, ultimately, God's business, not mine. God happens in me, whether I know it or not, whether I wish it or not. In order for this to be my business something more is needed: it is necessary that I make it mine. And this *making it my business* is the acceptance, the surrender. This is what I expressed earlier when referring to the access of humans to God as something different than the access of God to humans. The surrender consists in my incorporating formally and deeply into my happening, as *something brought about by me*, the happening through which God *happens in me*. That God occurs in me is a *function of God in life*. But the surrender to God is to make *life into a function of God*. And under these conditions, knowledge and faith are not only different but separable. We can very well know by demonstration the existence of God and His grounding characteristics, and yet have an attitude other than surrender. For example, we can demonstrate and admit the existence of God conclusively, and then disregard it, dealing with God as he would with any other object in the universe. He may even reject His intervention in life and rebel against it. Between both extremes there is a complete gamut of intermediate attitudes, despite the presence in all of them of an admittedly conclusive demonstration. None of them is surrender and therefore none is faith. In those cases, the lack of faith does not stem from the presence of a demonstrative knowledge making faith impossible because it is useless, i.e., because a proof is already in hand, but because it is demonstrative knowledge without surrender. {234}

There are cases of a type where knowledge is insufficient in itself, but in which, nonetheless, the surrender is total. This is what occurs, as I mentioned above, either when dealing with truths which exceed the natural capacities of intelligence, like the truths of Christianity, or dealing with the existence of God, when no proof of His existence has been found. But in all these cases there is some intellection of the reality to which a human surrenders, at least an intellection of the auditive type, as announcement.

Regardless of the perspective one may choose to approach this question, there is a knowledge (demonstrative or not) and in addition a surrender, or an absence of surrender. In other words, there is knowledge without faith, or knowledge and faith. Therefore, there is an irreducible distinction between the two terms. Because of this, I consider it a serious error to say, "if there is proof, no faith is possible, and if there is faith, the proof is not possible without faith ceasing to exist". Both affirmations are false. No knowledge, demonstrative or otherwise, entails surrender within itself: there is faith in addition to knowledge. On the other hand, any surrender presupposes knowledge (demonstrative or not): there is knowledge in addition to faith. Returning to the usual formulation, the fact of the matter is that the problem of reason and faith is not a problem between two *criteria* of knowing but a problem between two *attitudes*, knowing and surrendering in the face of the same one reality-ground, the personal reality of God *qua* true.

In summary, when dealing with a reality-ground, knowledge and faith are essentially different not only when it is the case of non-demonstrable truths, but even when dealing with truths rigorously demonstrated. {235}

b) Nevertheless, though essentially different, the two attitudes are not disconnected from each other, even in the case of truths that are not demonstrably knowable. Actually, any surrender, as we have pointed out, presupposes, or if one wish, carries in itself, a certain intellection of that to which each human surrenders; any faith entails a non-visual intellection, an intellection of the auditive type as announcement and "as towards". Otherwise, there would be no possibility of surrender. This issue comes to a head when dealing with truths of which there is precise demonstrative knowledge, as in the case of the existence of God. Therefore the connection between reason and faith is found to be formally anchored within intellection and not outside it. Hence, faith and reason do not primarily constitute two diverse domains, the domain of reason and the domain of faith, but two different functions of intelligence itself. What are they?

As we have discussed, intellection consists in the actuality of what is intellectively known in the intelligence. And therefore, the function of intelligence always depends upon the characteristics of that which is known intellectively. When that which is known intellectively is a reality-object, the function of intelligence consists in discovering it and "leaving it" in front of us, according to what it is in and by itself. But if that which is known intellectually is reality-ground, the intelligence has a dual function, or better still, a complex function. On one hand, it discloses reality to us, and on the other, it not only leaves it in front of us, but opens for us the whole realm of grounding, that realm where I can and must anchor my reality in its ground, i.e., it makes it possible for me to make that grounding mine. Strictly speaking they are not two functions, but the complexity of a function determined by the grounding characteristics of that which is intellectively known. They would be two functions if {236} grounding were a characteristic extrinsic to the presence of reality-ground. This is what might occur if it were the case, for example, of supporting oneself upon a reality-object in order to do something with it in life. Then reality is object and in addition it is useful for doing something. But this is not a reality-ground. Reality-ground is not a reality present as an object that in addition to, and extrinsic to its mode of presence, may have a grounding characteristic. Reality-ground is a reality whose own mode of presence in intellection consists, formally and intrinsically, in being that of grounding. Then its actuality in intellection discovers for us reality on one side, but on another it places us *eo ipso* in the realm of grounding. The unity of the functions does not lie in their convergence on the same object, as is the case with the reality-object, but is a unity in the intellection itself: the discovery of reality is formally the outline of the realm of grounding. Such is the case with the intellection of God. God is present to us in intellection, in the "towards" of the religating power of the real. Intellection has "hurled us towards" Him as *realitas groundalis*, as absolutely absolute reality, foundational of my relative absolute being. Intellection, therefore, discovers God for us in and by Himself, but does so by opening the realm of the grounding of my *I*. Hence, I know in a rigorously intellectual way, the reality of God; but this knowledge is in itself the opening to the realm of grounding. To be sure, it is not by such knowing that I make this grounding mine—that would be faith—but the knowing, inexorably, is what I make of God, in and by Himself, as the ground of the construction of my *I*, what makes {237} a faith possible. Whence the possibility of this faith is not something we have "in addition" to knowledge of the reality of God; rather, that knowledge is intrinsically and formally the opening to the realm of a possible faith. It is not the convergence of two attitudes upon the same object, but the unity of two attitudes *qua* attitudes. It is knowledge that *qua* knowledge constitutes the realm of the possible faith *qua* faith. Knowledge of God is already in itself, *qua* knowledge, a possible faith.

To be sure, we said earlier that faith and knowledge are two different attitudes that are so distinct as to be separable. This would seem to contradict what we have just said, i.e., the affirmation that knowledge is in itself and formally the opening to the realm of surrender, of faith. But the contradiction is only apparent. Formally the knowledge and the opening to the realm of faith are one. Yet the realm of faith is not faith itself. This and the other possible attitudes of humans when confronting God are irreducible to knowledge; but it is essential to knowledge to make them possible. All of them are inscribed in the same realm, and in this sense knowledge and realm belong to each other inexorably. So much so, that humans may be able to take many attitudes in it, but must inexorably take just one, after they have known God. Each may choose not to concern him- or herself with God, but this non-concern is a positive act; it is not a mere abstention from acting, but an act of abstention, and therefore an attitude. The realm we have been discussing is not faith, but is the possibility of faith and any other attitude. What is consubstantial to the knowledge of God is the possibility of faith. The truth of God is the real truth of an absolutely absolute person, and {238} therefore knowledge of Him is *eo ipso* the realm of surrender, of faith.

This is why I reject as inadequate classical conceptions of the connection between reason and faith (as it is usually termed), which have been circulating since the times of Tertullian and St. Augustine. One side has placed the accent on faith, *credo ut intelligam*, I believe in order to (*ut*) understand; the other has placed more emphasis on reason, *intelligo ut credam*, I understand in order to (*ut*) believe. But regardless of how one chooses to weigh these two, the question still remains: is this what is primary in the connection between knowledge and faith? From my point of view it is not, because in those conceptions it is presupposed that "connection" means "way": faith as the way "towards" (*ut*) knowledge or knowledge as the way "towards" (*ut*) faith. But to be a "way" is not the primary connection between knowledge and faith. If we place this question on a somewhat external plane, it is true that when dealing with mysteries that intelligence does not reach demonstratively, one might be able to refer to this as a "way". But beneath this consideration more radical questions appear. In the first place: How is that "way" possible? Upon what is the unity of the "way" based? We are not told. Indeed, it would be impossible for a term to connect to another if a common dimension did not exist in which the "way" in question could be traced. But then it becomes clear that it is within this common dimension that we find *eo ipso* that which is primary about the connection we are seeking. Now, this common dimension is the intellection as "towards", the presence as "towards" of God. From this it follows that the connection between knowledge and faith is the unity of two functions, or better still, the unitary complexity of one self-same function of intellection. And the proof resides in the fact that the problem of the {239} connection between knowledge and faith is not posed only with respect to incomprehensible truths like the mysteries, but most radically and basically, from my point of view, with respect to truths like the existence of God that *can* be known demonstratively. The radical connection between knowledge and faith with respect to the truth of God's existence is found in a simple fact: *because it deals with a reality-ground, the proof of God's existence establishes the realm of possible surrender to God*. It is no longer the case of a "way" which goes from knowledge to faith and from faith to knowledge, but of the unity of the groundal characteristic of the reality of God present in one self-same intellection. And in this unity is founded the connection having the type of a "way", i.e., of the type "*ut*" (in order to) when dealing with undemonstrable truths. In them there is always an intellection; and if faith is the way "towards" knowledge or the latter "towards" the former, this unity of "viability" is only possible when grounded upon the most primary and radical unity I have just presented: the unity of knowing and the realm of surrender in the intellection of the reality-ground in which God consists for us. Any truth of religious mysteries, however "mysterious" it may be, is always presented to us as a truth from God to human beings; therefore, the unity of knowledge and faith in these truths is inscribed and grounded in the unity of knowledge and faith such as it exists in the truth about God.

In summary, intelligence and faith, or rather, knowledge and faith are essentially different, but are essentially connected in the intellection of God: this is the unity in God as reality-ground, the unity of knowledge and the realm of surrender. But this realm of surrender is not the surrender {240} itself; it is only the possibility of the surrender. It is certain by virtue of this unity that each human being inexorably finds him- or herself compelled to assume an attitude with respect to God, whose existence he or she knows demonstratively. But this attitude, as we have said, is not necessarily the attitude of surrender, of faith. A human being can assume and in fact does assume other attitudes. With respect to all of them, the unity of knowledge and realm of surrender is just their most radical possibility. Hence we can do no less than ask ourselves the question of the radical characteristic of that forcefulness, i.e., of that which determines the step from its possibility to the reality of an attitude. Only then shall we be able to fully state the truth of the existence of God as simultaneously a truth of reason and a truth of faith. This is the second of the two important questions concerning intelligence and faith that we posed at the beginning of this paragraph. The first was the question of the difference and unity between intelligence and faith. The second is the question of the radical characteristic of the simultaneous truth of intelligence and faith.

2. *Actual radical unity of intelligence and faith.* We have just seen the radical unity of intelligence and faith, but only as a possibility. Therefore, the radical unity we have been describing is only a possible unity. We need to take a further step. We need to proceed beyond the possibility of surrender to the actual surrender. That is, we must describe precisely the characteristic of that by virtue of which the possibility takes on reality.

Clearly, the character of this factor depends essentially upon the nature of what we understand by "possibility". And although we have already made reference to them in some form throughout the last few pages, it will not be superfluous to collect carefully some of the concepts that have been appearing along the way, {241} orienting them towards the theme that concerns us now. Although that theme is the knowledge of God, what we are going to develop is neither exclusively nor preferentially proper to the knowledge of God, but concerns all knowledge as such.

As we have just said, the intellection of any reality is always, in some form, the intellection of reality "as towards". And the terminus to which we proceed in this "towards" is never univocally determined by reality itself. Unless the question is clarified further, several different forms of termini for the "towards" present themselves. From this it follows that what an intellection as "towards" formally does is to open in front of one's intelligence a realm of different possible determinations of the real. The indetermination of the terminus of the "towards" consists in being a realm. The real correlate of the "towards" is, therefore, a realm.

But this is not enough. What type of realm is this "towards"? Above all, it is a realm of several termini. And these termini are, thus far, just possible termini. Here "possible" means that unless the matter is not "resolved", these termini are *possible real things*. The realm, therefore, is a realm above all of possible real things. But not only this, because reality as "towards" not only *opens* the realm of real possible things, but *hurls* us to it. Intelligence, actually, has to move in this realm. These motions are, therefore, my motions; each one with its own direction. And insofar as this direction is not univocally determined, it is not only a possible direction in the abstract, so to speak, but is a possibility of mine for direction. In this aspect, the realm offers several possibilities of intellection {242} from my side. The terminus of the realm is not only possible real things, but also simultaneously *my own real possibilities*. We shall soon see the characteristic of such "unity". Therefore, a possibility of mine is a possibility to realize myself in a certain way, i.e., a possibility to realize my own being. The possibilities offered by the intellection as "towards" constitute a possibility of my self-realization. No knowledge, regardless of how remotely placed it may be from human reality—for example an abstract theorem in mathematics—is exempt from this condition. Real possible things open the realm of my real possibilities, and at the same time these possibilities can determine, in one form or another, the real possible things.

What is essential for us now are these possibilities and the characteristic of the realization of the possible *qua* possible. There is a different characteristic depending on whether we are dealing with possible real things or with my own real possibilities. Concerning a possible thing, its realization depends purely and simply upon the *actualization* of those potencies thanks to which the thing in question is possible. But when dealing with possibilities of mine it is not enough with the actuation of potencies. Between these and actual reality something different mediates: my appropriation of that possibility. The possibilities turn into actual reality not only by the actuation of previous potencies but above all by *appropriation*. If can also be stated this way, actualization incorporates in the potencies an intrinsic moment of appropriation. On the previous pages we spoke about acceptance, to make a possibility mine, etc., adding that in this consists surrender. We were doing nothing but anticipating the more precise concept of appropriation. The very essence of surrender is appropriation, and conversely {243} appropriation is the surrender of personal reality to a certain type of possibility, and therefore, to one's own particular way of being.

And so, each human not only *de facto* appropriates possibilities, but inexorably has to appropriate some, because every appropriation is one determination of my mode of being instead of others. And in this volition formally consists. Volition is ultimately and radically the determination of one possibility as a mode of my being. That upon which volition formally rests *qua* volition is the possibilities, and to desire them is to appropriate them. In this dimension the possibility involves and goes beyond the distinction between ends and means. The realm of possibilities is *eo ipso* a realm of volition. And since the possibilities are diverse, any appropriation is necessarily a *choice*. Thus, the *forcefulness to make my being* opens the realm of the possibilities of being; this forcefulness then carries a *choice*; and the choice realizes the possibility by *appropriation*. Forcefulness, choice, appropriation: here we have the formal structure of the step from possibilities to actual reality.

But let us not forget the point of departure of these considerations. We started from the intellection of God, and we inquired about the actual radical unity between knowledge of God and free faith in Him. At bottom, we now realize, is the problem of the unity of intellection and of appropriation in the determination of my being. And though it may seem paradoxical, this unity is found precisely in free choice. The choice, actually, is a choice of something intellectually known, and intellection is intellection of something being chosen as a possibility of mine. A possibility of what? We have just mentioned it: a possibility of my being, therefore, relatively {244} absolute. Consequently, if we call a choice, as it should be called, "will", it follows that the radical unity between knowledge of God and faith in God, is inscribed precisely and formally in the *will to be*. Let us be clear: this is not something that belongs exclusively to the theological problem we have been studying, but rather *is an essential structure of any knowledge, be it or not a knowledge of God*.

What is this will? It is not the mere tendency to be or the mere appetite of being. Certainly, not all my being is determined by choices; all my substantive reality, my appetites and all tendencies configure my being—not just what is chosen. But the fact of the matter is that just as stimulation itself opens the door to the awareness of reality for the intelligence, so also the tendency to be opens the door at certain levels to the function of choosing. To choose is not only a question of tendency, just as intellective knowing is not only a question of sensing. And as intelligence is sentient, in like manner the will is tending. Nonetheless, sensing is not intellective knowing, nor is tending or having appetite willing. Now, to choose is only possible by virtue of the function of the intelligence. Hence even though choosing is compulsory by the necessity of being relatively absolute, nonetheless, the terms of volition are opened by intellect. And since what is proper to intellection is to actualize the real in which real truth consists, it follows that what the will-to-be has of volition (and not of appetite) must be based in one form or another upon truth. The will to be *qua* will is, therefore, formally *will to truth*. Therefore, the radical unity of knowledge of God and faith in Him, consists in the *will to truth*. To understand this we must examine three questions:

A) What is this will to truth? {245}

B) What is the unity of knowledge and faith in God in the will to truth?

C) What is the will to truth in human reality?

I will repeat this *ad nauseam*: these are questions that do not belong exclusively to the knowledge of God, but concern the essence of any knowledge as such.

A) *The will to truth*. We must to conceptualize with some rigor what this will to truth is. Otherwise the second question runs the risk of loosing itself in empty vagaries. Therefore, I ask forbearance for this somewhat detailed explanation of purely philosophical character.

The expression "will to truth" has several meanings. In the *widest sense*, "will to truth" means what we have just indicated: the fact that our tendency or appetite moves within what intelligence proposes, and which in the widest sense may be called "the true". Here "true" means that whatever determines the will is known intellectually as "being" in one form or another, ignoring whether it actually is so. Therefore, in this context, "truth" means only that in some measure or another, the will determines itself by knowing that about which it determines itself, and that this knowledge counts as one of the essential motives for the determination. For this reason I speak about "the true", without further qualifications, as a synonym for "the known", and as a synonym for knowing that something "is". In this widest sense, will to truth is a pleonasm, because the will formally consists in determining itself within "the true". More than will to truth, this is the very definition of will as differentiated from mere tendency. It is, groundally, the idea which classical philosophy formulated about the will: rational appetite. I consider this concept of {246} will to be inadequate; however, we need not enter into a discussion of the matter here.

Although not the widest, there is still a *wide sense*, according to which the will to truth does not merely consist in moving within the realm of the true, but in proposing to itself something that may "truly" be. Above, truth was realm; now it is terminus of volition. Truth consists here not in merely being known but in "truly" being as distinguished from what is only "in appearance". To wish appearances only is to wish deceit. Humans can very well have the will to deceive others or to deceive themselves. Thus, the will to truth consists in *veracity* as opposed to *deceitfulness*. This is, in the deepest sense—and only there—what Nietzsche understood by will to truth (*Wille zur Wahrheit*): veracity (*Wahrhaftigkeit*) towards others or towards oneself. This second meaning presupposes the first: clearly veracity and deceit are possible only within what we have called the realm of the true.

The expression "will to truth" is nowadays employed everywhere with these two senses mixed indiscriminately. But there is a third sense which, I think, is the *strict meaning* of the will to truth. Here, "truth" does not mean either what is true or what is truly, but something much more modest, though much more radical: the actuality of the real in intelligence. This is what I have repeatedly termed "real truth". What is "true" and what is "truly" are inscribed in real truth. Only because the real is actual in the intelligence, i.e., only because apprehending the real as real is the essence of intelligence, it can and must elaborate ideas, assemble arguments, delineate projects, etc.; "the {247} true" presupposes real truth and is only possible through it. Likewise, the difference between being "truly" and being only "in appearance" is only possible because of real truth: to be truly and to be appearance are differences of the real actually present in intelligence. Therefore, the will to truth is primarily and formally *will to real truth*. What is this will?

In order to clarify it, let us recall that real truth, despite the simplicity of its definition, has an enormous inner richness. This is because real truth, i.e., the actualization of a real thing in intelligence, has three dimensions. Above all real truth consists in the *patency* of the real thing in the full richness of its notes. In the second place, we say that a real thing is true when we can depend on it, because its truth consists, in this dimension, in the fact that the thing is and operates in accordance with the being of what its notes offer: this is the *firmness*. Finally, truth means that the real is *in fact* real when it is in a certain way, commonly referred as "real and effective". Patency, firmness, and facticity are three different dimensions to be sure, but essentially inseparable. We may pay more attention to one than the other two, but the three of them always exist because their intrinsic unity constitutes the very essence of real truth.

Granting this, we ask, what is the will to real truth? At first sight, such a will may appear as something impossible because it concerns the structure of the intellectual act itself and therefore of something prior to any volition. Nevertheless, it exists, because real truth is not just a *beginning* of an intellectual process, but a *principle* of every act of intelligence of that process. If it were nothing but beginning, real truth would {248} only belong to a very remote past. But as principle, real truth is always present: every act of an intellectual process is supported by the presence of real truth. Reality, in fact, is present to us in primordial apprehension and in the whole intellective process in a variety of ways, and one of them is "as towards". Thus, reality itself in its real truth propels us to "ideate", encompassing in this term "ideate" all the many types of intellective processes that humans have to perform (conceive, judge, reason, plan, etc.), and the real truth which propels us to ideate *eo ipso* opens the realm of two possibilities. One, is to fall back upon ideas by themselves as if they were the canon of reality; taken to the limit, one ends by making ideas the true reality. The other is the inverse possibility, to address reality itself, and take ideas as organs which hinder or facilitate making reality ever more present in the intelligence. Guided by things and their real truth, intelligence enters deeper and deeper into the real, and achieves an increment of real truth. Each human has to opt for one of these two possibilities, i.e., he or she has to accomplish an act of the will: this is the *will to truth*. Real truth is certainly a constitutive moment of intellection as such; but takes us inexorably to the will to truth, precisely and formally because actualized reality in primordial apprehension is reality "as towards". In such manner the will to truth bases itself upon real truth. But then, this will to truth takes two different forms depending upon the choice made. If it opts for the first, we have the *will to truth of ideas*. If it opts for the second, we have the *will to real truth*. This is precisely what {249} we were searching for. Truth makes the will to truth necessary and makes the will for real truth possible. Human beings, in fact, can very easily drift into the option of the will to ideas. More difficult and less brilliant is to hold sternly to the will to things. Therefore it is urgent that we reclaim it vigorously.

The will to real truth seeks more presence of reality in humans. Because of this the will to real truth is the very condition to reach real truths, if not of the elemental or simple ones, at least of those founded upon them. Real truth, as I said, is certainly a characteristic of reality *qua* actualized in intelligence. But the nature of this actualization makes the will for truth inexorable. Now, *qua* terminus of the will to truth, the possession of real truth involves essentially not only the presence of the real but *eo ipso* the realization of my possibilities. It is, in fact, a choice for the possibility of real truth as different from the possibility of mere ideas. And like every volition, this choice among possibilities is an appropriation on my part, i.e., involves my own being. How does it do so? Not indeed because real truth consists or is grounded upon my own being; rather, it is my being that is grounded upon this truth. The will to real truth is not a question of *authenticity*; on the contrary, that will chooses because it is real truth that configures my being. The will to real truth involves my being not as an authentic expression of it, but configuring it by appropriation of the possibilities that real truth offers. In its apparent simplicity, real truth is filled with immense possibilities not only with respect to intellection {250} of things but with respect to realizations of my own being. In his or her will to real truth, each human being therefore appropriates the possibility for truth which reality offers, and surrenders to this truth, i.e., makes with it the figure of his or her own reality. In the surrender to real truth there occurs simultaneously the presence of reality and the realization of my own being in surrender to that truth. The will to real truth is thus the radical unity of the intellective process *in actu exercito*.

This unity has several characteristics, because the possibilities that real truth offers are in turn different depending upon the type of reality. I do not refer, of course, to the fact that human beings may take different attitudes when confronting the same reality, depending upon their particular interests, but to something prior, to the ways in which reality presents itself to me. These ways are all different. And this means that the radical unity of the intellectual process is also differentiated in the will to real truth.

If reality is present as reality-object, its real truth is certainly the actualization of what its reality is in and by itself. But its mode of actualization is most precise, consisting in the actualization of reality in and by itself, and nothing but this in and by itself. However, that "nothing but" is not just a negative moment. It is something eminently positive: the very definition of *a possibility of mine*, that of going to reality only for the sake of reality. The will to real truth is in this case will to reality, searching for reality itself. The appropriation of this possibility is the surrender to reality *for the sake of* reality. This "for the sake of" is what specifies my possibility and my option when confronting a reality-object. The option for real truth is now {251} an option in which I only wish to be the natural place, so to speak, of the truth of reality. It is, among other things, the birth of science (in the widest sense of the term). Scientific knowledge, of whatever type, owes its existence to the will to real truth. It is a free option: I might have chosen to surrender to reality not for the sake of reality but for its utility, application, etc. of realities (we are not now concerned with terminology). Let us call this the "will to the elaboration of reality." It follows that in the will to real truth, when dealing with a reality-object, what is present as act is the intrinsic and radical unity of intellection, plus an option of my being: it is simultaneously the presence of reality-object, and the realization of a mode of my being, i.e., my being as surrendered to reality for the sake of reality. This unity is that specific form of will to real truth expressed in "for the sake of": the surrender to reality for the sake of reality. Here is the will to real truth when that which is present is the reality-object.

But when reality is present as reality-ground we find ourselves in a different situation. Certainly its reality is also reality in and by itself, because if it were not it would not be a ground. But its mode of actualization in intelligence is very different from that of a reality-object. In a reality-object its reality is present in and by itself, and "nothing but". However, just the opposite occurs here, because the mode of actualization is "grounding", specifically, my grounding. Therefore, I am myself a moment of that actuality. The reality-ground is reality in and by itself but "*for* my sake". It is not the case that besides being real the reality ground may be something else that could be used to serve my interests, necessities, or conveniences. Rather, the very mode of presence {252} of this reality *qua* reality is to be what it is as a ground; the very mode of presence of this reality is "presence-for my sake". What is this *my*? Any act of mine certainly constitutes a characteristic of my being. And in this sense any act constitutes *velis nolis* the determination of a characteristic of mine, of a characteristic of my being. But in the actualization of the reality-ground we are not dealing with making a characteristic of my being possible, however important it may be, but with making possible the constitution of my entire being *qua* my being. The "my" of "for-my-sake" is my entire being as such, my *I*. And this being is what constitutes a moment of the actualization of the reality-ground in my intelligence. Now, actuality of the real in intelligence is precisely real truth. And this is also intrinsically valid for the grounded real truths. It follows that in this "for-my-sake" of a reality-ground we have simultaneously the real truth of reality and the real truth of my person, my real truth. This truth has, as we pointed out before, three dimensions that in the case of personal reality are manifestation, fidelity, and unquestionable facticity. And it is in accordance with these three dimensions that the grounding of the reality-ground is present to me: it is grounding with regards to manifestation, fidelity and unquestionable facticity.

By virtue of this, actualization along the lines of "grounding" constitutes a radical actualization for *my possibility*. It is not the possibility of reality for the sake of reality, as in the case of reality-object, but the possibility of reality "for my sake" of real truth. This is the possibility of being my own being, but of being so, in a grounded sense. The actualization of the reality-ground is simultaneously presence of the fundamental ground and possibility of radical realization of my own being {253} in truth: I proceed towards reality "for my sake". And this "for" is what specifies this new possibility.

What is the characteristic of this possibility? A possibility is so only if it is *one* possibility *among others*. What are these others? That is the question. As we already pointed out, the actualization of the reality-ground is actualization not only of a *reality*-ground but simultaneously actualization of a reality-*ground*. In other words, one aspect of it is knowledge, i.e., the terminus of allowing that its reality be what it is in and of itself; but another aspect is terminus of allowing that this reality occur in me grounding me *qua* reality. From this I obtain a double possibility for myself. One is the possibility of making it ground me within myself; another, the possibility to leave this grounding in suspense. In such case the reality-ground is still known in its reality, but ceases to be grounding, i.e., remains reduced *eo ipso* to a mere reality-object. It is not the case that it has presented itself as a reality-object, but that it remains, by suspension of its grounding characteristic, *reduced* to a reality-object. A reality-ground can be turned into a reality-object, but only by reduction. These are the two possibilities. This is different from the case of the reality-object, where we found the possibility of real truth on one side and on the other the possibility of elaboration of reality; now we have, within real truth, the possibility of reality-ground on one side, and on the other the possibility of reduction to a mere reality-object. These are the two possibilities inscribed in the real truth of a reality-ground.

Each human has to choose between them. But before we delve into this choice, let us review at least very briefly the conceptual scheme {254} we have just presented to avoid losing our way. Intellection is formally the actualization of something in its naked reality. *Qua* actualization, this is its real truth. Reality is actualized in many ways; one of them, especially important for our problem, is the actualization of reality "as towards". This form of reality hurls us towards a realm of reality, a realm, above all, of possible termini having different characteristics. Here we are concerned with two: reality-object and reality-ground. Naked reality then, opens before us the realm of these two types of reality. But this realm is not only of possible termini, but is "at one and the same time" of *my possibilities*, because the termini have to be determined by me and therefore their determination is *eo ipso* a possibility of realizing myself in one form or another. Among these possibilities each human has to choose in order to appropriate them, i.e., he or she must act on a volition. And inasmuch as this volition falls upon a reality "as towards" it is a will to truth, to a truth which is not the elemental real truth of first intellection, but the will to grounded truth. Real truth takes one inexorably to the will to grounded truth. This will chooses between two possibilities: the possibility to ideate reality (will to truth of ideas), and the possibility to increment the presence of reality in each human (will to grounded real truth). This last will in turn opens new possibilities depending upon the type of terminus upon which it falls. If it concerns a reality-object there are two possibilities of the will to real truth. One, to proceed towards reality to "do" something with it. Another, to proceed towards reality "for the sake" of reality. Both possibilities are grounded upon the will to real truth. If it is the case of reality-ground there are two other possibilities. One is {255} limiting myself to knowing its reality, i.e., reducing it to reality-object; another, letting it ground me, i.e., for me to proceed towards reality as "for-my-sake".

As I said, each human has to choose between these two ultimate possibilities. I can choose grounding itself, i.e., the possibility that the grounding of the reality-ground happens in my being as such. What is this happening? When surrendering to reality "for my sake", the "my", i.e., my whole being, *eo ipso* acquires the figure of reality-ground, because my being has appropriated it, has made it its own, i.e., lives in the figure of its ground. Therefore, to happen is here to allow the reality-for-me to be formally the "my" for which it is the ground; it is the actuality of grounding in me. The real truth of my person, in its three dimensions of manifestation, fidelity, and unquestionable facticity, is configured on the real truth of the reality-ground: my manifestation as a relatively absolute being is the manifestation of the absolute of a ground, my fidelity is fidelity in the absolute, my facticity is the unquestionable facticity in the absolute. Then the will for real truth is *will to grounding*. This is what we were searching for. My being is thus being *in truth*, something quite different than being *truly*. "Truly" actually expresses authenticity. On the other hand, "to be in truth" expresses that my entire being is such in and by the truth of a reality "for my sake". To surrender to a reality-ground as such is to surrender to my own grounding, to make my own its grounding. This is to make that grounding become the *formally* and expressly desired structure of my own life, to make me live in a grounded way. {256}

Each human carries out this option more or less freely, but always with freedom. He or she could have chosen for the other possibility, that of suspending the grounding of the reality-ground. Under the latter option, it is not the case that I have placed myself in a different way with respect to the same reality as before; despite appearances, what has occurred is a change in the characteristic of the mode of presence of the thing. The latter continues being the same materially, so to speak, but formally its type of reality has changed: it is no longer *ground* but *object*. And this is the essence of the matter: one has made the reality-ground into something else, a reality-object. Then my surrender to it is a surrender to the reality of that object for the sake of its reality itself; but it is no longer reality for me. This does not mean that knowledge of that reality, or its cognitive value, is annulled. On the contrary, such knowledge is preserved. What it means is that simultaneously with the objectification of the reality-ground, the human being remains *eo ipso* distanced from it. This distance is, actually, the very definition of something being *ob-jectum*, ob-ject. By virtue of this, the human being has become a mere natural place for his or her own truth. I do not surrender to my ground now, but find myself distanced from it. To distance myself from my ground is simply to reduce it to the condition of object. That is the reason for that paradoxical situation in which a human knows the reality-ground perfectly, but yet does not surrender to it. The fact is that a human *reduces* grounding to mere objectuality. This reduction is a possibility which the human chooses freely. It is commonly thought that in order to surrender to the ground a human has to choose, but not to surrender him- or herself, as if reality began {257} by presenting itself as object and only afterwards was discovered to be ground. No, a reality-ground presents itself *a limine* as reality-ground. In the case of reality-ground, the choice for objectuality, i.e., the reduction to reality-object, is not less optional or less free than the surrender to grounding itself.

In the will to grounding a human wishes to know, surrendering him- or herself to the grounding of the known, in order to let the known be what it is (i.e., a ground), and to let me be what I am (i.e., a being grounded on it). This is, therefore, the radical unity of the intellective process and my being as such. My intellection and my freedom of choice are not only not incompatible, but have an intrinsic unity: this is the will to grounding.

What is its nature? The will to grounding is not merely an act following upon the intellection of a reality-ground; it is a will that starts the intellective process (to discover the possibilities of the "towards"), and makes the intellectively known into the real, actual ground of my substantive absolute being, in which my life consists. This will is, therefore, as any will to truth, a will antecedent in some measure to the truth known intellectively. This "antecedence" does not consist in being *act*. Were that the case, it could be thought that it is a will that exerts pressure so that the known may appear to me as that which I beforehand wish it to be. Neither as consequent to knowledge nor as antecedent to it is the will to grounding an act of the will. Primarily and radically the will to grounding, as any will to truth, is not act. It is more than mere capacity, but is less than {258} act: it is *attitude*. It is the attitude of surrendering my own being to that which may show itself intellectively to be its ground. The will to grounding is principle of attitude.

With these quite summary concepts, sufficient for our purpose, we can confront the problem of the radical unity of knowledge of God and faith in Him.

B) *Unity of knowledge and faith in God.* Let us revisit the issue. We already saw that knowledge and faith are essentially different: knowledge is an intellection of the reality of God, and faith is the personal surrender to Him *qua* true. But we also saw that they are essentially connected: all knowledge of God traces out the realm of a possible faith, of a possible surrender, because God is the grounding reality of our *I*, and therefore His knowledge opens in and by itself the area of my ground. Between knowledge and faith in God there is, therefore, a unity which is not one of mere convergence but an intrinsic and radical unity. In this sense the same truth, the existence of God, can be simultaneously a truth of reason and a truth of faith: the "simultaneously" is precisely that radical unity. Yet, it is a unity that is only possible, or better still, it is unity only of possibility. We need something that will make it actual as reality. And in this "something" is what the "simultaneously" we seek for formally consists. This something is the will to grounding. How?

Let us remember that a human being is a reality whose being is relatively absolute, an acquired being supporting itself in a religated fashion on the power of the real. This is not a theory but an incontrovertible fact, something immediate, a radical fact {259} concerning my entire being. Religation to the power of the real is, therefore, something inexorable. In this religation everything real shows itself to me as constitutively enigmatic, and therefore problematic; i.e., everything real, simultaneously, real things and my own *I*. My person finds itself, therefore, religated in its own *I*, but in a problematic way. This means that I am relatively absolute, and that my *I* is not only acquired; indeed, in order to be so, it is radically in need of a ground in order to be. And it is such, inexorably, because to acquire my *I* is something radically inexorable. In such a fashion, the power of the real is not speculatively but physically and really that which hurls me inexorably towards the real ground of the power of the real. This is what we call "God". Therefore, God is a reality-ground as terminus of the "towards" to which the power of the real inexorably hurls us.

I have repeated the term "inexorable" monotonously and insistently. I have done so with the clear intent to show that that reality-ground that is God is not something that a human may or may not concern him- or herself with, as with so many other things in life; but *velis nolis* is something towards which we are physically hurled not accidentally, but constitutively. Hurled: that is, the power of the real inexorably opens the realm of grounding. God is, for us, *quoad nos*, reality-ground, with respect to which, therefore, each person not only can choose but has to choose; moreover, each person is inexorably so choosing in all the constitutive acts of his or her own *I*, i.e., in all the acts of his or her own life. In other words, with respect to God the *I* inexorably has with respect to God a will to grounding, primarily and formally because in every moment the *I* needs a ground. God is the real ground of my *I*. {260}

At this point an observation will suddenly strike the reader; I am aware of it and will discuss it a little further on.

The reality-ground is not only real, but is simultaneously a possibility of mine and my own possible way to be absolute. This possibility is divided in two. Let us investigate each half by itself.

One is the possibility of considering God as a reality in and by Himself and nothing more; i.e., God, merely as supreme reality in Himself. This is God, reality-ground, reduced to reality-object. Then *eo ipso*, we have already explained it: God remains distanced from humans, and humans are separated from God. This is not just a mere concept realized more or less dialectically; it is the very reality of what, throughout the history of religions, comprises the *dii otiosi*, the otiose gods. They are realities, without doubt, and supreme realities, but otiose with respect to humans who in general have no relationship with them, either of supplication or of support. An otiose god is a real god but one that does not intervene in the life of the person; in such case the life of a human being is not traced out as a function of God. This is the reality-ground of God reduced to reality-object. And we should not think that this is only proper to primitive mentalities. fundamentally, the *theós* of Aristotle is a super-otiose god: not only does he not bother with humans, nor they with him, but he cannot have any relationship with the cosmos. And this is not the case for Aristotle only. Basically, this is the situation today for a large percentage of mankind in ever increasing numbers. Their atheism is rather the theism of an otiose god. They admit the existence of God, of a first cause, and they even admit His strictly demonstrative knowledge; but for them He is only a mere reality in itself, which does not intervene in {261} life, with respect to which the consideration of a surrender in faith makes no sense. This is a rigorous knowledge of God but without faith in Him. From this fact spring most of the considerations we have been presenting in the preceding pages. Here we have, thus stated, one possibility. God real reality but otiose; this is the *otiosity of God*. The realm which it opens for us is the emptiness of distance. And the appropriation of this possibility is an alienation from God.

The other possibility is to opt for the grounding nature of God as such, *qua* reality-ground. It is, throughout the history of religions, the case of all the other gods. God is then not just a supreme reality, but an ultimate reality, possibilitating, and impelling: this is what I have called "God *qua* God". He is certainly a supreme reality. But His "supremacy", so to speak, with respect to us reveals Him as absolutely absolute reality. That upon which our *I*, our relatively absolute being, is grounded positively is an absolutely absolute reality, and therefore, something that for us is formally grounding. In that case, together with the reality of God, humans have the possibility of being relatively absolute in Him. Besides knowledge of God, indeed, there is faith in Him. This is the *grounding nature of God* as differentiated from the otioseness of God. The realm which it opens for us is not the emptiness of distance but the field of our dynamic tension in God. The appropriation of this possibility is the surrender of our person to the personal reality of God, the donation of our person to Him in faith: this is life in function of God.

Here are the two termini of the choice: otiose God or grounding God. And precisely because it is a question of choice, it is in *both cases* a free choice. Certainly it is {262} inexorable that we choose, but the termini of the choice with respect to my possibilities are free. Yet, free choice does not even remotely mean that it is arbitrary. Just the opposite. It is an option of the will for truth and, therefore, a constitutively grounded choice. My freedom to opt for an otiose God or for a grounding God is a decision not about what I believe but about what the reality itself of God is. It is, therefore, a grounded option. Grounded on what?

The will to truth, we have already pointed out, is not only a series of acts, the acts to choose for one terminus or another, but primarily a principle of attitude. For us, the choice we shall freely carry out is grounded upon this attitude. And this attitude has two moments. One consists, of course, in wishing to discover the ground towards which we are hurled. But in addition it is an attitude of self-surrender, to make our *I* accept what we have discovered to be our ground.

a) Above all, the will to grounding is the attitude which sparks the march of the intellective process towards intellectively knowing what the ground is, that ground to which our relatively absolute being is inexorably hurled by our constitutive religation. This is the will to grounding as motive force of the intellective process. We have reflected on this in the previous chapter. There, we had to prove that the power of the real is grounded on an absolutely absolute reality, on God, who by reason of being ground of the power of the real is the ground of this power being an ultimate, possibilitating, and impelling power. And as ground of this power, God possesses those same three characteristics. He is, {263} therefore, *eo ipso*, not only a supreme reality but a grounding God, whose character as personal we also had to prove. By all this the possibility of an otiose God is rationally excluded, and the reality of a grounding God rationally justified. The choice for a grounding God is, then, grounded in turn upon *rational* explanation: this is the demonstrative knowledge of the reality of a grounding God.

b) But the will to grounding as an attitude not only motivates intellection; it is something more. It is the will to make my *I* accept that which reason has proven to me is the reality-ground. This is the attitude of surrendering to the ground which reason discovers. And this is not itself rational, but a desired congruence with the rational. It is a congruence which has a precise name: the *reasonable*. "Reasonable" does not necessarily mean that it is a truth not sufficiently proven, but rather that it is in conformity with reason, which primarily means that it is congruent to accept in life that which reason knows, be this knowledge sufficient or not. And the acceptance of the matter will become more reasonable as its knowledge becomes more rigorous. What is reasonable, in this sense, is more than the rational; indeed, this is the rational transfused into the whole being of humans. Even if we were to be presented with a mathematical demonstration for the necessity of the will accepting and incorporating into the being of the

UNFOLDING OF THE PROBLEM: HUMAN ACCESS TO GOD   193

person whatever reason discovers, still, the real and effective acceptance would always remain open to choice. This is why the will to grounding is necessary. Present day humans are more in need of it than ever before. The vital acceptance of the rational in its turn is not rational; it is more than rational, it is reasonable.

From this stems, on one hand, the possibility of a dissociation {264} between knowledge and faith: this is the lack of will to grounding. God is known, and there is no faith in God, his grounding is not accepted. With this the reality-ground, God-grounding, is left *eo ipso* reduced to a reality-object, to an otiose God.

But, on the other hand, the possibility exists to have actual unity, rational knowledge of God and faith at one and the same time: this is the will to grounding as an attitude of the reasonable. The attitude of the reasonable is based upon the rational part of reason. This is the rational as something offered, which is precisely what the reasonable is. Thus far, reason shows that it is reasonable to accept reason. And from the point of view of surrender, reason makes of the rational something acceptable for the will. This is what in a very imprecise way and in a different conceptual context (the context of the so called "proofs" of the supernatural) was called *credibility*. But not only this. Reason would not be acceptable if it were not in itself acceptant. And that it should be such just expresses the inexorability of choice. This is what sometimes, in the context just referred to, used to be called *credible*. They are not two unconnected concepts. From my perspective, reason is acceptable because it is acceptant; I maintain that all credibility is founded upon a previous state of being credible. But underlying both credibility and state of being credible is the will to grounding as a firm attitude.

The will to grounding as an attitude to proceed towards the ground of my *I* in religation sparks the intellective process. This process itself constitutes the realm of a possible surrender to God. But this same attitude of free and reasonable will to surrender to whatever intelligence shows me to be the ground of my *I*, is the principle of my real {265} surrender to what intelligence knows. By virtue of this, the surrender, which was a simple constitutive possibility of the knowledge of reality-grounding, converts itself, by the same principle, into free realization of that possibility, into faith. Thus, the will to grounding as an attitude is the unitary principle of the intellective process about God and of the personal surrender to Him *qua* true person. We are not dealing with the question of whether faith leads to intellection, or intellection to faith, but rather with the fact that both aspects constitute a *radical unity*. That is, their unity is in the very root from which the movement of the person towards God emerges: in the will to grounding as the principle of attitude. Knowledge and faith are but two moments of this unitary movement. The will to grounding as the principle of attitude is therefore, in itself, the radical unity that is not only possible but real, of knowledge of God and faith in Him as a free choice for the reasonable person. This is what we have been arduously searching for.

However, it is not something as univocal as might appear at first sight, because this attitude of grounding, however well established, does not always lead to what we have just discussed. There are, actually, great numbers of humans who despite their will to grounding have no strict knowledge of God and do not surrender to Him. This is precisely the observation I had in mind above, which surely and with reason must have struck all readers. It is necessary for us to be concerned about it, because until now we have only posed to ourselves the problem as to how knowledge and faith in God are radically "unified" in the will to grounding. And this has left the reverse question standing, i.e., not the question whether knowledge {266} and faith are *rooted* in the will to truth, but the question whether this will *unfolds*—and under what conditions—in knowledge and faith. That is the question concerning the will to truth in human reality, the third of the three great questions which the will to truth posed to us.

C) *The will to truth in human reality*. Strictly speaking this question is already settled from everything we have said. Free choice, I have argued, is a choice grounded upon a demonstration of the reality of God that we set forth in Chapter Three. And consequently the will to truth unfolds into strict knowledge and faith. To be sure, this is only speculation. But let us not forget our purpose. We were not attempting to outline the way by which a person reaches God—these ways are infinite. The only thing we were attempting is the *intellective justification* of all these ways and of all these arrivals. As soon as we have provided this justification, the purpose has been achieved. But such considerations might seem merely dialectical to many, because intellective justification involves something intrinsically problematic. I had already warned about this expressly when I began the exposition of the justification for the reality of God: this justification "is the explanation of an experience we are experiencing physically; therefore, always has that resonance of problem proper to the character of the progression of personal life". The justification we have found preserves all its value, but precisely because of this it forces us to question that problematic resonance.

UNFOLDING OF THE PROBLEM: HUMAN ACCESS TO GOD 195

The problematic character appears concretely in three facts which concern the two {267} moments we described when dealing with the will to grounding as an attitude. First and foremost, there is the start of the "intellective process" set in motion by that will. The fact is that intellectual justification of the reality of God has been carried out in multiple ways; as a result, we have numerous so called "proofs" of the existence of God. But this multiplicity is not simply "multiple", because "new" ones have repeatedly been attempted largely because the previous ones, for a variety of reasons, did not appear quite satisfactory. And of course, I do not think the proof outlined here is exempt from this condition, though I consider it rigorously conclusive. This is a first fact we must keep in mind. However, there are two other facts which refer to the will to grounding with respect to the "choice" occurring in it. First is the fact that countless persons ignore the question. The inexorable characteristic of having to choose is seriously affected by indifference. But beyond this there is a second fact, namely that many persons—whose numbers are ever increasing—do not even reach the point of ignoring the question, because they never felt it as a question in the first place. That is, not only does it not seem inexorable to choose one terminus or another, but it does not even appear inexorable that the will to grounding is actually constitutive of the human person. This is the third fact to which I referred. Under these conditions it seems as if the will to grounding were somehow in suspense. Such is the way which these three facts, in a concrete way, frame the question of what the will to truth may be with respect to human reality.

Let us begin by reflecting upon each of the three aforementioned facts separately. Only in this way we will be in {268} a position to conceptualize in a unified way the problem they pose.

a) Above all else, there is the undeniable fact that the validity of rational proofs for the existence of God, presented throughout history, has not been admitted by everyone—not even by all those who admit, or are willing to admit, the reality of God. This would seem to reveal the inanity of the will to truth with respect to knowledge of God. The first moment of the will to truth, i.e., that this will leads to the knowledge of God, appears to be "refuted" *in vivo* so to speak. But here there is a serious misunderstanding that we need to resolve. Proof of the existence of God, i.e., intellectual demonstration, even when set in motion by the will to truth, has a scope and a value which do not depend on the will but exclusively on the intelligence itself. Discussion about the validity of the proofs is a matter of intellection and nothing else. Following this line of reasoning, I have proposed a proof in Chapter Three of this book. I consider it rigorously conclusive (if not, I would not have proposed it) and together with the other proofs it is subject to argument. But, is this to what we refer when we say that the will unlocks and puts in motion the intellective process of the knowledge of God? That the will to truth, as will to grounding, may set in motion the intellective process is something that belongs intrinsically and indisputably to that will. What has not been claimed is that an intellective process is identical to a demonstration. This is the mistake that must be dispelled. Demonstration is only a mode, though the most strict and stringent of intellection. But it is not identical to an intellective process; rather {269} such a process is prior, even chronologically, to any possible demonstration. Demonstration is the most rigorous form this process can acquire. Because of this, discussion about the rigor of the argumentation does not affect the existence of the intellective process; such discussion always arises from within that process. Hence two things must be considered in the intellective process. One is that which intelligence manages to know intellectively through a process; another, the aspect by which the intellective process is anchored in the will to truth. "Demonstration" only concerns the first point, but does not touch the second, which is the prior and radical one. The multiplicity and possible lack of satisfaction of the proofs in no way "refutes" the fact that there is a will to truth to which an intellective process essentially pertains.

Nonetheless, this does not exhaust the "real" question, because while distinct, these two points are not absolutely independent. What, in fact, is this process? My person, insofar as it has to construct its relatively absolute being acquired in religation to the power of the real, is, as we saw, in need of a ground because the power of the real is intrinsically problematic. This is not a speculative problem, but a "real" problem *qua* problem, the problem of personal life. With respect to this problem, in fact, we are not directed towards an object that may be terminus of a theoretical consideration; rather, in all our acts we are physically *hurled* "towards", i.e., towards the realm of grounding. And in this opening "towards", intelligence itself is included. Therefore intellection has two aspects. Primarily, in this "hurling" it sketches out what grounding is. We saw this at the beginning of the {270} third chapter: the idea of God Himself *qua* idea. But, in the second place, that realm is something more: a realm as a moment of the reality of the power of the real. And under this aspect we here have something more than an idea; we have, so to speak, the perimeter which outlines an area of reality, that area called "grounding". It is nothing more than the perimeter of a realm, but it is a real perimeter of reality; it is, therefore, a moment of reality. This is not a question of argumentation: it is the very structure of my *I* in reality, to the power of which we are religated. And this structure is formally intellective; it is the intellection of something real, of the realm of the grounding of the real. Naturally, as I just said, it is nothing more than a real realm in reality, which is most imprecise. But this imprecision is not the imprecision of an idea but the indetermination of a real realm. Thus the will to grounding moves intelligence in order to determine this realm more precisely; this is just what the intellective process is. To the will to grounding essentially belongs, therefore, an intellective process making intellectively known a moment of the reality that is realizing itself as a process.

This process is a process of intelligence *in reality itself*, in that mode of it which is "reality as towards," because the realm of grounding, as I just mentioned, is not a mere idea, but a moment of reality itself. Therefore its intellection is always an intellection of something real; real "as towards", but still real. And this is essential, because inside this real realm in reality, the intellective process can adopt the form of a conclusive argument; this is the proof or demonstration that this real realm is constituted by an absolutely {271} absolute reality. The demonstration of that reality is not just a mere transition from idea to reality, but the discovery of the very structure of the real *qua* "as towards" real, of that reality in which we already are and which we already know intellectually. Any demonstration of the existence of God is thus an intellective process from within reality itself.

However, not every intellective process is demonstrative. And this is so for several reasons. In the first place, the validity of the proofs is always debatable; on the other hand, from the point of view of a will to grounding, the intellective process of a realm of the real is a fact perhaps much in need of clarification, but a fact nevertheless. In the second place, it might happen that a particular person is unable to arrive at a proof that is self-convincing. Nonetheless, an intellection of something real, i.e., of the realm, always exists. And in third place, and most importantly, the intellective process can lead to something quite different than a demonstration.

In fact, a human being can more or less spontaneously lodge (so to speak) the absolutely absolute reality of God in the realm of the real we are considering. If for such a person there were no "demonstration", this admission of the reality of God would not be intellectively justified; but it would be an authentic faith. Then there is an intellection, a *gnosis* (in the etymological sense of the term and not as a designation of Gnosticism in the history of religions). This is the intellection of the *real* realm of the grounding of the real, an intellection which does not yield strict knowledge but faith. Such is, definitely, the case of nearly of all men who believe in God: they do not try to {272} prove or rationally justify the reality of God to themselves. To discover God does not mean to demonstrate His existence. Conversely, to demonstrate the existence of God does not mean that reasoning is "the" way to discover God. Demonstration of the existence of God is not primarily a logical requirement waved only in front of those who do not believe in God, but a logical requirement addressed equally to the believers, a requirement that demands from the latter a strict justification of that in which they believe.

Nonetheless, faith is only one possible terminus of the intellective process without demonstration of God's existence. It is also possible that humans may not only not attain to a proof, and moreover that they may even suspend belief. In such case there is, strictly speaking, no gnosis but *agnosia*; this is *agnosticism*. Even though it may seem like a paradox, agnosticism is an intellective process; the agnostic intellective process. What is, actually, agnosticism? It consists, of course, in placing oneself in the *ignorance* of the reality of God: "I do not know if God exists". But insofar as it is ignorance, agnosticism is *eo ipso* a mode of the intellective process, because ignorance is not just mere lack of a knowing. Every case of ignorance, on the contrary, is always ignorance of something quite precise. In other words, the one who ignores knows in one form or another what it is that he or she ignores. The man of Altamira[7] was not ignorant of what a differential equation is, because he lacked any possible reference to such equations. Only someone who is told about differential equations, and does not know what we are talking about because he or she does not understand the meaning of the words, only this person is ignorant of what a differential equation is. The mere expression "differential equation" means, by the fact of being a mention of *something*, what it is that is ignored: *that* (the differential equation) is ignored. Without the "that" there is no ignorance but merely a lack. {273}

Ignorance is, therefore, a mode of the intellective process. And so, agnosticism is not lack of information, but ignorance, in which, therefore, one knows what it is that one ignores. Yet agnosticism is more than that. It is not mere ignorance but ignorance of something that is ignored because it has not been intellectively found. Only this type of ignorance is the one proper to the agnostic: the ignorance of what has not been found. Where has it not been found? In reality. But in reality not like that in which our ideas are realized, but like that which, being a moment of the real, appears indeterminate to me. The realm of grounding is a moment of reality. Therefore, although not known specifically as being God, God is indeed a real moment. He is known intellectively as really a being that, though we do not yet know what it is in reality, the agnostic knows intellectively He is real in a mode not yet well known. Therefore, agnosticism is not fully alien either to the reality of God or His intellection. It is rather alien to the strict knowledge of God. With respect to God or to any other reality, to know it intellectively, i.e., to apprehend it as real, is not the same, by any stretch of the imagination, as to know it. To hear a sound is not to know what the sound is. Hence, the ignorance of the agnostic is not lack of knowledge of God but an intellection more or less specific of Him, i.e., with no strict knowledge. This is the *unknowability* of God, quite a different thing than His non-intellection. However agnosticism is goes beyond this. It is not only ignorance and unknowability, but the ignorance and unknowability of something that the agnostic searches for diligently but does not find. He searches for God, because God, although unknown, is something in which the agnostic lives as it were touching his {274} naked reality. The realm of grounding, I repeat, is a moment of reality. And this real moment is not alien in its reality to the reality of human beings themselves. It is an absolute moment that, as such, the agnostic like any other human not only knows intellectively but "touches". It is a probing, which however does not yet reach the precise figure of the *eidos* of the moment of reality—let us state it thus. And in this sense it is probing without a precise encounter. From this point of view, agnosticism is a *frustrated* intellective search. It is in this frustration where unknowability and ignorance of God take on their figure, where the suspension of faith occurs. But as ignorance, as unknowability, and as frustration, agnosticism is a strict form of intellective process which rests upon a real moment of reality known intellectively as such.

Both faith which is intellectively insufficient, and agnosticism, shed a positive light on the essential nature of one aspect of the will to grounding. A strictly intellective process formally and essentially pertains to this will. Inasmuch as this process is not identified with a proof, i.e., with a rational justification for the existence of God, it follows that this first fact of the three we are studying discloses that the will to grounding is essentially a *will to search*. And it is in this will, in a variety of ways as we have just seen, that intellection and choice are radically "united", because the very suspension of faith of the agnostic is a positive mode of choice. The will to grounding is, therefore, not only that in which knowledge and faith are *rooted*, but that which *unfolds itself* into intellective search and option. {275}

But not every human is a searcher after God. This takes us to the other moment of the will to grounding, to the choice itself. It is there that the other two facts we must now consider are inscribed.

b) Firstly, there is the fact that a very large number of people live completely unconcerned about the question with which we are wrestling. We pointed out above that humans find themselves inexorably forced to proceed "towards" the reality of God, choosing, also inexorably, between God as *reality-object* and God as *reality-ground*. However, it is an undeniable fact that many are unconcerned with any choice. Therefore, they are neither involved in an intellective process towards God nor do they make any choice with respect to Him. And since these two moments are the ones that constitute the will to grounding, these people live heedless of the problem of their ground, and *eo ipso* their lives are without any will to grounding.

We are not trying to underestimate this attitude—just the opposite. To be unconcerned about the problem of the ground of life is not synonymous with *frivolity*. To be sure, it can be and in many cases is frivolity; but frivolity has nothing to do with what, in itself, is the attitude of the person who is unconcerned with the problem of his or her ground, especially since frivolity may affect everything, including admission of the reality of God. We are concerned here, therefore, with an absolutely serious attitude. We shall soon see how it differs from frivolity.

And indeed, it is precisely when taken with full seriousness that this attitude displays its nature to us. What, in fact, is it to be unconcerned? Let us consider what this attitude is with respect to the intellective {276} process. Here we encounter again, although in a different dimension, the same situation we examined concerning the rational proof for the existence of God. As the intellective process is put into action, intelligence encounters two types of reality, reality-object and reality-ground, and therefore two conceptualizations of God: the otiose God and the grounding God. And the proof, via religation, has taken us to God as grounding reality. I repeat: this aspect of the conceptualization of the reality of God is an exclusive matter of intelligence; something, therefore, completely alien to any possible will. But, as we have already mentioned, "intellective process" is not synonymous

UNFOLDING OF THE PROBLEM: HUMAN ACCESS TO GOD 201

with "demonstrative process". The human being, actually, is hurled intellectively "towards" the grounding of his life, religated to the power of the real. And then, as we have also shown, in this hurling the human encounters not only the outline of the idea of God, but also the realm of grounding as a moment of reality itself. This is an intellective process. Now, it is *within this process* that the intelligence takes a decisive step: it examines the nature of this realm as a moment of reality and discovers the polar *difference* between reality-object and reality-ground. It is precisely at this point when the intelligence demonstrates that this realm is real only because of a reality-ground. But the reverse is not true: even though intelligence did not to discover it as such, there would always be an intellective process inexorably unlocked by virtue of being hurled, also inexorably, "towards" grounding. In what then would this process consist? It would be really and truly the intellective process of a moment of reality, but a process which does not arrive at that difference: {277} this would be *indifferent* intellection. Then it is not the case there is no intellective process, but rather that there is an intellective process which arrives at *indifference*. Here we have, with respect to the intellective process, the essence of the attitude which is unconcerned about the reality of God. The one who is unconcerned is indifferent towards an otiose God or towards a grounding God. We shall soon refine the sense of this phrase which in itself is not rigorous. It is a suspension of conclusion. The agnostic suspends faith; he who is indifferent suspends the intellective conclusion. He does not even question whether he knows the existence of God, nor what He might be if He were to exist; his attitude across the board is "Let God be as He may"; I am not concerned. In this "be as He may" we have the very essence of what I have called "suspension of the intellective process". This suspension is not a cessation of intellection, but a strict intellection of what grounding is as moment-type realm of reality: it would be something *really* indifferent. This indifference has many shadings, from admitting the reality of God known intellectively but indifferently, to the opposite extreme, a certain indifference with respect to the reality of God Himself, passing through the idea of divine otiosity. At this point I must correct the expression I employed before: it is not exactly the case that he who is indifferent may admit that God is an otiose God, but that it is otiose to be concerned about God..."be as He may", i.e., be God otiose or not. The realm of grounding is always known intellectively as "whatever He may be". But since this realm is a moment of reality, the "be as He may" always involves the undifferentiated reality of God: this is the undifferentiated intellection of a moment of His grounding. Consequently, {278} despite appearances, whoever is unconcerned with the reality of God, has in his or her attitude a strict intellective process which knows God intellectively as "be as He may". Indifference is a mode of intellective process different from demonstration. What occurs is that intellective demonstration is *eo ipso* the radical overcoming of any possible indifference: God is reality-ground.

Nevertheless, this does not exhaust the attitude of one who is unconcerned about the reality of God. Because in this attitude not only is the intellective process suspended by reason of indifference, but at the same time one lives unconcerned about the reality of God. Intellective *indifference* is simultaneously *unconcernedness*. On this basis it would seem that one who ignores these matters lives without making any choice regarding God. And yet, this is but an appearance. Just as indifference is not lack of intellective process, so unconcernedness is not absence of choice. Unconcernedness is not no-choice. Anyone who ignores, I said, knows in some measure that which he ignores. Similarly, one who is unconcerned senses that behind his lack of concern there throbs the mute presence of what he is unconcerned about; therefore, he is subliminally directed towards it. Because of this, unconcernedness is a positive state; it is not no-choice but strict choice, the choice of not being concerned about that which "is there" indifferently. Therefore, one chooses *for* indifference: this is the moment of the "un". The one who ignores concerns himself unconcernedly about what he knows intellectively as indifferent. Whoever disregards the problem of the reality of God has, therefore, not only intellective process but also choice. The realm of grounding is known intellectively as indifferent, and humans by choice appropriate the possibility of living in fundamental indifference: this is unconcernedness. To {279} intellective *in*-difference there corresponds the *un*-concernedness which has been chosen: the "un" life is life in "in".

In-difference and un-concernedness, in their intrinsic and radical unity are, therefore, the two moments of a unique attitude, a very precise attitude with respect to the grounding of life. Even to disregard the problem of grounding, the problem of God, is therefore, a will to grounding. And in its apparent negativity, this attitude reveals something essential for us in the will to grounding, because a person does not disregard God as he or she might disregard a scientific or speculative problem or perform a task, such as undertaking a voyage, e.g., due to a lack of curiosity or capacity. The turning "towards" grounding is, actually, something inexorable. Consequently, to disregard it is a positive way of living. And as a way of life it has two aspects. On the one hand, unconcerned with God, i.e., with the grounding of life, one lives abandoned to "whatever" might happen. Therefore, strictly speaking, it is not the case that one may live without grounding, but that one may live in a fundamental indifference, which is a different matter. This living in such indifference is precisely what we call "let live", i.e., to allow oneself to be grounded. And here we find the difference between disregarding God and frivolity. Frivolity is lack of seriousness. On the other hand, whoever disregards God lives seriously based on his or her ground, even though it may be conceptualized as indifferent. The indifference of let live is anything but frivolity; it is a mode of grounding. Therefore, the will to let live is a will to grounding. It is a kind of indifferent surrender to the grounding of life, a non-blind faith, but one which is indifferent and unconcerned. Yet on the other hand, there is something {280} in a way more decisive in this attitude, because it is certainly a let live, but a "let" only with respect to its ground. In itself this attitude is a resolute *will to live*. One who is unconcerned lives and lets live because above and beyond his fundamental indifference, what he does is to affirm forcefully that he lives and wants to live. His disregard of the problem of God is taken for the sake of life. He opts for being unconcerned with a God whom he knows intellectively as indifferent, precisely because of his will to live: he wants the indifference of fundamental reality not to be an impediment to life.

The two aspects of this attitude, to let live and the will to live, taken unitarily, define one unique will: a will to live that we might call "penultimate": the *penultimateness* of life. It is a will to live, but allowing oneself to be borne along wherever by the ground. One who is unconcerned with God lives superficially: it is a constitutively penultimate life. And that manifests its principal limitation: this will to grounding does not go beyond indifference. But it also manifests something essential: that the will to grounding is not a will to truth in some theoretical way, but is, constitutively, the will to live. And it is this will that unfolds into intellective process and option. Though limited and penultimate in this attitude, still, intellective process and option are a fundamental unfolding of the will to live.

But not everyone seems to possess this will to grounding, because for many of them their will to live is not even penultimate: it reposes upon itself *qua* will to live. This is the third of the three important facts we are addressing. {281}

c) There are not only those who are unconcerned with the problem of the reality of God, but an increasing number who are not even unconcerned about the problem because it has never been a problem for them. Their lives, like all the rest, are woven of securities and uncertainties, easy times and difficult times, achievements and failures. Therefore, this life presents problems, and very serious ones, but all within life itself. Taken as a whole, life for these persons does not present any problems: it is what it is and nothing more. This is a life which reposes on itself. Consequently, there is no occasion to talk about choice, indeed not even about will to grounding: this is the atheist life. It is not the case of an atheism placing itself "against" the reality of God. Being "against" is not essential to atheism. Every day sees the increase in the numbers of those whose atheism does not go against anything or anyone. It is also not the case that atheism is unconcernedness and still less agnosticism, but that it is a case of life lived in and by itself, "and nothing more": it is *a-theist life* in the merely privative sense of the prefix "a". And for such a person, since life is something which undeniably exists, any appeal to another grounding reality, outside or above it, would have to be the responsibility of the non-atheist. Atheism would be, therefore, the primary attitude, and any other attitude to refer to God in any of its forms (belief, agnosticism, unconcernedness) would need justification: the *conditio possidentis*, as a jurist would say, would be the fact of a-theist life. All the rest are options, and as a consequence, only "the rest" is optional.

Is this the case? To profile a-theism with precision is more difficult than it might seem at first glance. In the first place, What exactly is understood when it is said that life {282} taken in and by itself is not a problem? We have already pointed this out: it is not a question of problems within one's life but of problems taken in their entirety. And that is the question. Life taken in its entirety is life insofar as it is the constitution and construction of my being, of my *I*. Every one of the acts of life, and *a fortiori* the entire course of them, concerns not only what things are, other men, and even my own individual characteristics, but where in the midst of all this the person is "in reality". Things (in the widest sense of the term, including all men and my own individual reality) are certainly what configures my life. But this life is the act of making my *I*, of making my being by confronting all of reality. Things, therefore, configure the being of my reality precisely by their character of reality. This character of reality is thus what, in things and through them, determines my being. And as such it is a power to which I am religated: this is the power of the real. It constitutes the grounding of my life. Regardless of what vocabulary may be employed, this is a fact; moreover, it is "the" fact of

UNFOLDING OF THE PROBLEM: HUMAN ACCESS TO GOD 205

life. To say that life is taken in its entirety consists, therefore, in saying that personal life is taken in religation, i.e., determined by the power of the real. But, this power of the real is nothing outside real things. Now, this is quite enigmatic; indeed, it is a serious problem. And it is so for all men. It is a problem that arises prior that of whether this enigma is grounded in the reality of God. That is why we find ourselves inexorably hurled to know intellectively what that power, that grounding, might be; this is indeed the dawn of an intellective process. And how do we know it intellectively? Some in fact have intellectively known this power, therefore the grounding of life, as {283} a function of an absolutely absolute reality, of God. Others intellectually know that the power of the real in things is a fact and nothing more than a fact, without need of an ulterior ground: that is the *pure facticity* of the power of the real. And it is in this that atheism consists. It is not only life in and by itself, but life resting upon the pure facticity of the power of the real: this is grounding as pure facticity. It is then clear, in the first place, that in the atheist person an intellective process occurs about the entirety of life, and therefore, for that person life is as problematic as it is for everyone else. What happens is that—perhaps without being aware of it—the atheist gives a solution to this problem; he or she gives it by means of facticity. Hence, and this is the second thing that must be pointed out, to resolve the problem of the grounding of life with pure facticity means *eo ipso* that the facticity of the power of the real is an interpretation, just as much an interpretation as the admission of the reality of God. The problem of the power of the real needs to be resolved, and to accomplish this it is necessary to give reasons, any kind of reasons, but to give reasons. Whoever admits the reality of God has to offer his reasons (we have done this in Chapter Three); but they must be given also by the one that sees the power of the real as pure facticity. Atheism is not, therefore, the primary attitude, the *conditio possidentis*, with respect to which one who admits the reality of God must justify himself; rather, atheism needs a homologous justification, since it is not a primary attitude. Theism and atheism are two modes in which the intellective process comes to a conclusion with respect to the problem of the power of the real. The facticity of the power of the real is not a pure *factum* but an intellection, and like any intellection is in need of ground. This ground must {284} be achieved through the intellective way. Atheism consists, therefore, not in having no problem but in understanding the power of the real, i.e., the grounding of life, as pure facticity.

In addition, however, the atheist makes a choice. The facticity of the power of the real is a personal possibility, and its appropriation by choice is just living life as something which is sufficient unto itself, so we have the *self-sufficiency* of life. It is self-sufficiency not in a pejorative sense, but in the etymological sense of something that is enough in its own line: a life that is what it is, and how it is, and nothing else. Self-sufficiency of life is the choice for the facticity of the power of the real. And by being a choice it is personal surrender to facticity, it is faith in facticity. Atheism is just the faith of the atheist. Faith, we saw, is formal surrender to a person as true. Hence, the atheist formally surrenders to his or her own formal reality as unique and sufficient true personal reality. And it is in this surrender that the faith of the atheist consists. The atheist understands him- or herself as surrendered to him- or herself and accepts it as such. Therefore he makes a choice; atheism is no less a choice than theism.

Consequently, atheism as a way of life has, despite what we are told, an intellective process with respect to the power of the real, and a choice with respect to it; these are the two moments of the will to grounding. Therefore atheism is the setting in motion of the will to grounding. This will *unfolds itself* into intellection of the power of the real as pure facticity, and into choice for the self-sufficiency of personal life. It therefore is not an exception to anything we have discussed.

But just as in the foregoing cases, and {285} independently of this self-sufficient facticity, the atheist's will to grounding displays an essential characteristic of every will to grounding. What is, actually, this self-sufficient facticity? It is not the fact that one may be sufficient unto oneself for one's own life, if by "life" one understands the interactions of the progress of life's actions, of situations, etc. Because living (as we have already indicated) does not consist in the occurrence of vital acts, but in the very simple act of possessing myself as configured in reality. And atheism refers, as we have already indicated, to this aspect, according to which throughout the whole of life I advance by configuring my *I*, feature by feature. And about life so understood the atheist informs us that it is something that ends in itself, and is the act of an *I* which ends in it: self-sufficiency is a mode of being absolute in its own line. This is what we must first draw out, that atheism is a will to grounding which rests upon the *I* as absolute being in its own way. But this does not mean the atheist is not aware that he or she was born on a certain day and will die some day. On the contrary, the atheist believes that his or her own being is pure facticity and nothing more. Facticity is a mode of relativity of being: my *I* is something absolute, but only relatively absolute. This is the second aspect we must stress: atheism is a will to grounding that concerns the *I* as something acquired in life, i.e., as something relative. And these two aspects simultaneously constitute the will to grounding of the atheist as a will to be relatively absolute. Atheism is the interpretation of the relatively absolute being as self-sufficient facticity. But this is just an interpretation; self-sufficient facticity is only a mode of being relatively absolute. And because of this atheism reveals to us that, as radical principality, the will to {286} grounding is a will to be relatively absolute. In order to will oneself as self-sufficient facticity, one must begin by willing oneself as relatively absolute being. The will to grounding is, therefore, *will to be*, to be relatively absolute, but to be.

d) Let us return now to the starting point of these analyses. We were attempting to conceptualize the "relation" between intelligence and faith. We recognized that intelligence and faith are essentially different acts: intelligence is apprehension of the real as real, and faith is personal surrender to a personal reality *qua* true. But these two acts are not disconnected; rather, are rooted in a unique attitude: the will to truth, which in our case is will to grounding. It is the will to discover the ground, making of what is discovered the express ground of my life, i.e., of the configuration of my *I*. Intelligence discovers the ground to us and with it the possibility of my personal life. In order to incorporate it into my life, the will must choose to appropriate this possibility, and that is what faith is. Therefore, in the will to incorporate its ground into my life, intelligence and faith are one at root. Intelligence is the intellective process, and faith is the foundational or grounding choice. We next ask, What is the characteristic of this radicality? We said that these two acts, intellective process and choice, are not only anchored in a will to grounding, but that this will is the radical principle of an attitude unfolding into intellective process and choice. Radicality is unfolding. Therefore, the will to grounding is essential to the human person as such; it is the origin of an attitude we inexorably have by the mere fact of being persons, and which unfolds itself into intellective {287} process and choice with respect to the ultimate ground of life, in the constitution of the *I*.

Nevertheless, three facts seem to contradict this assertion: the agnostic, who does not find reasons and suspends faith in God; the one who ignores the problem altogether; and the atheist, who does not go beyond his immediate life. We therefore had to examine each of these three facts separately, and have been able to discover that agnosticism just as much as unconcernedness and atheism consist, despite appearances, in an intellective and choosing process regarding the ground; and therefore they all possess a true will to grounding. But this examination has uncovered something else besides: it has put before our eyes in a preeminent fashion the will to grounding as *originating principle* of the constitution of the *I*. The agnostic has allowed us to see that the will to grounding as a principle of attitude is *the will to search*; the one ignoring the problem has allowed us to see that the will to grounding as a principle of attitude is the *will to live*; and the atheist has allowed us to see that the will to grounding as a principle of attitude is the *will to be*. As a principle of attitude, the will to grounding is, therefore, will to be, to live, and to search. And now we shall be able to conceptualize in a unified manner these three characteristics of the will to grounding. In what does the principal unity of these three moments, and therefore the turning towards the reality of God, consist? At the risk of monotonous repetitions, we shall state it very concisely because it has been more or less expressly mentioned in the preceding.

To do this let us tackle the question at its very root. Even though it may seem that we are returning to points already quite {288} remote in this study, it will be necessary to utilize them precisely in order to apprehend faith in God in all its human concretion.

A human being, as we have said, from the beginning, is a living and personal substantive *reality*. Its life consists in possessing itself, affirming itself (let us put it this way) as an *I*. The *I* is not my substantive reality, but the being of my substantive reality. The progression of one's life is nothing but the configuration, feature by feature, of this *I*, of this being. In constituting oneself as being of the substantive consists living. This is the intrinsic and formal unity of the human being and living: to live is to autopossess oneself as "being", i.e., as an *I*. This being has two sources. One is that according to which each human "is" a reality which possesses itself, which belongs to itself, which is "its own". It is in this that being a person consists. The *I*, the being of each human, is a personal being. According to the other source, a human by "being" affirms its reality as its own in the process of confronting all real things *qua* real. Therefore, belonging to itself is a belonging with respect to everything real; it is an absolute belonging. Personal being is, therefore, an absolute being. But since it is something realized, this *I*, this being, is only a relatively absolute being. A relatively absolute personal being is that in which to be *I* consists.

Each human realizes him- or herself as a being supported by real things and by other humans encountered during the course of life, and by his or her own individual characteristics. This means that in this its personal being, a human certainly is *with* real things (we now use "thing" for anything with which humans lives), but that *in* which he or she is with them is reality itself. To have or {289} to desire a real thing is to have or to desire a mode of being in reality; that mode is precisely the characteristic of that real thing. Therefore, it is reality itself, when living with things, that dominates me and determines my relatively absolute being. Reality, as that which is dominant with respect to the constitution of the *I*, is the power of the real. To be inexorably dominated by this power is what constitutes religation. Through this power we find ourselves, therefore, religated to reality itself. And reality itself present to me in this religating power constitutes the grounding of my personal being.

When I actually become aware of reality, several possibilities intervene between things and their realizations. In fact, to be aware of reality is *eo ipso* to sketch some possibilities of responding not only to this or to that, but of responding *really* by means of this or that *to* reality itself. Humans have to sketch the mode of being *with* each thing *in* reality: these are the possibilities. To respond, therefore, humans have to appropriate some of them. This appropriation is *will*. Will has an essential moment of reality; that which the will desires is always my mode of being in reality, i.e., my mode of being real in reality. Therefore it is a feature of my *I*, of my relatively absolute being. Because of this, that which the will desires is always, ultimately, my relatively absolute being, not only materially (to realize my relatively absolute being in the material sense only is proper to every act of life, including the merely vegetative), but formally as well. That which determines my act is reality. And it is religation to this power of the real that now determines me to desire {290} formally in each thing known intellectively as real, my relatively absolute being. And since the actuality of the real thing in intellection is its real truth, it follows that the tendency that has taken me to the willing of my relatively absolute being, has taken me to desire my being in real truth. Every will starts from and is nourished with and issues forth in my real truth. The will to be *I* is essentially the will to real truth. Therefore, my relatively absolute being incorporates in its very entity my own real truth. Therefore, it follows that the will to real truth is the will to be a relatively absolute being, living from reality and grounded in it. It is radically and unitarially the will to be and to live.

Each human, therefore, determines his or her personal being in a will to real truth, i.e., by the presence of reality as ground of his or her life. Inasmuch as reality is present to me as ground of the personal being of my life, it constitutes a reality-ground. Thus, any intellection of a reality-ground is *intrinsically and formally* the outline of the possibility to live in a grounded way; i.e., it is the realm of a possible choice. Concerning reality-ground there is no separation whatsoever between intellection and possible choices. Such choice is an appropriation of possibilities. And in this choice-based appropriation formally consists surrender as such. To surrender oneself to something is to appropriate, through choice, that something as possibility of my self. Essentially, willing is surrender.

What happens is that the power of the real determining me by religation is only in real things, though not identified formally with any of them nor with all of them together. This is reality itself as enigma. From this it follows that {291} humans are religated to reality itself by the power of the real is so in a problematic way. In order to determine themselves by the power of the real, they cannot allow themselves to be dragged along by the real things with which they are, but must try to be in reality itself with respect to which each thing is a mode of it. Therefore in each thing humans must search for the reality in which to be. So it emerges that the will to be relatively absolute in the process of living has to be a will to search. To search for what? Not for the reality of an object, for *its own* reality, but the reality *for me*, i.e., the reality constituting the ground of the power of the real that holds me religated and that opens for me the realities among which I must choose in order to be living. As long as this ground is not intellectively known these possibilities for choice remain in suspense. To desire a thing as mode of being here-and-now in reality is, in fact, something depending essentially upon that which in itself is actually constituting the power of the real as a moment of it. And since this power is the grounding of my being, of my personal life, it follows that to search for that constituting the power of the real to be here-and-now in reality is nothing but to search for the ground of grounding. Grounding is a characteristic of reality *given to me* in religation and therefore, in reality itself, but in reality "as towards". The terminus of reality "as towards" is something not yet determined. Consequently the terminus of this "towards", i.e., the ground, has to be searched for. Humans have to search, indeed, for this ground, and therefore, the will to real truth is a will to grounding. As such it is a will, not only to be and to live, but also to search. It is will to be living in search. The unity of these three moments is thus {292} conceptualized, and is the essence itself of the will to grounding.

It is in this problem, indeed, where the configuration of my relatively absolute being, of my *I* moves, not only in fact but constitutively. What is problematic about the power of the real is *eo ipso* problematic about my own personal being: the constitution of my *I* is formally and inexorably problematic. And precisely because of this the will to grounding is the free surrender to what intelligence knows intellectively as ground. It is a free surrender, i.e., grounded. The will to grounding is will to ground surrender. The will to grounding is the will to reasonable surrender. The will to grounding is in a radical sense a will that from the ultimate root of my reality unfolds itself as being, living and searching for a surrender, however deficient it may be, but a true surrender. It is the will to affix my being vitally and firmly on the power of the real, which, though inseparable from things and from my own person, cannot be identified without any further ado with things or with my person. And in this consists what I call "transcendence of the human person": the characteristic by which the human person cannot be a *real* person unless including in his or her reality, as a constituent formal moment of it, a power of the real that is more than the person and all real things. It is, ultimately, that characteristic by which the relatively absolute being of my reality incorporates in itself formally and constitutively the very happening of its grounding. It is not *transcendence to* the person but *transcendence in* the person. Because of this, to surrender to the ground of the person is not to go outside the person but to surrender oneself to one's own constitutive transcendence; and conversely, to surrender to the {293} transcendence of a person is to surrender oneself, in the person itself, to his intrinsic and formal ground.

This surrender is the radical choice of the will to grounding, and has two aspects. On one hand, it sets in motion the progression of intellection towards that ground to which we are physically hurled. And in this aspect, it is intelligence that has the last word. Its intellective process can reach a certain level of intellection of the absolutely absolute reality, of the personal reality of God sufficient for life, either to know it intellectively as inscrutable or as indifferent, or rather to submerge ourselves without God in the pure facticity of my relatively absolute being. Only intelligence can decide it. And in making a decision it gives reasons. Ranging from the one that more or less vaguely knows God intellectively to the atheist, with the agnostic and the unconcerned person somewhere in the middle, all without exception have to justify intellectively the terminus of their intellection. Here we have provided those reasons that, from my perspective, conclusively lead to the reality of God, and consequently determine the truth of that reality already known intellectively in mere intellection. So intellection is more than mere intellection: it is knowledge. Any demonstration of the reality of God presupposes in the human person a previous intellection of His reality. The proof is just the foundation of this intellection, and of that which is known intellectively in it: it converts this intellection into a demonstrative intellection. Due to this, no one is exempt from the necessity of providing reasons. Whether from the viewpoint of the agnostic, the unconcerned person, or the atheist any alleged proof can easily be regarded as an audacious and useless dialectic game. But this is beside the mark, because often it only means that one has abandoned oneself to the easier way {294} in order to avoid the effort of the proof. On the other hand, when these positions are viewed from the perspective of the proof, they appear as essentially incomplete intellections. Thus, it is not a question of arbitrarily choosing between audacity and incompleteness, but to choose in a grounded way. And this grounded option is the result of intellective discussion.

With that we come to the second aspect of the choice. Depending on the type of terminus of the intellective process, the choice will be the self-sufficiency of facticity, the unconcernedness facing the indifferent person, or the surrender to the personal reality of God. But the essential point is that this choice is always physically necessary and therefore always exists, first, by reason of the characteristic of the reality of its terminus (it is reality-ground); and second, because the will to grounding is not just some desire to arrive at the ground, but a desire such that in it, precisely because what is desired is a ground, the person is gambling physically and really the card of his own relatively absolute being. It is from this that the will to grounding acquires its exceptional seriousness. Theism just as much as agnosticism, indifference or atheism, is a mode of the same will to grounding. Anything less, even if it were theism, would be radical frivolity. This will is the one that, as an attitude, constitutes the originating principle of an unconditional surrender to the real ground at which the intellection arrives. The will to grounding is thus the *originating principle* of my personal life understood as constitution of my *I*. This attitude is, therefore, the one that unfolds itself into intellection and choice.

In Chapter three we expounded the reasons that demonstratively justify the intellection of God and {295} force us to admit the absolutely absolute reality of a personal God as reality-ground. This is the personal reality of God as the possibility to realize myself as a person. The appropriation of this possibility is therefore the surrender to a personal reality *qua* true: it is faith. Faith in God is, consequently, the surrender to the transcendence of my person; and conversely, the surrender to the transcendence of my person is faith in God. This "reciprocity" is precisely the sense and scope of the proof I proposed. The will to grounding is, then, the originating principle of an attitude which unfolds itself into knowledge of God and faith in Him. When one reaches a personal God, the will to grounding is the attitude of being a relatively absolute person "in" the absolutely absolute person that God is. It is the will to seat the real truth of my person in the real truth of the person of God, transcendent in all things and in my own person. It is not a question of going outside real things and of my own personal reality, but of being in these things and in my person fully, i.e., of reaching that in which their reality ultimately consists. If we were to see integrally the reality of a grain of sand, we would see God in this grain in His personal reality including the Trinity. It is in the attitude to reach a God, transcendent in me, that the principal unity of intelligence and faith consists.

And so we have seen, in the first place, what faith as such is, and afterwards we have examined the "relation" between intelligence and faith. These were the first two questions that faith posed for us. But there still remains a third question which is inevitable given the conception of faith which we have been expounding. Faith, in fact, is the personal surrender to a {296} personal reality *qua* true. And surrender is appropriation through choice, i.e., willing. But then will is not a mere intentional determination, as the enunciation of a judgment might be; rather, willing, by reason of being personal surrender, involves the totality of the person. Therefore, faith, like the surrender that it is, involves the entire concrete reality of the person who surrenders, and its own mode of surrender is also concretely personal. Thus faith has a characteristic of essential concretion. What might the concretion of faith be? This is the third and last of the questions we proposed to examine.

III

Making faith concrete

Faith, we say, is the surrender to a personal reality *qua* true. And surrender is appropriation of a possibility through choice. It is the very essence itself of volition. Because of this in each act of will we must distinguish two aspects. One is that aspect by which I appropriate a possibility. Under this aspect, appropriated possibility is that which has the determining characteristic of my person. Willing is, under this aspect, an act of the person. Yet there is another aspect inseparable from the previous one, but different from it in a certain way. It is the aspect according to which, when opting for the foregoing possibility as my determination, I surrender my person to be in one determinate way rather than another; willing is surrender and it is such by being appropriation through choice. In the case of faith in God, it is the act {297} of surrendering myself to be *I* in God in a grounded way. In this aspect, willing is not determined by possibility; rather, it is the person who determines the realization of the possibility. Then willing is not "an" act of the person, but is "the" act itself of realizing oneself as a person. Whoever desires something, even to take a walk, is surrendering him- or herself as person to be personally a walking or ambulating *I*, to realizing him- or herself as walking person. These two aspects are but the two sides of a selfsame act: every appropriation is surrender and every surrender is appropriation. Volition, on one hand, is the person as "subject" of the appropriation of possibility; it is, on the other, the desired "object" itself, because it is the surrender of the person to be one way rather than another. All of which allows us to see that a person is not only a subject of volition (first aspect), and object of it (second aspect), but is identically the latter as much as the former. In what sense? Of course, it is not a merely formalistic identity as Kant would think—as if the identity of both aspects were that which constitutes personal reality, i.e., as if being a person consisted in self-determination. On the contrary, it is the personal reality, already real as person (reality which is "his-own" or "her-own") occurring in an occurrence, which consists in that this reality making itself *I*, makes itself the being of the substantive of my person. What constitutes the identity of self-determination is personal his-ownness, not the identity constituting the person. It is "my" reality *qua* "mine" which, by reason of being mine, is subject "and" object of the will itself. Therefore, surrender is not self-determination as formalistic identity of subject and object, but the reality already personal in its-ownness which surrenders in appropriation {298} through choice. Now, it is thus clear that surrender is of the person with all the characteristics it already possesses. It is not an *I* which desires, but that what desires is *I*. Therefore, surrender is an essentially concrete act, where "concrete" means that in it reality is involved, reality *qua* its-own, in accordance with everything it already is and has become.

And this is essential for the problem of faith in God. Faith in God is my surrender to His personal reality *qua* true. Hence, it is always and only concrete surrender, and consequently, concrete faith. Until now we have seen in what faith formally consists as such. Still, this leaves unanswered what faith is, what the surrender itself is in its concretion, in the same way which the formal explanation of being a person leaves unanswered the concrete question of what each human is as a person. By "concrete faith" I mean the modes, shades or qualities (the term is not important) according to which faith is not only faith but "my" faith. What is this concrete faith?

We are not dealing with the case of a merely practical concreteness—as if the differences under question were minor variations of how persons "function", so to speak, in their faith. Much deeper than the *functional*, it is something *constitutive* of the believing person. But this still needs further clarification, because it is not the case of differences consisting only in the personal mode of being of each person, but extraneous to faith itself. In that case these differences would be something concerning faith only *concomitantly*, something similar to the way an epoch, for example, accompanies scientific research, but does not form part of it. In concrete faith we are concerned with more than mere concomitance because concomitance is in fact always something [299] *extrinsic*. But the concreteness in question concerns the very structure of faith *qua* faith. And this is because faith is not the mere admission of truths, but the surrender of the entire person; and therefore the modes of being a person not only "accompany" faith but are an *intrinsic* moment of its constitution: they are precisely its positive and intrinsic concretion. Faith is an act of will to grounding. And this will is lived by each person in his own way. Each person surrenders to the occurrence of his own grounding in his own way. And in this is what the concretion of faith formally consists. To be sure, faith is always the same in some ways, but never the same *thing*: "my" faith is not "your" faith, not *qua* faith, but because in one case it is mine and in another it is yours. The unity of faith is not something that *concretizes itself* in different persons, but is the identical meaning of *radically concrete* persons. To be "mine" is a formally constituting moment of faith in God. Put in a deliberately exaggerated way, the problem is not how the same faith is lived by different persons, but in what measure and up to what point different persons have the same faith. And this is not a subtlety: history bears indisputable testimony to what we are referring. That is the radical concretion of faith; it is not an adventitious concreteness added to faith but makes faith concrete *from within faith itself*. Faith has personal modalities; there are many personal modes of the same faith. This is a significant problem because it requires maneuvering between two dangers that have usually damaged the conceptualization of faith. One is the danger of considering faith as something resting upon itself, and which therefore only applies externally to the concrete situations of the person; the ingredients of this concretion would {300} simply something earlier vital in one's life, namely faith itself. This is on all counts a monstrous extrinsification of faith. The other danger is just the opposite. It consists in supporting itself only upon the mental structures of each person; in this case faith would be a blind impulse, or at best a subjective attitude emerging from psychic structures. In fact, however, faith is neither the one nor the other. Faith emerges from personal structures and possesses the sense and extent of truth in these same structures and from them. This intrinsic articulation is precisely the problem of making faith concrete as *mine*. It is a problem concerning principles.

And in this concreteness, faith is mine in several dimensions. Above all, faith in its radical concreteness is so by reason of the individual characteristics of the person who surrenders him- or herself. Faith is the surrender of my person to another personal reality *qua* true. The person who surrenders in faith is not just "a" person, but "this particular" human person in his or her intrinsic concretion. The one who believes is not a human being in the abstract but "this particular" human being; not "the" abstract person but "this particular" person. And this is something essential for any faith; it is not something exclusive to faith in God; but acquires its maximum expression concerning such faith. In addition faith is concrete because of the different modalities that the surrender itself incorporates. And above all, faith is concrete by virtue of how God is seen in it as ground of my *I*. To see God concretely as the ground of my being is something depending essentially upon the concreteness in accordance with which I am turned towards God.

I am turned towards God from my concrete personal reality, because faith is the surrender of *my* person, mine—not the faith of a person, but my surrender, of my person—which forces one to ask about the concretion {301} of this faith. This is not merely a fact but something that is a formal and essential constituent of faith as such. No faith is faith unless it is *my* faith. The moment of faith is *my* belief, *my* surrender to the personal reality of God, which is not only manifest to men and humanity, but to me as a person. Faith is essentially personal. And the person is always *my* person, mine, untransferable and unchangeable for others. Faith is mine for several reasons.

In the first place, faith is mine by reason of the person, by reason of my own person. But this would be a unity of mere singularity. And in fact there is more to it. Each person is a person *in his or her own way*. And if the reality of being a person is always one, the individual way of being a person is the individual way in which I am one. And this, which is true from the point of view of personhood, is even more visible as true from the point of view of personality, i.e., from the being of the substantive of my person. My reality *qua* person, as personhood, makes the configuration of its *I* in the course of my life.

This is absolutely essential for faith. The correct intellection is that the type of the person must be considered as a constitutive ingredient of the act of faith. This would uproot, or at least would put into its proper place, many considerations made based on the particular characteristics of persons. It is said, for example, that such-and-such a person believes because he is neurotic; but this only means that he will be a believer neurotically, not that he may not be a believer personally. It is a different personality, but it is a personality which is *mine* with its neuroses, with its imperfections, with its qualities and dispositions, and it is *this* personality that decides. It is *my* faith, the faith of *my* person. It will be the same faith which another person has with a different personality, {302}, but it is so by reason of the terminus upon which faith rests.

But let us add that this concrete person, by reason of his or her personality has, besides his or her own particular concretion and dimensions, social and historical dimensions as well. The faith of any religion is not the same in different societies, or even in the same society as it changes and varies in space and time. The belief that it remains the same is chimerical. The people of Israel certainly believed in Yahweh, but did so with respect to a set of particular social conditions; theirs was a theocratic nation. Other societies are not. Now, not only is this not alien to faith, but without that there could be no faith. The social conditions are formal and constitutive ingredients of faith. And, above all, just as there is immersion in societies, there is also immersion in history. The people of Israel felt itself to be a chosen people, but only after a long history and not from the beginning; they reflected upon many isolated episodes of their life as a people, and discovered in them the unity which could exist in all, and in this way appeared the idea of chosen people. That history is a concretion of faith. It is not fortuitous, therefore, that faith in Yahweh did not begin to be preached in a universal manner from the beginning, but only after a historical experience. In general it can be said that the history of religions is the experience that peoples have made of God throughout history, and in our case, is the history of the faith of those peoples.

What *my* person is, *my* personality with all its concretions, individual, biographic, with all my personal gifts and with my history, installed in a society, an installation which is not necessarily a limitation—all this is essential for faith. An intelligence installed in this way not a {303} limited intelligence. And, consequently, nothing this precludes the intellective activity that forms an essential part of faith, but rather demands it. Of course, such intellective activity is a function of the characteristics of my person.

In the second place, faith becomes concrete not just through me as a person; it is also connected with my mode of surrender. There are those who are eager and those who are procrastinators in surrendering themselves. There are those quite anxious to acquire faith; others are not. There are some who have an enlightened surrender. There are some who have a staunch faith, and others who display a weak faith. These are all different modes of surrender. And among these different modes of surrender is how the surrender of my concrete person to the personal reality of God *qua* reality precisely occurs.

But, in addition, faith is concrete through a more subtle moment, upon which we must dwell. Each may have or can have *his or her idea* of God, by reason of the terminus of his or her own faith. I do not refer to the case that one may be a polytheist and another a monotheist. But within Christian monotheism, for example, a saint can have an idea of God different than that of another. God is not only God, but is also my God. One sees God from the point of view precisely of the personal truth of God, but with essential reference (without which there would be no diversity), to those dimensions through which God makes a donation to me. In definition He may be the same to all, but the lived faith is not the same to all. There are some who see God, above all and primarily, as merciful, as charitable; there are some who see Him as Supreme Being. Each has his or her own God; and this is so *a fortiori*, if we consider the idea of God in different religions. {304}

However, this is not a relativism. It is an aspectualism, which is different. I see the reality-ground of God with different aspects. And this is so because from the point of view of humans, how can any particular aspect of that person to whom one surrenders in truth because it is true be absent from the unity of inter-personal causality we mentioned above? This moment of fidelity is not lived equally, for example, in the people of Israel and in our Christian society. Between the Israelite conception that Yahweh above all belongs to Israel, and the conception that to be a true Israelite one must ground oneself in Yahweh, there is an enormous difference. The collision of these two conceptions is precisely the crucifixion of Christ. The historical path of the idea of God in Israel and above all the idea of God in different religions and different peoples, manifests at what level it is essential that we give consideration to the concretion of faith.

If the encounter of humans with God, beginning with the accessibility of God to them, is grounded on the fact of religation, the ground of my personal being; and if the person is essentially concrete, the actual encounter of humans with God and of God with humans, the surrender of humans to God as truth cannot be anything but concrete. There lies the root of the concretion of faith, affected as much by the individual dimension of humans as by their social dimension and their historical dimension.

---

[1] [A fifth subsection is indicated at this point in the Spanish text, but there is no corresponding material in the chapter so the subsection title has been omitted here.—trans.]

[2] [English rendering of Zubiri's neologism *ensimismante*.—trans.]

[3] [Another neologism, *suificándolas*.—trans.]

[4] [*Facticity* (or *Effectivity* which is sometimes used by Zubiri) in this context means the ability to bring about an action or result.—trans.]

[5] [In Spanish, *donación* comes from the verb *dar*, to give, in the expression *dar de sí*—trans.]

[6] Tract. in John. XXIX, 6.

[7] [Reference to Prehistoric man (c. 14,000-c. 9,500 B.C.) who left cave-paintings near Altamira in northern Spain.—trans.]

PART III

HUMAN BEINGS, EXPERIENCE OF GOD

{307}

CHAPTER 5

GOD, EXPERIENCE OF HUMAN BEINGS

Of the three parts I intended to develop, the first comprises the reality and being of humans. The second develops the subject of what divine reality is as the ground of human reality, and the access of the human person to the divine reality. And so we have human beings "and" God, God "and" human beings. What now remains is to observe and analyze the singular and *sui generis* unity between God and humans. Since God is found at the terminus of personal religation, In what does this "and" consist when we say God "and" human beings? What do we mean by God "and" human beings?

In order to pose the problem in a satisfactory manner, and not as some mere abstraction with a more or less ontological character, let us review some of the points already covered.

In the first place, humans in their religation are precisely and formally religated in their being to the power of the real, supported by which each makes his or her own I. In the second place, the power of the real is a power which is *in* real things. Religation is then a manifestative experience of the power of the real, and of the real in itself. It is an experience that is a physical test of reality, but also a manifestative and ostensive experience in some form of {308} that power of the real, and of the reality that has that power. In my religation, therefore, there is going to be a manifestation through experience of what reality is and what the power of the real is. We continually apprehend *in* and *by* reality itself what reality itself is about. In the third place, the power of the real is not real unless grounded upon a reality-ground, the absolutely absolute reality with respect to which my personal reality, made with the power of the real and religated to it, is only a relatively absolute reality. The human person, by virtue of the structure of the power of the real itself to which it is religated, actually finds itself remitted to a grounding reality, to a reality-ground, i.e., to an absolutely absolute reality. In the fourth place, this power is a transcendence of God in things. God is not a thing which is beyond things themselves, or only a type of efficient cause, a *natura naturans*, underlying all of them. He is, from my perspective, something more elemental and prior to any theory: He is God transcendent *in things*; He is not transcendent *to* things, but transcendent *in* things. And among them, transcendent *in* the human person. And here our problem begins.

Since religation is a moment of personal reality, insofar as it makes its own being, and insofar as it makes its own I, it follows that the actuality of God (in one form or another that we will have to determine precisely) is in some way included in my personal and human reality, insofar as that person is religated, and therefore, inasmuch as it makes its own I. And this is despite the fact that the actuality of God is the actuality of an absolutely absolute reality, and consequently, *other* than all personal realities. {309}

Of course, one may ask in what way. To be sure, it is not in a merely copulative manner. God "and" human beings do not exist in the same way that the sun "and" the moon, "and" the earth, "and" the animals, "and" humans exist upon earth. Clearly, it is not a merely copulative "and" because it is God transcendent in things, and therefore, it is not a mere copulative summation. But neither is it purely and simply a kind of efficient causality, more or less *naturans*, naturing; rather it is a presence of God in things, constituting them formally, constituting them as realities. And in the case of human persons, it is something that constitutes my remission to the divine ground of my own personal reality in the configuration of my own I. He is a reality which is precisely grounding. It is as grounding that God is in the ultimate depth of things and especially in the depths of the person.

We may then ask about the characteristics of this grounding presence.

Said *in genere*, God is present to me, grounding me in my religation, which is a moment of my own I. He is religating me precisely at that moment in which the power of the real is at its greatest, so to speak—precisely when, and to the degree in which, the power of the real is something we experience in religation. Therefore, God and the human person find themselves bonded; they are bonded in this experience of the real. Since religation is a formally constitutive moment of my person, it follows that God and the person are determined *in* and *by* this experience of God, at least insofar as grounding is concerned. A human being, to put it in terms of a thesis, is experience of God. Here lies the radical unity of God and {310} the human person. It is the moment of the "and". So far this "and" means that each human is experience of God. It is not a merely copulative "and" but an experiential "and". This affirmation is somewhat obscure at first, because the expression "God, experience of human beings" has two vertices. It incorporates one that opens onto God Himself *qua* reality. On the one hand, with respect to God, God is a reality that, regardless of what He may be, occurs in one form or another in an experience, and is thus bonded to being an experience. But, on the other hand, to say that a human is experience of God means that each human being, in his or her own personal reality, is experiencing the reality of God. Thus, there are two different aspects of the experience: one concerns God *qua* God, and another concerns humans *qua* humans. Each human is experience of God, or God is experience of each human. With respect to God, God is experience of humans; with respect to humans, each human is experience of God.

But this convergence of two experiences is not a sufficient explanation, because then another problem surfaces, namely in what does this unity ultimately consist, which apparently is not a convergence of God as experience of humans, and of humans as experience of God? Our question is thus divided into three parts:

1. With respect to God, in what does God as experience of human beings consist?

2. With respect to human beings, in what does a human as experience of God consist?

3. In what does the radical, ultimate, unity of God and human beings consist in this fundamental experience?

In this chapter we shall give an answer to the first of the questions. {311}

As we have previously said, God is *quoad nos et quoad omnes res* a *realitas fundamentalis*. He is not a supreme being but a fundamental reality, absolutely absolute. He certainly does not consist in being an Aristotelian formal cause of creation—that would be an enormous pantheistic monism. God does not consist in being a fundamental or grounding reality. God would be absolutely absolute reality even if He did ground us. And, conversely, if He had to be grounding in order to be God, He would not be absolutely absolute reality. He would then depend upon whatever He would have to ground. And this is not the case. God is an absolutely absolute reality, and therefore, God does not consist in being fundamental reality. But, given the fact that God is grounding things and particularly persons, then the primary and radical way God is God with respect to things, is to be *realitas fundamentalis*. He is ground inasmuch as He is transcendent to things, but in things. And He is transcendent in things, and is grounding them, inasmuch as He is absolutely absolute reality. It is not the case that God grounds things formally *qua* volitional intelligence.

God is absolutely absolute reality, and is grounding things insofar as He is absolutely absolute, even though in this grounding activity the characteristics of intelligence and will are not formally included. God is absolutely absolute reality transcendent in the real.

But then, What is the concrete figure of this constitutional transcendence of things?

In the first place, God is in things, in the manner I have just indicated, in every reality, in each thing. God is a grounding reality. To ground is a mode of dynamism, {312} and the dynamism in each being is formally identical to that in which its naked reality consists. Reality is not only—stated humanly and anthropologically—the set of qualities and properties that reality possesses, later put into act; but rather to be dynamic belongs to reality intrinsically and formally, i.e., to be self-giving. Reality is essentially a self-giving. God self-gives and cannot not give. God is a self-giving, and a self-giving of the self-same reality in which He consists; furthermore, precisely because He is something which self-gives reality, insofar as that reality is not God—and precisely due to that—He is grounding of all reality.

This giving, therefore, concerns reality *qua* reality; it concerns everything real. And the important point here is that it concerns the real *qua* real. This is the radical point; everything else is inscribed within it. But, in addition, this self-giving and constituting of reality is not as if a cause and causal process produced things, and afterwards in some form may continue producing or maintaining them in being. This is true, but I consider it grounded upon something more radical, i.e., that this self-giving of the real, *qua* real, consists precisely in the transcendence of God in that which He self-gives, i.e., the real. Consequently, God consists—from the point of view of grounding—in being the ultimate and radical depth from which the reality of each human emerges and where its reality is *qua* real. Actually, the ultimate depth of things is not a *phýsis* or a *natura* either *naturata* or *naturans*. It is rather just their reality, the characteristic of reality. And inasmuch as God is constituting *in actu exercito* and at every instant this characteristic of reality by His transcendence in things, {313} God is something present in the ultimate depth of all of them in a continuous, constant, and constitutive manner.

What qualifies the presence of God in things, in all of them without exception, is to be constitutive. And it is in this that the fountanality of God consists. God is ground and grounding reality qua fountanal reality—fountanal reality, I repeat, not in the sense of a *natura naturans*, but in the sense that it is something by virtue of whose presence reality is constituted, because that presence constitutes the reality of the real *qua* real. Of course fountanality, and not only fountanality but, as I see it, creation itself, depends essentially on the terminus to which it leads.

On the topic of creation, we are accustomed to consider creation as a univocal act. God has made things out of nothing and they are there in terminal fashion, and are terminally transcendent to God. This is inadequate. In my estimation, a precise idea of what creation is and the different modes of creation should have been posed in metaphysics and theology. If we rest content only with creation as production *ex nihilo sui et subjecti*, the conclusion would seem to be that all creative acts are equal. But it is a somewhat negative equality. Elephants are similar to stones in the fact that they do not climb trees. This is true, but does not tell us what the elephant and the stone are.

Creation must be conceived as the very life of God projected freely *ad extra*, consequently in a finite form. Therefore, this coefficient of finitude of divine life projected *ad extra* is precisely finite nature, i.e., things. The pure divine life *ad extra* in its finitude is the characteristic of reality as such. From {314} this perspective is how the different modes of creation have to be understood. And we cannot apprehend the different modes in any other way but showing that they depend upon the different types of metaphysical reality as such.

Now, in my estimation, the types of metaphysical reality are fundamentally two: on the one hand, there is the reality of those things which have certain properties by virtue of which they are in their own right that which they are in themselves: these are the so-called the 'closed essences', i.e., the case of the realities that are not persons. They are things which have their properties, which are the properties of their reality *qua* reality, and act according to them. In that case the mode of fountanality consists in the fact that God is fount of their being in their own right what they are. We may illustrate this with a simple example: it is not the case that God burns in fire but rather that He makes fire burn; He makes that fire burn by making fire be fire. We are not, therefore, dealing with coincidences and concurrences, which are something quite different from what we are trying to express here.

But there is another type of metaphysical reality, the metaphysical reality constituted not by things that are simply in their own right, but are so in such a form that, in addition, they are *their-own*. They behave with their own characteristic of reality—something that does not occur with other of cosmic realities. These are the "open essences," open to their own characteristic of reality. This is the case of human beings. Human beings not only act by virtue of the properties they have, or by virtue of the properties possessed by the things with which they make their lives; above all, they act in an absolutely real manner, however problematic and difficult. {315} Each human acts by being and in order to be a form of reality, i.e., from the perspective of his or her own characteristic of reality. This is appropriate for open essences. However, it causes fountanality to acquire a special characteristic. Fountanality is certainly a constitutive presence of God, a transcendence of God in things, by virtue of God giving Himself to them. When this terminus to whom He gives Himself is a person, then fountanality acquires a special characteristic. It is no longer a mere fountanal giving, it is a more intimate and more profound giving. It is donation. Only when that to which He gives is a person do we have a donation. For this reason, *a parte Dei*, His transcendence in persons consists in being donation. And by being thus, by God being that which is constituted in donation, it follows that the person himself is his or her own.

But then, donation of what?

Clearly we are concerned with an inter-personal relation, in which God's own reality in one form or another constitutes human reality. But this human reality is qualified as open reality. Then the mode of God giving Himself is just a *personal* donation, which makes this donation have a special characteristic. It is not simply the brute funneling—in some cosmic and mechanical manner—of a reality into something that did not previously have it; rather, it is something much more concrete: the fact is that what God actually gives to the human person in donation is precisely his real truth.

By "real truth" I understand—and I repeat it again—not something that simply consists in being true in the sense of an affirmation, of a true judgment. It does not consist in being a truth in some way ontological; rather, it consists in something more elemental, and for our problem {316} more decisive: the very actuality of the real in an intelligence, but *qua* reality. By virtue of its actualization in intelligence, we say that the real is true. Truth is not a kind of extrinsic relation to the real. It is extrinsic in a certain sense, because it might not be actualized in an intelligence. But supposing that it is, it is not an extrinsic relation but the mere actualization of the real in that intelligence. This is real truth. Let us remember that this real truth has at least three dimensions. One, truth in the sense that it is a showing, a manifestation; in the second place, truth in the sense that it is a kind of security or firmness with which the real is actualized in human intelligence; and in third place, the fact that it be *in actu exercito*, here and now.

And indeed, God gives Himself to human beings, to the human person, as real truth in that triple aspect, because in His transcendence and in His personal donation God is, in one form or another, an actualization of that donation consisting of the reality in which the being of humans is constituted; in the second place, it is a kind of presence—I shall develop this theme a little further down—of security and fidelity with respect to himself; and in the third place, it is something really and effectively in being, and without such being the human person would have no reality.

Therefore, it is with this true reality and in this true reality that each human being, with the donation of God, is making his or her own relatively absolute person. The reality of God is absolutely absolute; the being of human personal reality is relatively absolute. From this it follows that the theme of donation to a person coincides {317} precisely and formally, upon that common point, with absoluteness. God is absolutely absolute; in His donation each human constitutes itself as relatively absolute. The moment of the absolute is what constitutes the point—let us state it simply without qualifiers for the present—of convergence between God and humans.

But each human is a personal reality with a special characteristic, because each human is an animal of realities. And animality constitutes the particular version of this person which humans are, or putting it in a better way, this particular version is constituted by what we call "experience." From this it necessarily follows that the donation of God as real truth is precisely experiential donation. God gives Himself to humans, not in an abstract manner as a cause may give itself to its effect in order to produce it; rather, by virtue of that which He produces, i.e., a person who is an animal of realities, the giving is intrinsically, formally, and constitutively a giving in experience. To say, then, that God is experience of humans consists purely and simply in saying that He is giving Himself to humans in a giving which is experience—an experience that is not consequent upon the being of humans, but one in which at one and the same time each human is constituted as such. Each human is, in this sense, God giving Himself as intrinsic and formal ground of religation, in the animal of realities. This is the concrete form in which God gives Himself to us.

This formulation poses, however, three questions we must answer:

§1. In what does this experience consist on the part of God?

§2. Which are its possible modes?
§3. What are its dimensions?

§ 1

EXPERIENCE WITH RESPECT TO GOD

Experience is physical probing of reality. In God's donation, as real truth, we have an authentic experience, because in it we are acquiring that absolute characteristic that God gives us relatively; of course. It is not given as an absolute characteristic resting upon itself, but as a characteristic stemming from one of the fundamental modes by which reality is present to humans, i.e., directional reality, in the form of "towards". Each human being receives this donation precisely in the form of a "towards", and not purely and simply as something there in front of us. The experience of God is a real experience, *a parte Dei*, because it is real experiential donation; it is God really and effectively as an experiential person. In the case of a human being constituting him- or herself as a "principially" absolute person, God gives Himself to us as experientiable, as a ground which is experiential, experientiable, and experienced. It is God giving Himself as absolute so that each human is able to be a person, i.e., experientially.

God has given Himself as absolute in experience; it is God giving Himself or making Himself experienced as absolute. It is in this that the experience of God formally consists, insofar as it is experience, and insofar as He is giving Himself in experience.

{319}

§2

DIFFERENT FORMS OF DONATION

The donation of God to humans can take on very different forms, which is necessary to set down.

First, God is giving Himself as experiential absolute in a universal form. All persons are constituted, in one form or another, by this characteristic of absoluteness; and therefore, inexorably, with or without the knowledge of humans, God has a universal form of being experiential for all human persons, to wit, being the experiential absolute.

But, second, there are forms that are more specific. For example, there is that form by virtue of which donation, and therefore each human, is an absolute reality, something grounded precisely upon the transcendence of God in things. This is something different than what I just indicated. It is, for example, that which entails the idea of the presence of God in persons, when one talks about grace. Grace is not a mere quality. It is a dynamic moment. This dynamic moment may be interpreted as the presence of God in persons (uncreated grace), and as the type of quality which that presence impresses upon persons (created grace). But this dualism, independently of any other formal theological considerations, is not sufficient. It must be absorbed into something more radical and primary, such as the transcendence of God in persons in the form of constitutive donation of their relatively absolute being.

Third, there is a more intimate and absolute mode. That mode is the presence of God in a person, making {320} and formally constituting therein at least its relatively absolute dimension. It is that presence by virtue of which the relation is so intimate that it is precisely the real truth of God in person. This is what happens in the Incarnation, just as it is accepted by the Christian faith, but which as a possibility can be thought of by human reason. Jesus-Christ is the truth of God in person. This is how the *Verbum caro factum est* must be interpreted. *Caro*, flesh, in this case means precisely the form of being experience, the experiential form in the person of the real truth of God. And the *factum est* means precisely to make itself experience: Christ Himself is making Himself in a certain way human, and more than humanly, although not as Word.

At least, therefore, we have these three forms of transcendence of God in things as donation: the universal transcendence in the form of giving Himself as experience of the absolute; in the second place, the presence in grace; and, in the third place, that presence in the form of being the very its-ownness of the human reality of Christ which is, according to the Christian faith, the Incarnation.

§3

DIMENSIONS OF THE EXPERIENCE OF GOD

In this experiential donation, donation concerns all the dimensions of the being and the reality of the human person.

In the first place, it concerns persons individually as we have just seen; but in the second place, {321} it concerns human persons inasmuch as they are making themselves socially and historically. God gives Himself to humans as experience—we are not talking about humans but about God—in the form of sociohistorical experience.

Hegel started from the idea that since God is absolute spirit and in the form of absolute reason, what we call society and history are moments of that absolute giving of Himself in the dialectic of being, in the dialectic of the absolute spirit which is the dialectic of reason. From my perspective this is absolutely untenable. In the first place, the function of God in history is not, as Hegel maintains, to be the presence of reason in history. No. It is to be the presence of real truth in history. Real truth is not to be identified with reason. Certainly, there is a presence of God as reason, but that is not the primary and formal form of the way God is present in history. He is present as real truth. And, in the second place, it is untenable because we are not dealing with the becoming of God, but with His giving of Himself, with His real donation. And this donation is not a dialectical unfolding but something different: an experiential unfolding. History is not dialectical, either in this case or in any other. History, in the problem we are studying, is the absolute as human possibility; it is absolute reality made possibility in human experience.

History is essentially experiential; it is God giving Himself as historical experience. And this is clear in the history of religion. We have, for example, in the Old Testament, that God founds or establishes the people of Israel, the chosen people, in a *berith*, in a covenant. In that covenant the initiative lies with Yahweh, with God. But that initiative consists, on God's part, in giving Himself {322} to the people of Israel precisely as origin, as agent, and as the medium of an historical experience. Really and effectively, God gives Himself as real truth in the three dimensions of real truth, but above all in that one to which humans are most sensitive, i.e., as fidelity. The covenant is an experiential initiative of the fidelity of God with the people to whom He offers it. This is the form in which real truth is in the people of Israel. In this manner one can interpret a good portion of the history of Israel, through the covenant, which itself is historical, from the accounts of paradise to the culmination of the prophets. This is the ratification of God giving Himself under the form of covenant, of *berith*, under the form of historical experience, to the people of Israel.

It is also the case with Christ. His historicity—God has an historicity, Christ has an historicity—grounds and constitutes the religious movement called "Christianity," whose history starts from Christ Himself. It is precisely God giving Himself as son of Mary, and giving Himself as absolute Truth of the Word, experientially, as son of Mary and Joseph.

If someone wishes to reflect upon the idea of providence, I consider it unnecessary to locate providence purely and exclusively in the arrangement of reasons and dispositions on God's part, some for approval and others for permissibility, anthropomorphically speaking. There is something much more radical: that upon which divine providence rests is the experienced transcurrence of God in the history and life of each human being. It is an unfolding, an experiential disposition. These are the particular modes, the particular dimensions, according to which God gives Himself to us, on His part, as something experienced by humans. He gives Himself to us in a universal form {323} as an absolute that is going to be experienced or, at least, that may be experienced. He gives Himself also in that other distinct form, although not equally recognizable, which the experience of grace is, which is also common to each human being. And in the third place, the supreme case, He gives Himself in that greater degree of unity and of presence which the Incarnation is. From this perspective, the Incarnation is the willful incardination of God in history as something that is going to be experienced throughout its whole course. God grounds Christianity in a more radical form than becoming "Christian." He grounds Christianity when entering history itself to be part of it. Humanity is thus initiated into an historical experience of the absolute.

Greek metaphysics here encounters significant limitations, stemming from the idea of the possible actuation of a potency by an act, or of a possible Platonic participation of some realities with respect to others. But above all it has a fundamental and serious limitation: the complete absence of the concept and the very term of "person." It took the titanic effort of the Cappadocian Fathers to divest the term *hypóstasis* from its characteristic of pure *hypokeimenon*, from its characteristic of *subjectum*, and of substance, to bring it near to what the juridical sense of the Romans had given to the term *persona*, as differentiated from the pure *res*, the thing. It is somewhat facile in the history of philosophy to speak of what the person is, in contradistinction to the *res naturalis*, for example in Descartes and above all Kant. But forgotten all to often is the fact that the introduction of the concept of person in its own peculiarity has been the work of Christian thought, and of the Revelation to which this thought refers. {324}

Be that as it may, God, giving Himself as experience, is precisely what He is for humans. God is an experience of human beings in a precise sense. On the one hand, He gives Himself to them to constitute each as a human being, a human being who is personal animal of realities. On the other hand, and as a consequence of this, He gives Himself to humans to be experienced by each human himself, who is personal animal of realities. It is here that the second question surfaces: In what does this experience of God consist with respect to humans?

CHAPTER 6

HUMAN BEINGS, EXPERIENCE OF GOD

In the previous chapter we have seen, from the point of view of God, what is the problem of God "and" human beings, of God giving Himself to humans as experience. In this chapter we shall concern ourselves with the second point: What are human beings themselves insofar as they, in their reality, are experiencing God?

The first thing we must point out when affirming that each human is experience of God, considered *a parte hominis*, with respect to humans, is that this does not primarily mean, much less formally mean, that each human *has* experience of God. This is not the ultimate truth. We must add something else: it is not the case that each human *has* experience of God; rather it is the case that each human *is* experience of God, in the formal sense. And, of course, one may ask, what does it mean that human *is* experience of God?

§1

WHAT IS EXPERIENCE OF GOD?

The issue is, then, what this experience of God may be.

We are referring now to what experience of God is *a parte hominis*, on the part of humans. Before anything else we must say that experience of God is not the experience of an object called "God", not only because humans are incapable of that, but because this is not even how one should conceive of what an intuition of the divine would be, were something like that even possible. God is not a reality-object, as we explained in the previous chapters.

Also, "experience of God" is not to be understood as some state in which humans are. At the beginning of the [twentieth] century, the invading avalanche of books about religious experience all started from the assumption that religious experience is something that affects a certain state of humans. Nonetheless, God is neither an object-like terminus for nor a state of humans. What happens is that humans are grounded, and that God is the *realitas fundamentalis*, the grounding reality, which is the reason why the experience of God on the part of humans consists in the experience of being fundamentally grounded on the reality of God. It is by making my being in a fundamental or grounding sense that I attain the experience of God. What there is in the experience of God is the experience of the welling forth and grounding reality of God in religation as ultimateness, as ultimate possibility, and as supreme impellence. This, together with what was said in the previous chapter, is what opens the door for us to understand with greater precision what the experience of God is on the part of human beings.

Actually, humans are one finite way, among many other possible ones, of being God really and effectively. And what we call "human nature" is nothing but this moment of finitude, which can be multiple and various, but in the case of humans is of a particular structure. The animal of realities is the moment of finitude, in accordance with which humans are God. Humans are a finite way of being God.[1]

This finitude is formally experiential. Every human is an animal of realities, and in that condition of its own animality its experiential mode is incorporated. Consequently, humans are an experiential mode of being God. God is an absolutely absolute reality and in this consists His metaphysical reality. On the other hand, I am, confronting God or with respect to God, a relatively absolute reality. "Relatively absolute reality," because I have acquired this absolute characteristic in the face of reality by making myself a person, by making my own being, by making my own *I*, by making and fabricating my personality. Therefore, the experience of making myself a person is experience of the absolute. I am not absolute as a substance is; I am absolute by making myself a person and by constituting myself as an *I*. In constituting myself as an *I*, I have and formally am the experience of the absolute. This experience is precisely the experience of God; the experience of the absolute inasmuch as it is experience of my personal being. God not only is not a being but with respect to our problem, He is not even a first efficient cause. He is *quoad nos* fundamental or grounding reality, *realitas fundamentalis*. And, therefore, one "is" by apprehending this formally transcendent characteristic of the grounding of God in the human person, in my own personal being. {328}

This is why God is neither object, nor a state, but that which is the absolute of my being. He is that which is grounding and making possible the absolute of my being. The experience of God is but the experience of the absolute acquired in the constitution of my being, the experience of being grounded upon a grounding reality. Consequently, God, absolutely absolute reality, is inscribed in relativity, in what is absolute of a relatively absolute person, in my own personal reality. Whence this presence of God in persons, and correlatively, the mode in which humans are partially experiencing God, may have different characteristics.

§2

MODES OF THE EXPERIENCE OF GOD

We have seen that human beings are experience of God. And they are experience of God formally, inasmuch as they are relatively absolute beings, so that the experience of their own absolute relativity is precisely the experience of God because it is the experience of the absolute. But this can have different modes.

In the first place, there is a mode that is radical for every person. It is the case, in fact, that the turning towards fundamental reality, towards reality-ground, is a moment of the will to truth. The will to truth, we said above, is precisely that moment by which each human is author of its own personal being, which can only "be" by acquiring support or true ground in the power of the real, {329} which it is experiencing as a relatively absolute reality. The radical mode of the experience of God is the will to truth—truth not in the sense of sincerity, not in the literal sense of the word, but in the sense of real truth. *The radical mode of the experience of God is will to real truth.*

This will is formed, as we indicated, in an intellective process, one which opens the realm of ultimate grounding. This intellective process offers humans several different possibilities for being a form of reality in the realm of reality and real ultimateness. Therefore, each of the forms that humans adopt in their choices, each one of the forms of their own absolute being, is precisely the terminus of an appropriation, of a will which is constitutively choice-oriented.

Now, choice is the real and concrete way to be free, to be absolute. This is freedom. Hence, the experience of God in a radical and ultimate way is the experience of my own freedom, insofar as God is ground of my own absolute being. Freedom, in fact, may have different aspects. Freedom is, in a first sense, "freedom from." Each human can be free, feels free, and is free inasmuch as he or she is free from particular coercions, from particular impulses, from the weight of a tradition which is not reflexive but received routinely, etc. To liberate oneself from this, in one way or another, is what belongs to one aspect of freedom, this is the "freedom from".

There is, however, another aspect of freedom. Each human is free from all this, having freedom in the sense of liberation. For what? Precisely, to be him- or herself. This is the "freedom for being". Each human is not only liberated {330} *from* things, but is inexorably "free *for* being", free to be precisely a form of reality confronting any other reality.

Nonetheless, there is still a third ultimate and radical aspect of freedom, because when all is said and done, freedom "from" and freedom "for" affect the modes of exercising freedom. There is something prior that consists in being free, before to any exercise of freedom. This is precisely freedom "in". Humans are free "in" reality as such. Being of a condition by virtue of which I am mine, I belong to myself and to no other reality. Freedom in this sense is or can be identical to the person. That is not so in the two first senses, but is radically and eminently so in this third aspect. This is what it is *to be free*. And it is in this third aspect of freedom where the root of my relatively absolute being is found, and therefore, where the radical experience of God is. The radical experience of God is the experience of being free "in" reality. To be free is the finite manner, concrete, of being God: to be free in an animal sense. The experience of this freedom experienced in the animal sense is precisely the experience of God.

In addition to this universal mode of experience thus described, there is another mode to which I had alluded previously. It is the experience of grace or of God as grace. In what measure can humans have an experience of grace, unless it is an intellectual certainty metaphysically deducible from the possession of grace? That is a matter which belongs to theologians and to the historians of dogma. Here it is a much simpler and elemental question. Each human has an experience of grace, even though he or she may not know it, because there is no one exempt from this presence {331} of God. Rigorously speaking it is not a presence; it is in the very projection of the Trinitarian life *ad extra* that the formal explanation of the creation of humans consists, as we pointed out above.

But there is a third mode of experience, and it is the supreme example: the human life of Christ. It is not a question of only seeing the mysteries we can observe in the life of Christ, but of seeing the very life of Christ as a mystery, not in the sense that Christ is the Son of God, but in a different sense. If one contemplates His life, Christ shows Himself as a person who is hungry, needs to sleep, has sorrows, sheds tears when a friend dies, etc. And one may ask, what were all these acts of the life of Christ to Him? One might think that they have a pedagogical function, that with them He wished to teach something. But the issue is *how* He taught it. He taught it by doing it Himself, but doing it *truly*. In other words, the concrete way He had of being the Son of God was precisely to feel hunger, to eat, to talk to friends, and to cry when He lost them, to pray, etc. This was the concrete way. He was not a man, in addition to being Son of God; rather, that was the concrete way in which He humanly lived His own divine filiation. It was the experience of His own divine filiation.

The opposite would be what I have often called in my conferences a "gigantic biographic docetism," as if Christ had an experience in the sense that He had to behave like other men, without this affecting Him as Son of God. In this "biographic docetism" would consist. In the same manner that God had in Christ a human body and psyche, He also had a strictly human biography, which affected His {332} own condition of being the Son of God. God desired to feel in His nature not only that He rendered homage from finitude to divinity, to Which He was united hypostatically, but He desired something else: He desired to live biographically the vicissitudes of a man who feels needs in His own personal characteristics, to have to confront all kinds of vicissitudes, and even assume, at least in His human intelligence, some aspects of His mission on earth while in it. The idea of *kénosis* explains or points to this dimension in Christ, which consists in that concrete annulment to be finitely and humanly, as a Palestinian, at that time, a son of Joseph and Mary, a carpenter who walks on the streets of Nazareth, to experience in that way His own divine filiation. We are accustomed to think that "the other life" is no longer what this life is; but it is unnecessary to assume that there is fundamentally more than one life, divinely lived in two different ways: one having hunger, thirst, etc., and another contemplating God for all eternity. They are not two lives; it is the *same* life lived in a *different* way. To live is to possess oneself. Here, it is to possess oneself in grace; in heaven, it is to possess oneself in God. It is not one life after another; it is one self-same divine life.

This manner of experientially living His own divine filiation was in Christ the secret of His own personal intimacy. In reality, He did not reveal this to men. When the exegetes speak about the "Messianic secret," they think this is an evident fact that can be taken from the text of St. Mark itself. But there is a subjacent fundamental theological problem: In what does this Messianic secret consist? It consists precisely in that, in being the experiential manner of His own divine filiation. Christ {333} communicated to others in some measure, inasmuch as personal intimate biography can be communicated to others, what was essential about His life. And He did it precisely so that men, adding themselves to it, and uniting themselves to it, and surrendering themselves to Him, would be able some day to ascend to that constitutive secret of His own divine filiation, which was the secret of His personal life.

And this, despite being a theologic postulate from the perspective of the Christian faith, is not an exception to everything I have presented thus far. I indicated that each human has an experience of God as a relatively absolute being, inscribed in a reality and in a power of the real. Christ not only had this religation to the power of the real, but was something else: the subsistent religation. And precisely by virtue of being so, He founded a religion, one which in a certain way is the religion of religions. Christ is the subsistent experience of God. To be sure, the subsistent experience of God is not an experience outside the limits of daily existence: walking, eating, crying, having children. It is not an experience outside such limits, but is precisely the manner of experiencing in all of it the divine condition in which each human consists.

It is not the case that in this world human beings in fact have to deal with things *and* in addition with God, when they concern themselves with God. No. Humans concern themselves with God purely and simply while concerning themselves with things, with other persons. Each human has to be concerned in this world with everything, even the most trivial. But each has to be concerned with everything divinely. There is where the experience of God is, exactly.

As subsistent religation and experience of His own divine filiation, as experience of grace, and as {334} experience of freedom—three essentially united things—is how the forms of the experience of God are given. The intrinsic unity between freedom as absolute experience of the absolute of God, the experience of grace, and the unfolding of that presence in divine filiation comprises the theological unity upon which, in my estimation, this complex and rewarding theme must be erected.

But the presence of God in the experience of the absolute not only has these different forms but also has different dimensions.

§3

INDIVIDUAL, SOCIAL, AND HISTORICAL DIMENSIONS OF THE EXPERIENCE OF GOD

In the three dimensions of human beings—individual, social, and historical—each human has an experience of God. Leaving aside the individual dimension, which is the one that has appeared mostly in the previous consideration, there is an historic experience of God, and a social experience of God.

In the first place, humans have a social experience of God. And they have it even when living in a society that has no God or does not wish to have one, because this not-wishing and this not-having constitute a precise form of experience of God, as we shall immediately forthwith.

This experience of God is not the result of a kind of syllogism: God is present in each human and each experiences God as absolute in everything; but {335} he or she lives in a society, and therefore, experiences God in society. But we are not concerned with this; we are trying to see in what the social dimension of the experience of God consists. The social experience of God, precisely because it is social, is multiform and varied, just as diverse as the manners of living the absolute in the freedom of each one. Each person creates in his own way the experience of the absolute. But in addition humans have a social experience of God as multiform as the individual one, a social experience with all the concretions, vicissitudes and limits of the societies to which *humans* can belong. In reality, the experience is not an attribute of *each human*, but of *humans* in its concrete form.

For example, in the people of Israel, a Semitic people is the experience of the true God as fidelity, as fidelity not only offered by God in a *berith*, in a covenant—as I explained above—but as an experience which humans make of the divine fidelity. Here "truth" means fidelity. Although the term used is "truth," the word "truth" is in this case something more than intentional conformity. The word "truth" is the fidelity of God. Thus, a person will ask mercy from God, will ask that God have mercy on him or her, precisely so that God Himself should faithful to the fidelity He has offered.

The examples can be multiplied. Among others, there is the episode of Elijah in his struggle with the prophets of Baal. Baalism is an historic form, an historic experience of God; the intellection of divinity as Baal was the product of an evolution within Phoenician thought, which originally had "El," supreme God, at the head of the Ugaritic pantheon. Only afterwards {336} did Baal acquire a certain supremacy, leaving "El" relegated to a subordinate divinity. The reason for this stems from the fact that the early Phoenicians were nomads, and a nomad is accompanied throughout his migrations in the desert by the divinity understood as "El" until his establishment in the country where he is going to become sedentary. But once becoming sedentary, what is essential is not that God accompany him through the desert, but that there be sufficient rain for the crops. It is then that Baalism appears. Elijah argues with the priests of the Canaanite God, but at that time this Canaanite God is now Baal. And the dispute occurs also in the form of a social experience, appealing to the fidelity of Yahweh with the trial of fire.

The people of Israel had had other forms of this experience of God before; for example, the experience of God in the desert, an experience that was an enrichment of the experience of God. The determination is maintained that Yahweh is the same God as the God of the fathers, and the fact that God is the God of the fathers is a form of social experience. The fathers are the ancestors of the family: this is the God of the family. It would be chimerical to impose on the mind of Abraham and the patriarchs the idea of only one God that Israel itself has in the last years of its pre-Christian existence. He is still the God of the fathers. The well-known text of the contracts signed between the gods of the others and the gods of the Hittite fathers clearly shows that the God of the fathers continues living in the Israelite society.

With Moses, however, there is a point of inflection. The God of the fathers changes into something more radical, into a jealous God, which is a social form of living the absoluteness of God. It would be an exaggeration to pretend that Moses was a monotheist {337} in the sense that he did not admit any other divine reality but the one of Yahweh. But the Yahweh of Moses did not admit any other divine reality next to Him; not only was He jealous, but He was solitary, even though this solitude may have only consisted in the solitude and real truth of Yahweh. This will require prophetic preaching to assume a different social form, which is the authentic and rigorous monotheism wherein the other gods are nothingness; the *elohim* have now turned into *ililim*.

There are, then, different social forms of the experience of God. I have mentioned a few as examples. They are social forms of the experience of the absolute. The Israelite did not feel himself to be an Israelite, or being what he had to be absolutely, like something constituting a dialectic of the exception; but leaving aside his sins, the Israelite felt himself truly Israelite when he was a faithful servant of Yahweh, a fidelity which had very different aspects in the different social eras of Israel.

In addition there is, nonetheless, an historical experience of God which is not identical to the social experience, to wit, a true historical experience of God.

It has become customary to consider history as a kind of chronological museum of human and social forms. But, is history a museum of social forms, even if they are chronologically connected? This seems to me radically insufficient. History, primarily and fundamentally and within the limits of its historicity, is properly and rigorously speaking an experience. It is not universal, and was not such until the beginning of the twentieth century, because what went before is not a universality but a synchrony of different individual histories. As experience history is physical proof of {338} reality. Humanity has not only been taking on different forms over the course of history, but in fact has been experimenting. Our era, for example, it is physically testing many things which for Aristotle were just a catalog of empty forms, and for us are experiences. History is constitutively experience. But, Experience of what? Precisely, experience of reality. Yet, history is not, contrary to what may be thought at present, the last word on human reality, because history is constitutively penultimate; ultimateness only belongs to the person *qua* person of each human being.

However, history has implied an experience of God. And in turn the experience of God has configured history. As such monotheism is one of the factors which have led to the universality of history. Whether seeking it or not, monotheism has had a great deal to do in the universal constitution of history. Regardless of the people adopting it—in Israel, in Islam, in the Christian peoples, etc.—we can detect how in the course of history the various polytheisms vanish in the face of monotheism. Humanity has been building a fabulous experience throughout history, the monotheist experience. It is a strict and rigorous experience, and not simply a theologic and metaphysical argument.

And this mode of experience is proper to the history of Israel. We have pointed to this before as social experience, but now we should return to see it as historical experience. When the God of Israel appears, Yahweh, who according to the earliest writers was invoked by the ancient fathers, God appears as the God of the fathers. This God of the fathers appears in a concrete form: not simply {339} offering His fidelity, which was the constitution of the covenant for Moses, but as historical experience. That form is the one of *being now with them*. This historical experience assumes different forms, from the most elemental form, His accompanying them across the desert to the borders of Canaan, to the constitution of that which has been called the "amphictyony" of the tribes of Israel. Regardless of how this may have come about historically—that is not our point—God then appears in another form: He is the God of the pact of the tribes. Later, in connection with the monarchy that was imposing itself, there appears another historical form of the experience of God: Yahweh as king. And in a still more particular form: the God of the armies, Yahweh Sabaoth. This is the historical experience of God as chief of a State, in this case theocratic.

Further yet, one can appreciate a true theology of history in the inspired preaching itself of the Old Testament, which is the supreme expression of this historical experience of God: God offers His fidelity under the condition that the Israelites be faithful. This is followed by the defection of Israel, then the punishment of God arrives, and finally the repentance with the return to God. This theology of history in four acts is precisely the theology of the historical experience of God. It is an experience lived by the people of Israel in different historical phases, the historical experience of God as fidelity, a fidelity which is the real truth of God, and never canceled regardless of any infidelities by men.

When reading the Old Testament it may seem that a unitary line is being offered. God creates human beings in His own image and likeness; they commit the original sin, corrupt themselves, then came the deluge, etc. The Red Sea is crossed...and {340} the lineal narration of a history continues. But the Israelites did not live it that way. They lived each of these episodes in and by themselves. Israel did not have from the beginning the idea of being a chosen people. How could they have had it, since they had started by not being a people? Israel has gone through all these historical vicissitudes and only when a theologian, the priestly writer, reflected with inspiration from the theological and theologic perspectives about these experiences of Israel, was he able to see along these diverse experiences the links of a unitary chain, which is the experience of God, unitary in different phases of manifestation, of that which is precisely to be the chosen people of God.

The being of the chosen people is the structure of their theology of history, in a unity which goes back to the earliest times of Israelite humanity, and which continues up to the time of Christ.

As the chosen people of God, the people of Israel have lived the experience of God as something absolute and something which, in a way, has made them feel absolute in the face of all other peoples, because those peoples pass on, and in the end, only Israel remains. However, this happens in such an obscure way that not even Job dared to answer the question which that experience poses. Such, then, is the historical form of the experience of God.

Nor is this extraneous to the New Testament. Christ did not found Christianity by organizing some institutions and saying "this is how one has to live". He did some of that. But Christ founded Christianity in a much more radical and intimate way. Christ founded Christianity by making Christians, i.e., setting in motion the movement of Christianity in the course of history. Christ wished to be experienced by His followers so that {341} they, associated in Him, could be in Him the historical experience of God. The historical experience of His divine filiation is continued precisely in the very expansion of Christianity. It is the real subsistent truth of Christ which runs through the river beds of a history.

This is not exclusive to Christianity, even primarily. In Christianity there is all of this, because it rests upon a universal augural truth, the historical experience of the absolutely absolute Being with respect to the human being, insofar as it is an *I* which advances by grounding itself as absolute upon the One Who is absolutely absolute. I am grounding myself as absolute upon the One Who is absolutely absolute. And only because of this are there all of those structures I have just recalled. If one wishes to employ the usual classical terminology, we could say that this structure of the experience of the absolute, the historical experience of the absolute, is the dynamic and obediential base, thanks to which it has been possible to have structures like the Israelite and the Christian in history. History is an experience, and a dimensional experience of the absolute.

Contrary to what Kant and Hegel said, history is not the unfolding of reason, of a logos; it is the unfolding of an experience of God. Hegel, who did not see in reality anything but a decanting of reason, failed to find a way of conceptualizing history except as the form of objective spirit, of objectivized reason, above persons, who, as Hegel says, disappear into the objective spirit which, in its turn, is the ultimate march towards absolute spirit. This is absurd. Hegel thought about how men could be God; Christianity taught them to think how God could become {342} man, and then precisely learn to be God. This is the anti-Hegelian or para-

Hegelian vision of history, a history which is, indeed, an historic experience of God.

§4

OTHER ATTITUDES WITH RESPECT TO THE EXPERIENCE OF GOD

There are other attitudes towards the problem we are discussing. In the first place, there is the attitude of the agnostic and the person who is indifferent. The frustration of the agnostic and the unconcernedness—if not, it would not be indifference—of the indifferent person are in reality modes of the experience of God. Without this the agnostic would not be an agnostic, and the indifferent person would not be indifferent. Each would be something else.

A more serious problem arises, on the other hand, regarding atheism: the problem of one who faces the theological question of the ultimateness of the real, and yet does not reach the existence of God. But this problem has to be approached clearly by saying that atheism does not enjoy the *conditio possidentis*. It might be thought that humanity is without God, and then whoever claims that God exists is the one who has to prove it. This is not true. The truth is that each human is religated to the power of the real in all of us. Whoever proceeds towards God admits the existence of God reasonably. And whoever does not so proceed has to prove why he or she does not. This person has to give reasons. What is primary is not to be without God; what is primary is to be religated to the power of the real. Atheism just as much as theism is the conclusion of an intellective and vital process within that aforementioned religation when one confronts the ultimateness of the real. {343}

So then we must ask, in what does the attitude of the atheist consist with respect to this line of thinking? I already indicated this before: it consists precisely in that the atheist, who undoubtedly would admit that in some way we are relatively absolute persons, has an attitude based on the pure facticity of the absolute, and he remains in that facticity. He would admit that, but would not admit that we can proceed beyond it. Now, the intent of formulating it this way is to provide a more careful exposition of atheism: the ultimate essence of atheism consists in this and in nothing else. When confronting this attitude, the reply does not consist in "proving" through an intellective process that God exists. No. Here we have to confront atheism directly. And then, from the reality of God, one thing is clear: if humans discover the fundamental reality in an intellective and volitional process, from the will to truth, and the atheist does not, it is because the atheist, in contradistinction to the theist who has discovered God, finds himself with his own pure facticity concealing God: this is the "covering up" of God confronting His "dis-covering". It is not a lack of experience of God. It is an experience in a certain way "covered up".

The experience of God may assume various forms. One of them is to discover it and another one to keep it under cover. This is not a dialectical metaphor to avoid the issue, because the atheist who is so sincerely, and finds himself resting upon his atheism (just as we believers find ourselves resting upon our faith without great theological arguments that may have brought us to it), this atheist, I say, just as the believer, is the terminus not only of the good will of God but of His supernatural graces, at least from the Christian point of view. At best, in this case, humans are in God. {344}

In 1936 while in Rome, I wrote the following: "It is probably necessary to activate experience even more. The time will surely come in which human beings, in their intimate and radical failure, will awaken as if from a dream, finding themselves in God and becoming aware that in their atheism they have done nothing but be in God. Then they will find himself religated to Him, not in order to flee from the world, from others, and themselves, but just the opposite, to be able to withstand and support themselves in being, because God does not manifest Himself primarily as negation but as grounding, as that which makes existence possible". The experience of God, consequently, *a parte Dei*, is God giving Himself as absolute to human experience; *a parte hominis*, it is to incorporate the experience of the absolute in the constitution of my person. A human being does not encounter God primarily in the dialectic of necessities and indigencies. A human being encounters God precisely in the plenitude of its being and its life. Anything else is to have a sad concept of God. Of course—all of us are victims of inelegancies—we appeal to God when it thunders. Indeed, no one is exempt. But this is not the primary form in which humans proceed towards God, and are now actually in God. Humans do not proceed by the way of indigence but of plenitude, the plenitude of their being, in the plenitude of their life and their death. Humans do not advance towards God in the individual, social, and historical experience of their indigence; this intervenes secondarily. They proceed towards God and must proceed above all through what is most plenary, in the plenitude itself of life, i.e., in making themselves persons. In the personal being, in the relatively absolute being of the person, is where each person finds God, giving Himself to humans in their experiences. This donation of God is precisely the reality of the person. And this {345} human experience of the absolute is experience of this donation of God.

But, what is the unity of these two moments? Is it enough to appeal to the concept of experience as physical proof of reality in order that this experience of God—God giving Himself to humans in experience—and this experience of humans, experimenting and searching individually, socially, and historically with his freedom that is the relatively absolute of his being? Is it enough with this convergence in the concept of experience to resolve the problem? Not in the least. We must then ask: in what does the intrinsic and formal unity of the human person "and" God consist, in this experience of God, now bilaterally considered? That is the issue of the next chapter.

---

[1] [The meaning of this paragraph may be unclear. In the context of Zubiri's philosophy, humans are God in the sense that they are absolute, but differ from God in that they are only relatively absolute.—trans.]

CHAPTER 7

UNITY OF GOD "AND" HUMAN BEINGS

Human beings are religated to the power of the real in a manifestative experience of the reality of this power. The power of the real is, in each real thing, more than its particular reality. And because of this it is grounded upon a grounding reality. Since this reality determines my *I* as relatively absolute, this grounding reality is an absolutely absolute reality, i.e., God. Therefore, since this power of the real is conveyed in and by real things, God is *in* reality constituting them as real. This is the transcendence of God not beyond things, but *in* things. With respect to this particular reality which the human person is, i.e., an animal of realities, the transcendence in it is a constituting presence in religation. And since religation in this case occurs in an animal of realities, it follows that the presence of God in the constitution of the personal *I* is a matter of experience. Humans are, in this sense, an experience of God.

We then asked ourselves, first, What is this experience of God *a parte Dei*? What is God as experience? And we saw that it is God as Self-giving, and {348} Self-giving-Himself not to reality, to produce it in some way, or to ground it; but Self-giving-Himself formally to a person, in the case of humans. Therefore this giving has quite a unique metaphysical and theological structure: unlike other sort of giving, it is a donation. It is a donation of God Himself to that which is at the root of the *I*, to that by virtue of which each human is a person, i.e., to its intelligence. And this actuality of God in intelligence is precisely His real truth. Consequently, the donation of God is donation of God as absolutely absolute reality, giving Himself as experience of His absolute characteristic under the form of real truth.

In second place, with respect to human beings, they do not have this experience only. It is not the case that each human *may or may not have* an experience of God; each is formally, *qua* person that makes its *I*, formally I repeat, experience of God as ultimateness, as possibilitation, and as impellence. Each human is, in its religation, experience of the absolute. And this experience is precisely the experience of God.

But then a third problem arises, to which we are going to dedicate this chapter: What is the unity of these two experiential moments, of God giving Himself in experience, and of humans experiencing God? That is the issue of the unity of God and humans. What is this "and"? For the purposes concerning this presentation, the problem unfolds into four questions:

§1. What is the characteristic of the unity between God "and" humans?
§2. What is the particular characteristic of this unity in the case of human persons? {349}
§3. What is the experiential unity of God "and" humans?
§4. What is the unity of humans "and" God as metaphysical transcurrence of religation?

§1

GENERIC CHARACTERISTIC OF THE UNITY OF GOD "AND" HUMAN BEINGS

From the side of God, His donation of Himself is a constituting donation to the human person, and is a donation inasmuch as this substantive reality of humans makes their *I*. Therefore, it is a real donation of the reality of God to the reality of humans in order that each human being should be an *I*. From the side of human beings, it is a manifestative experience of reality, *qua* moment, an act by which each affirms itself as relatively absolute reality in the depths of the real.

From this we obtain a first immediate consequence: the second aspect depends on the first, inasmuch as humans can have experience of the absolute and be relatively absolute, and inasmuch as they are constituted in some form by the donation of God. But this donation is a donation that concerns God as reality, and humans as reality. So ultimately it is just the case of a functionality of the real as real, with respect to humans insofar as they makes their *I* with God Who is present in them formally, making them be *I*. And since the functionality of the real as real is what constitutes, in my estimation, the very essence of causality, it must be said that in the unity between {350} human beings and God we are dealing with a strict causality. It is a unity of causality, but of a constituting causality, one which formally constitutes, not merely one which is efficient and productive. We are thus dealing with a formal constitution. It is the functionality of my reality in its formal constitution as *I*. And it is precisely there where the causal functionality to which I am referring lies.

But, even from the point of view of causality understood in such a way, the question is not exhausted, because the functionality of the real, as real, actually concerns all things. However here we are referring to human persons, and therefore, this functionality also has an absolutely unique characteristic: the functionality of the real as real, inasmuch as God is absolute person and inasmuch as each human is a relative person, whose relative and formal act is to be *I*.

For this reason the type of causality we are discussing here is what earlier we called "personal causality". It is a type of causality different from the type of causality canonized in the history of philosophy after Aristotle. Aristotle, with his division of the four causes, classifies causality from the point of view of what causes are insofar as they produce some reality: the cause which is efficient, material, formal, and final. In my estimation, we should make the decision to introduce into metaphysics a type of causality I would call *personal*, by virtue of which the functionality of the real as real concerns persons as persons. Persons are "who", and any individual "who" is not a numerical determination of the "what". The "who" is an irreducible and ultimate metaphysical mode of reality, proper to open essences in contradistinction to closed essences. {351}

From this perspective of personal causality we should be able to see that many things we tend to consider as the complement, the embellishment, or the consequence of causality understood in the Aristotelian sense, such as prayer, the love of God, and help from God, in reality are not just purely religious things without metaphysical importance. No. I believe this is an absolute error. All these moments belong to a personal metaphysical causality, with as much causality as the fall of a stone can have under Aristotelian causality. From our perspective we are not dealing with an efficient, material, formal or final causality, but of a personal causality befitting an open essence.

This makes us realize that the unity of God "and" humans is definitely a causal unity, though a unity of personal causality. And naturally this leads us to the second question.

§2

TYPE OF UNITY BETWEEN GOD "AND" HUMANS

In what does the unity stemming from personal causality consist?

To be sure, in this personal causality the distinction between God and human beings is maintained. Regardless of how greatly personal this causality may be, I am not God, and neither is God, formally considered, an *I* which might not exist. Therefore, the strict distinction between God and humans as personal realities is maintained.

Nonetheless, this distinction is not the same as separation. One might tend to think that since God is what He is as {352} person, and since each one of our meager realities is what it is with respect to God, there would be a possibility at least in principle of tracing a kind of perimeter for each human being, delimiting on one side the territory of God, and on the other the territory of humans. This is an absolute fantasy, not because of any general metaphysical reasons, but really and concretely because of personal causality. It would completely erase and annihilate the very idea of personal causality. Persons are not, not even at the human inter-personal level, facing each other, as stones do in an electro-magnetic or gravitational field. Persons in their human relations are implicated in one form or another among themselves. It is a structure of implication. This is even more true in the case of the Divine Person.

The distinction between God and humans, as persons, is something completely different. In the first place, there is a given presence of God, formal to be sure in my person, constituting me as His donation. And there is also the presence of myself as formally constituted in God by the donation of God. God is certainly God without the need to be constituting any personality in any reality grounded on Him. But I would not be *I* if I were not formally grounded in the formal reality of God, present in me and constituting me as such an *I*. This is an incontrovertible truth. It is one thing that God may not need humans to be personal, quite another that the reverse be true. The *I, qua I*, is not formally what it is except in and by God. *I* am not *I* except for the formal and constitutive presence of God in me as personal reality. {353}

Still, *I* am surely not God. But then one may ask: What is this "not"? That is the question precisely.

One might tend to think that I am not God just as a dog is not a cat, or as the planet Jupiter or the Moon are not the Sun. It would be a distinction indeed somewhat numerical, grounded upon numerical multiplicity. This is absolutely not the case concerning the human person.

It is not so because this "not", according to which *I* am not God, is precisely one of the intrinsic and formal moments of my constitution, of my *I*, by God Himself. In other words, not to be God is a formal way of being here-and-now in God. It is an active moment. The "not" is precisely the donation of His reality in order for each human to be an *I* that is not God, so that this "not", as moment of the *I*, is absolutely positive and active. God makes that *I* be a person without being God. It is a question, therefore, of a unique type of implication. It only appears between persons, and in a special way between the Divine Person and human persons. It is a formally active "not". Without God *I* would not be what *I* am, i.e., absolute. But if this not-being-God were not to have an active characteristic, then *I* would not be relatively absolute. If the formally active characteristic of the "not" is not affirmed, one would fall into one of the forms of pantheism, or into one of the forms of extrinsicism between God and humans. But, if it is affirmed, we have the formal presence of God in things from the point of view of reality, and we have the ground of the relativity of the absolute. The "not" has the characteristic of being essentially positive and a constituent of the *I*, insofar as it is not God. And this is why not-being-God is precisely, with regards to a human person, a real and {354} positive way of being here-and-now in God. Therefore, between God and humans there is a real distinction, but one which is not only no-separation, but a formal implication.

It is a formal implication not a delimitation. It is a way of my being implicated in God and of God being co-implicated or *complicated*—if we could put it this way—with me. When all is said and done, God has somewhat complicated—expressed anthropomorphically—His own divine reality "with" having given Himself *ad extra* to human persons. And this being-in-God, but not-being-God (with the "not" as a positive moment of being in God) is precisely a type of implication we shall call "tension". The implication between humans and God, as a type of personal causality, is precisely tension. The unity of God and humans is, therefore, theological tension. The concrete type of formally personal causality in our problem is precisely this: the case of an inter-personal tensive unity.

Here the word "tension" does not have a psychological sense, as if humans were pretending something. It has a metaphysical sense in the form of implication, as I have explained. How this tension is lived is a separate question. Here, we are affirming the metaphysical characteristic of tension, and it is not to be construed as a psychological or anthropologic structure.

In this tension the donating moment of God, as a constituent of my personal reality, in the relatively absolute act of my *I*, is preponderant and initiating with respect to whatever the *I* may be as constituted person. Consequently, from the point of view of tension, in this inter-personal unity between God and humans, God has a strictly pre-tensive function. {355}

This is precisely the pre-tensor of what is going to be the tensiveness of humans with respect to Him. And, on the other hand, each one of our personal realities is not pretensor but only tensive or tensoral. And this tensive unity is precisely the metaphysical essence of the theological unity between God and humans.

This tension is precisely the formal constitution of the *I*. God, absolute reality, is formally in my reality causing this reality to make itself *I* in the divine reality, without being the divine reality. And in this unity is in what the experiential characteristic of the "and" consists.

§3

EXPERIENTIAL UNITY OF GOD "AND" HUMAN BEINGS

Viewed from the tensiveness, In what does this unity consist, that experiential unity by which God gives Himself as experience of absolute reality to me, constituting me in my relatively absolute reality?

The tensiveness, I said, is formally the experience of humans as experience of God. And the experience of God is ultimately and radically experience of this tensiveness. God, giving Himself as experience, is an eminently active moment on the part of God. It is, to be sure, God giving Himself in experience. But with respect to humans, this which we have called "the experience of humans", is not experience in the same sense as it is in God, because in the case of God, it is God giving Himself as experience to a human being. But, on the other hand, in the case of humans, they are experiencing that which God {356} has given them. Each human being is experience of God in the sense of experientiality, an experientiality of the donating reality of God as absolute. It is an experientiality of the absolute. And, therefore, since the experientiality of the absolute in God, as formal constitutive of the *I* is a donation, a unity is given between donation and experience. And in this unity is in what the unity of theological tension concretely consists. My absolute has a tensive characteristic. Each human is God finitely, tensively.

Naturally humans can be God tensively in several different ways.

There is in first place, a tensive unity proper to every personal reality, by virtue of the fact of being an *I*. The *I*, let us repeat, is not the substantive reality of humans. Each human being is a substantive reality, provided with an intelligence, by virtue of which he or she possesses a characteristic, which when activated will exercise the relatively absolute being. Prior and independently to its exercise, each human is a person in the sense that he or she possesses that characteristic I term "personeity". However, what we call *"I"* is not this reality but the act in which this reality affirms itself as such a reality, i.e., as person. Confronting what? Confronting everything real *qua* real. It then follows that the *I* is not the substantive reality of humans at all, but the act in which the substantive reality actualizes itself as its-own, the act of being

I. It is relatively absolute because it is an act in which my substantive reality is affirmed not confronting this or that person nor this or that thing, but confronting any reality whatsoever *qua* reality. This includes, in principle, as absurd as this emplacement may be, the case of the sinner, who confronts God Himself. The *I* is then not only a tensivity, but is {357} precisely the radical metaphysical characteristic of being a "tensal" act. It is an act in which my substantive reality affirms itself tensively, and constitutes itself as an *I* in which its-ownness, that in which its substantive reality consists, is reactualized, and therefore, is that in which the formal explanation of its personality consists.

But there may be other cases, other different ways of being God tensively. Once more I allude to things which transcend a strictly philosophical framework, but serve as a concrete example of possible ways of being God tensively.

Thus, we have the Pauline references to grace. The word *háris*, grace, is not limited in St. Paul to what theologians will later call "sanctifying grace", but refers to everything that is "gracious" from the side of God, gratuitous from the side of God, which translates an ambivalent term from the Old Testament, *hesed*. On the one hand it signifies something that has been translated as "mercy", a translation which can be correct, but correct in the sense of a contraction of what the word *hesed* signifies. Actually, this term means the good disposition, the benevolence with which God inclines towards human persons. From the point of view of humans the same word and the same concept do not mean benevolence, but rather the intimate attitude in which each human being places itself internally in the hands of God, and receives its *hesed* from God. This is not simply the case of a word that may have two senses but of something much more radical; it represents a typical case of "tensive unity". This is precisely the tensive unity of a *hesed*, which from the side of God is donation under the form of benevolence; but from the side of humans is what a Greek might call *eusébeia*, interior {358} religion. When Hosea placed on the lips of God that He wished mercy and not sacrifices, he was not referring to the mercy of God, of course, but to *eusébeia*, to the interior religion of humans. The term, however, is *hesed*. This is the expression of a concept that is really tensive of the unity between God and humans, from the point of view of what we call "grace".

Many other examples can be quoted. When the sacred texts make reference to "men of good will", or "men loved by God", we face a case similar to the above. The *eudokía* from the side of God is just the benevolence, love, and inclination with which He loves mankind. But with respect to humans, the issue is not the good will one has for doing this or that, but the will to place oneself in the hands of God. Because of this, it is good. The tensive unity of these two aspects is precisely what the word *eudokía* (Lk 2:14) expresses. It is not a question, in my estimation, of words that have polysemy, depending on whether they are referring to God or to human beings. It is not the case of two senses more or less analogical, more or less harmonized in a unity. No. We are concerned properly and rigorously with only one unique concept, which has the tensive unity of a donation from the side of God, and from the side of humans of an experience, of a surrender to God.

There can still be a superior mode, a superior manner in which a human can be God tensively. It is that mode in which the *I* is a reactualization of its-ownness, but of an its-ownness that does not belong to the human being, i.e., the substantive reality belongs to someone else. This case is precisely the case of Christ, the *I* of Christ. The reality of Christ is not his-own, but is of the Word mysteriously, {359} so mysteriously that not even the human intelligence of Christ Himself could have had a comprehensive and exhaustive view of this fact, which in its ultimate depth is His divine filiation. Christ is a reality that, as substantive reality, is not his-own. He exercises the act of being an *I*, and in this act He expresses his-ownness in second act. But it is not a his-ownness determined formally by His own human substantivity. It will be useful to pursue this example further.

One could very well ask, when Christ says *I*, Who is this *I*?

The interpretation has been given that Christ has two *I*'s, one *I* which is human, the son of Mary and Joseph, working as carpenter, suffering, etc.; and another *I* which would properly be the Word. This appears to me as something absolutely untenable, because in this interpretation one starts from a false idea of the *I*. What is an *I*? Is it a mere psychological structure? As we have just said, *I*, born of my father and my mother, cry, suffer...this is not the *I*; these are the features with which my own experience advances as it configures the *I*. The *I*, formally speaking, is not a psychological or anthropological structure; it is a rigorously metaphysical structure. It is the act by virtue of which it reactualizes itself—if it does so, that presupposes a prior act—in the form of an act of which the its-ownness is proper to the reactualized reality in that act. This is precisely the *I*. If this is the case, it is impossible to say that in Christ there are two *I*'s.

And this is so for two reasons. First and most fundamental, the Word is not an *I*. We are accustomed to consider that the three Persons of the Trinity are *I, You, He*. This is the ultimate expression of a destitute anthropomorphism. {360}

Anthropomorphisms are inevitable, as long as they are not empty. Formally speaking, none of the three Persons is *I*, not in the sense we are discussing. But, in second place, the *I*, as act in which a nature reactualizes itself in its-ownness, is an act which is performed. By whom? Precisely by the Incarnate Word. Then, the *I*, to which Christ refers, is neither the Word, nor His human nature: it is Jesus Christ in His unity. It is a grounded act, which is not the one constitutive of a theanthropic and hypostatic unity, but the act in which He reaffirms Himself precisely in His his-ownness; He reaffirms in a second act, so to speak, what His reality is in its-ownness in the first act. This occurs in the case of Christ, and in the case of any one of us. What occurs in the case of Christ is that his-ownness, which reactualizes as an *I* in His human nature, is not a his-ownness which pertains to Him by reason of human nature, but precisely by reason of the Word. And in this case, what we call the *I* of Christ is the actualization in a second act of the unity with which the Word and the singular nature of Christ really and mysteriously constitute only one reality.

In Christ, therefore, there are no two *I*'s, first because human reality and the reality of the Word are not an *I*. And, secondly, because the *I* is not one of a human reality. There is only one *I*, the unique *I* of Christ, which is precisely the reactualization of His his-ownness, of His human substantivity in a his-ownness, which in this case is a subsistent tensiveness, i.e., Christ, who is precisely the subsistent experience of God, as we saw earlier. The personal biography of Christ—not only the acts He performs but His internal mode of being—is {361} not extraneous to His own reality considered as Incarnate Word. This would be what I have called an "enormous biographic docetism". It could have been otherwise; but in fact it was this way. His biography affects Him and, therefore, Christ, as Incarnate Word in His unity, really and effectively wished to have experience of His filial condition, of His metaphysical filial characteristic with respect to God. That was precisely the "one", the supreme tensive characteristic of that in which the proper experience of humans consisted, on the part of humans, in his unity with God. Jesus-Christ is in this sense the very subsistence of the tensive experience of humans with God.

There are still other aspects of this tensive unity. We are accustomed to consider the situation of humans on earth as someone looking for God here, or there, or nowhere, or rejecting Him. Saint Paul put it in one sentence: humans search for God as if groping. From the point of view I am here describing, Christ is not only, in my estimation, a mere factual condition, which each human being possesses with respect to God, to an unknown God. With this "literary genre" some have wished to express something that is not simply a historical vicissitude, but the very structure of history, considered from the point of view concerning us here. It is indeed the historic tensiveness with respect to God, and the entire history of religions is a historic tensiveness with respect to God.

Therefore the metaphysical unity of humans and God is not a metaphysical transcurrence, but a metaphysical unity with a tensive characteristic, which may adopt diverse forms or different modes. But all these modes, of *hesed*, of *dóxa*, of *eudokía*, of Incarnation, {362} of searching like groping, of *pselafáo*, which St. Paul mentioned to the Athenians, are grounded in something which is prior to all of this: viz. the characteristic by virtue of which a human person is constitutively tensoral and, therefore, able to experience that something which God gives to it, namely, the donation of His absolute being, of the absolute reality of God which is given to each human being for him or her to be absolute.

§ 4

UNITY OF HUMAN BEINGS "AND" GOD AS TRANSCURRENCE OF RELIGATION

We began this book by referring to humans as substantive realities, who make their absolute being in religation. And now we find out that each human is a tensive experience of God. Indeed, these two aspects are precisely the same thing. This is the essential point.

In his religation to the power of the real, each human is formally sustained in God, grounded in God, transcendent *in* things. By virtue of this, religation is in reality a constituting support of humans as an *I* in God, since we have seen that the power of the real supports itself upon a God transcendent in things. This support is a tension—in the sense I have just explained. Thus, the theological essence of religation consists in that tension. In religation there is a dominance of the power of the real with respect to humans who make their *I* with that power of the real.

Hence, from the point of view of God, that dominance has a precise characteristic: the pre-tensor characteristic of God. {363}

And from the point of view of humans, who need to support themselves upon reality to make their *I*, that dominance is the tension with which each supports him- or herself precisely upon that pre-tensor structure, which the absolutely absolute reality is, transcendent in things and in a special and personal way in every human. The essence of religion is precisely the theological tension between human beings and God. This is why when in the previous chapters I mentioned that each human is restless in his absolute being, I was referring not to the restlessness for happiness—even though this may be one of the forms restlesness takes on—nor to the "irrequietum cor nostrum, Domine, donec requiescat in te" of St. Augustine, but to something much more radical. What St. Augustine says is true, but it is true because what makes each human being restless in its depth is precisely the figure of its own relatively absolute being, the "What is going to become of me?", and "What am I going to do with myself?" This is the true restlessness.

From the point of view of what we have just explained, the matter is quite clear: restlessness is the human and lived expression of the tensive unity between humans and God. Humans are restless, because their *I* formally consists in a tension, in a tensiveness with God. The tensive restlessness of the constitution of the *I* is the concrete form by which each human being finds itself in its being, which is the *I*, religated to the relatively absolute reality. This point is the culmination of the unity of the different issues studied in this book.

I said, in fact, that I was going to be concerned with the theological dimension of humans, understanding by "theological" a concept which expresses not something theologic, but something which is prior to any theology and which is the fundamental presupposition to all of theology. Namely, a dimension {364} of the very being of humans that faces God. Humans proceed towards God and encounter Him while making themselves persons. And in this making themselves into persons is where the theological dimension of humans is found. I have accomplished the exposition and articulation of this idea in three successive parts.

In the first place human beings: What is it to be a human being? How does a human being make itself a person? To this problem an essential and fundamental concept is addressed: religation. Each human makes itself a person by being religated in its very being to the power of the real as real, as ultimate, possibilitating, and impelling.

In the second place, in this religation humans find themselves hurled towards the ground of religation: this is the progress of humans toward God. In his personal religation each human possesses *velis nolis* a will to real truth, that is, to ground his own being in one form or another, perhaps even upon himself, as in the case of the atheist. Nevertheless, humans necessarily possess that will to truth. And this will to truth unfolds in an act which has two aspects. On one hand, it is to know intellectively in some form the characteristic of this ground, in such a way that this intellection is the intellection of the absolutely absolute reality of God; and on the other, it is to have access to it, in a precise from, appropriating to him- or herself that personal reality. This appropriation constitutes a surrender to the personal reality of God, and insofar as true, is precisely faith. It is the concept of intellective surrender to God as the will to truth.

In the third place, posing the problem of what human beings are and what God is leads us to discuss the problem of God "and" humans. In what does this "and" consist? This "and" does not have a copulative but an implicative characteristic. In {365} his intellective surrender humans discover that their being is formally and constitutively experience of God. To be a human person is a way to be an experience of God, i.e., a tensive experience, one which unfolds itself individually, socially, and historically. To be human is a finite way of being God. And it is in this *I* with a tensive characteristic that the ultimate and radical transcurrence of religation consists, for anyone who admits the reality of God.

Religation to the power of the real, intellective surrender to God in the will to truth, and the tensive experience of God: these are the three concepts which express three moments of only one phenomenon, of only one structure, whose intrinsic and formal unity constitutes the theological dimension of human beings, of them as constitution of the act in which each affirms him- or herself as relatively absolute in the depths of reality *qua I*.

BY WAY OF CONCLUSION

{368}
These pages comprise the Introduction to the course I gave at the Theology Faculty of the Gregorian University in Rome, in November of 1973, which will soon appear as a book in its entirety.[1] Despite its brevity, I can offer nothing better to the great theologian Rahner than these introductory reflections that I began to publish some thirty-nine years ago.

Madrid, 1974

THE THEOLOGICAL PROBLEM OF HUMAN BEINGS

These lectures are not just one more treatise about God, arbitrarily chosen from among a thousand possible ones about Him, because they concern not only the *content* of our knowledge about God, but what "the" radical problem of God is for us today. Present-day Western men and women, in fact, are characterized not just by having this or that idea about God, or by adopting an {370} attitude ranging from agnostic, denial, or belief, with respect to God. Whether atheists or believers, they have a more radical attitude. For the atheist not only does God not exist, but even the *problem* of God does not exist. It is not a question of the non-existence of God, but of the non-existence of the problem of God itself; and in the atheist's estimation the justification for the reality of God is something for which the believer must be held accountable. But the same happens with the theist. The theist believes in God but does not live God as a problem. His life, is oriented towards God with supreme firmness, but it obscures whatever in this belief may show up as a problem. At best he will try to demonstrate to the atheist the reality of the problem of God; *qua* problem, it would thus be a matter reserved for the concern of the atheist. But he himself—the believer—feels that it is almost a contradiction to think that his own faith might be the solution to a problem. Present day Western men and women, therefore, whether atheist or theist, pretend that they do not have in their lived reality a problem of God. They do not think that their atheism or theism may be a reply to a previous question, especially to a problem which underlies their beliefs. Conversely, by virtue of being a solution to a problem, theism has to justify its belief, but atheism is equally forced to it; atheism is no less a belief than theism. Neither theism nor atheism are in a situation of not having to ground their attitude, because one thing is the *firmness* of a state of belief and another its *intellectual justification*. And the ultimate root of this intellectual justification of what God may or may not be is found necessarily in the discovery of the problem of God in human beings. The fact of this problem and not some theory is what must constitute our point of departure.

But it will be more than a mere point of departure, because {371} "problem of God" and what we call "God" are not two termini of which the first may be extrinsic to the second. Rather in my estimation the elaboration of the problem of God, insofar as it is a problem, is precisely the conceptualization—agnostic, negative or positive—of what may or may not be God. The discovery of the problem of God, as a problem, is at one and the same time a more or less precise encounter with the reality or with the unreality of God. This direction of thought is what the title "Theological Problem of Human Beings" expresses.

What exactly does this mean?

The mere mention of the subject already indicates that we are analyzing human reality as such, aiming towards the problem of God. But it is necessary to avoid a serious mistake at the outset. It is not our purpose, in fact, to make of human reality an object of *theologic* speculation, among other (more profound) reasons because this would already presuppose the reality of God. Any theologic speculation at this level would be purely and simply a *theory*, however important and truthful one might wish, but pure theory nonetheless. On the other hand, what we search for here is an analysis of *facts*, an analysis of human reality as such, taken in and by itself. If in this reality we discover some dimension which *de facto* constitutively and formally entails an inexorable confrontation with the ultimateness of the real, i.e., with what we may in a merely nominal and provisional way call "God", this dimension will be what we call the *theological dimension* of man. {372}

The theological dimension is, thus, a constitutive moment of human reality, a structural moment of it. Here, therefore, at the outset of this analysis, the expression "God" does not designate any concrete idea of God (whether Christian or any other), nor does it even mean divine "reality". Given what we have said, "God" only means the arena of the ultimateness of the real. Pure atheism inscribes itself within the theological dimension of man, because atheism is an attitude towards this confrontation (with the ultimateness of the real), and by virtue of this it is only possible in what we call the "theological dimension". Atheism is a confrontation with the ultimateness of the real, a confrontation certainly not theologic but theological. The theological is, therefore, in this sense, a strictly human dimension, accessible to an immediate analysis. With it we shall be concerned. The elucidation of this dimension is the disclosure *in actu exercito* of the existence of the problem of God, as a problem. The problem of God, as such, is not like any other problem arbitrarily posed by human curiosity, but is human reality itself in its constitutive problematicism. It is from this dimension that we must start towards any further consideration of what God is. How should we approach the question?

I

We must start, as I have just pointed out, from an *analysis of human reality*. We shall accomplish this in three steps.

1) A human being is not a reality made and finished, but a reality which must continue to realize itself in a very precise sense. Each human is, actually, a reality {373} constituted not only by its proper notes (in this it resembles any other reality), but also by a peculiar characteristic of its reality. What occurs is that the human being not only *has* reality, but *is* a reality formally "its-own", as reality. Its characteristic of reality is "its-ownness". This is what, in my estimation, constitutes the formal explanation of being a person. A human being is not only real, but is "its own" reality. Therefore, it is real confronting *every other* reality but its own. In this sense, each person, so to speak, is a "sole" reality separate from any other reality: he or she is "absolute".

But only relatively absolute, because this absolute characteristic is acquired. Indeed, each person has to be continually making him- or herself, i.e., realizing him- or herself in different forms or figures of reality. In each action that a human being performs, a form of reality is configured. To realize oneself is to take on a figure of reality. And each human being realizes itself by living with things, with other humans, and with itself. In every action, a human being is, therefore, "with" all the things with which it lives. But that "in" in which he is, is in reality. That "in" which and from which each human realizes itself is reality. Therefore, besides their real properties things have for humans what I have called *the power of the real* as such. Only in it and by it can a human being realize itself as person. The forcefulness with which the power of the real dominates me and moves me inexorably to realize myself as person is what I call "seizing". A human being can only realize itself when seized by the power of the real. And this seizing is what I have called {374} *religation*. A human realizes itself as person thanks to its religation to the power of the real. Religation is a constitutive dimension of the human person. Religation is not a theory but an incontrovertible fact. Insofar as it is a person, therefore, each human being is constitutively confronted with the power of the real, i.e., with the ultimateness of the real.

But, How is the human religated? When realizing itself with things, with others and with itself (let us call everything "things"), the human being configures its form of reality not freely but constrained by the power of the real and supported in it, because only in things is the power of the real given. However, the power of the real is not to be identified with things: things are nothing but "intrinsic vectors" of the power of reality itself. And they are such by the mere fact of being real. From this it follows that there is always some inequality between what the things with which human beings live are, and what humans are forced to do with them. Indeed, here lies the question: each human realizes itself in a form of reality that things do not impose on it, but still the human being cannot realize itself except with and for things. Hence, in the power of reality that they convey, things do nothing but open different possibilities to adopt one form or another. Therefore, each human has to choose among them. To choose is not only "to choose" (opt for) a particular action, but is "to ad-opt" a form of reality in the action which has been chosen. In religation, therefore, each human is confronted with the power of the real, but in an optative or choosing mode, i.e., problematically.

And not only that, because all those foregoing possibilities, as the forms of reality that they are, ultimately rely upon what this power of reality is in things. But the lack of {375} identification of this power of the real with things themselves manifests that between them and that power there is a precise internal structure. This structure is what I call "ground". It is not a matter of being a cause or something similar, but of an intrinsic structural moment of real things themselves, regardless of what the structure may be. The mere reliance upon them factually would already constitute a ground: real things themselves, in their pure facticity, would be fundamental or "grounding-facts". Therefore, whatever their structure may be, the power of the real in things is nothing but the occurrence of the ground in them. That is why the possibilities of the forms of realization as a person rely upon the ground. For this reason each human being always finds itself inexorably hurled in and by reality itself "towards" its ground. The "towards", actually, is a mode of presence of reality: it is "reality-as-towards" in contradistinction to "reality-in-front-of" me. By virtue of this, the hurling is always a strict "progression". It is not a mere intellective process, but a real "motion". Each human finds itself hurled towards the ground of the power of the real, in the inexorable "physical" forcefulness to choose for a form of reality. Therefore, the progression is not a progression because it is intellective, but rather intellection is the moment of clarification of the real and physical progression in which each human is progressing by the power of the real. Hence, it is a real intellective progression. The problematic religation is thus *eo ipso* a real intellective progression from the power of the real "towards" its intrinsic ground: this is the problem of God viewed as a problem of ultimateness of the real *qua* real—exactly what we were searching for initially.

2) Owing to the fact that it is problematic, the progression towards the ground {376} of the power of the real in things is not univocal, precisely because the power of the real is only conveyed by real things *qua* real. To be sure, in this progression humans *always* accede to that ground, because it is a matter of a real and physical march and not of just reasoning or anything of that nature. Hence, the end point of this progression is always attained, but in a different mode depending on the roads taken; so what we (looking ahead) call "atheism", "theism", or even "agnosticism" itself, are already a form of access to the ground, a contact with it. But since we are dealing with an intellective diversity, the chosen way has to be intellectively justified. And this justification is at the same time the ground of the option itself. Every option is already an inchoate progression at the very least. The seizing of the human person by the power of the real is accordingly a seizing of it by the ground of this power. And in this seizing the intellection of the ground takes place. Every personal realization is therefore just the configuration, through choice, of the human person with respect to the ground of the power of the real in it.

Since the access to the ground is problematic, human beings, as I said, have to justify their mode of access. For us, the intellective justification of the ground of the power of the real is the one which hurls us upon a course leading from the human person (i.e., from a relatively absolute person) to an absolutely absolute person: this is what we understand as the reality of God. A human being finds God when it realizes itself, in relegated fashion, as a person, and finds God throughout the whole ambit of the power of the real, and therefore in all real things and in its {377} own person (which also conveys in itself the power of the real). The power of the real consists, then, precisely in that real things, without being God or a moment of God, are nevertheless real "in" God, i.e., their reality is God *ad extra*. For this reason, to say that God is transcendent does not mean that God is transcendent "to" things, but that God is transcendent "in" things. The seizing of the human person by the power of the real is then a seizing of each human being by God. In this seizing is where the intellection of God occurs. From this it follows that every personal human realization is just the configuration, though choice, of the human being with respect to "God in my person".

The discovery of God in the intellective progression of religation is the second essential step in our question.

3) The progression "towards" the ground of the power of the real is not only problematic, but the problem itself has a very precise character. The progression, in fact, is real and physical. And this establishes the problematic character as a strict "probing". The progression proceeds by probing. Religation, therefore, acquires the concrete form of a probing. But it is a probing that is in reference to the power of the real as such. It is, in each of its steps, an attempt at "testing". Hence, "physical testing of reality" is exactly what, in my estimation, comprises the very essence of what we call "experience". Thus, the problematic progression towards the ground of the power of the real in religation is experience of that ground, a real and physical experience, but still intellective. The seizing by the power of the real occurs in an experiential form. Religation is, therefore, an experiential progression towards the {378} ground of the power of the real. It is *grounding experience*. And in this experience the concrete intellection of this ground takes place. This character is essential to religation. Human beings, we said, always accede in relegated fashion to the ground of the real. Hence, they always have in their personal realization that grounding experience. Every human act, even down to the most common and modest, is in all its dimensions and in an express or muted way, a problematic experience of the ground of the power of the real. Atheism, theism, agnosticism are modes of experience of the ground of the real. They are not mere conceptual attitudes. This grounding experience is individual, social, and historical. By virtue of this the experience of the ground of the power of the real is an individual probing, but it is at the same time a social and historical probing. From this it follows that the ground of the power of the real belongs, in one form or another, to the person himself: to be a person is to be a "figure" of this ground, and to be such experientially.

Thus, the grounding experience, i.e., the experience of the ground of the power of the real by the path that intellectively leads to God, is *eo ipso* God experienced as ground, experience of God. And since by virtue of the grounding experience the ground of the power of the real, as we have just seen, belongs in one form or another to the person, it is evident that God, by being the reality-ground of this power, discovered *by* the person and *in* the person when realizing him- or herself as a person, is not something merely added to the personal reality of human beings, or something juxtaposed to it. It is not the case that there is a human person "and in addition" God. Precisely because God is not transcendent to things, {379} but transcendent *in* them, precisely because of this, things are not *simpliciter* a not-God, but rather in some way they are a configuration of God *ad extra*. Therefore, God is not the human person, but the human person is in some manner God: he is God "humanly". Because of this, the "and" of "human beings and God" is not a copulative "and". God does not include human beings, but human beings include God. What is the concrete mode of this inclusion? It is precisely "experience": to be a human person is to realize oneself experientially as something absolute. Each human being is formally and constitutively experience of God. And this experience of God is the radical and formal experience of human reality itself. The real and physical progression towards God is not only a true intellection, but an experiential realization of the human reality itself in God.

Experience of God is thus the third essential moment of the analysis of human reality.

In conclusion, religation, intellective progression, and experience are the three essential moments of the human personal realization. They are not three *successive* moments; rather, each is grounded upon the previous one. They constitute, therefore, an intrinsic and formal *unity*. In this unity is in what the ultimate structure of the theological dimension of human beings consists. The realization of human beings in it is what in a synthetic manner has to be called *theological experience*.

II

This dimension, by virtue of being individual, social, and historic, necessarily assumes a concrete form; such is the {380} molding of religation. Here, "molding" means the concrete form in which individually, socially, and historically the power of the real seizes man. Molding is, therefore, a form of seizing. This molding is *religion* in the widest and strictest sense of the term: religion is the molding of religation, the concrete form of the seizing of the power of the real in religation. Religion is not an attitude with respect to the "sacred", as is repeated nowadays monotonously. Everything religious is certainly sacred; but it is sacred because it is religious, it is not religious because it is sacred.

As the molding of religation as such, religion always has a concrete vision of God, of man, and of the world. And because it is experiential, this vision necessarily has multiple forms: this is the history of religions. But the history of religions is not a catalog or museum of coexisting and successive forms of religion, because that experience is, in my estimation, experience by probing. Therefore, I consider that the history of religions is the theological experience of mankind, either as individual or as social and historical, about the ultimate truth of the power of the real, of God.

III

In this experience Christianity is inscribed. Christianity is a religion, and therefore, a molding of religation, one form of the power of the real. Because of this, God, as ground of the power of the real, seizes human beings (in the individual, in society, and in history) experientially. The power of the real, I said, consists in that {381} things are real "in" God. And thus, for Christianity, this "to be real in God" consists in being *dei-formed*. Real things are, as I said, God *ad extra*; for Christianity, this *ad extra* is "to be like God". This dei-formity admits of diverse modes and degrees, but they are always modes and degrees of a strict dei-formity. Therefore, the seizing in which religation consists is concretely a dei-formity. The form of being God in a human way is to be such dei-formably. Each human being is a formal projection of the divine reality itself; a finite manner of being God. The moment of finitude of this dei-formity is what, in my estimation, constitutes that which we call "human nature". God is transcendent "in" the human person, whereas the human person is God dei-formably. The transcendence of God "in" the human person is then, I repeat, dei-formity. Therefore, to realize oneself as person is to realize oneself through the dei-forming seizing of the real. The seizing itself is the occurrence of dei-formation.

In my estimation, this is the essence of Christianity. Prior to being a religion of salvation (often repeated nowadays as if it were something evident), and precisely in order to be such, Christianity is a religion of dei-formity. That is why the experiential character of Christianity is the supreme theological experience, because there is no other possible greater form of being real in God than being such dei-formably. By virtue of this, Christianity is not only true religion in itself, but indeed is the "radical", and also the "formal", truth of all religions. This is, in my estimation, the transcendence of Christianity—not only historical, but theological. The theological experience of humanity is thus the experience of dei-formity in its triple dimension, individual, social, and historical: it is Christianity as probing. {382}

IV

And so, the theological problem of human beings unfolds into three parts: religation, religion, dei-formation, which constitute three problems: God, religion, Christianity.

At this point it is appropriate, before finishing, to return to something upon which I touched earlier, namely, the need to avoid a sad mistake that has managed to transform itself into a kind of solemn thesis: that theology is essentially anthropology, or at least, anthropocentric. This appears to me as absolutely untenable. Since the preceding exposition might give the appearance that it is inscribed within this erroneous thesis, it is necessary to clarify the ideas somewhat.

Theology is essentially and constitutively theocentric. It is true that I have affirmed that theology is grounded upon the theological dimension of human beings. But the fact is that the theological is not the theologic, and that, at least for two reasons:

a) The theological is only a foundation of theologic knowledge, but is not the theologic knowledge itself.

b) The theological is certainly a human dimension, but is precisely that dimension according to which humans find themselves grounded on the power of the real. Therefore each human is human precisely by being something formally grounded in reality. And this is something quite the opposite of anthropology; it is an immersion of humans in reality as such. It is only by virtue of this, that one is a human being.

If we reserve, as we should, the terms "theology" and "theologic" for what God, human beings, and the world are in all religions and especially in Christianity, then we shall have to say that knowledge about the {383} theological is not theology *simpliciter*. Knowledge about the theological is, as I said, a knowledge that occurs in the grounding experience. Hence, knowledge about the theological is *grounding theology*. The so-called "grounding theology" thus acquires its own essential content. In the midst of numerous discussions about the concept and content of grounding theology, I personally think that grouinding theology is not a study of the *præambula fidei*, or a kind of vague introductory study to theology properly so called. In my estimation, grounding theology is precisely and formally the study of the theological as such.

The three parts of this subject were developed for my course given at Madrid, in the Society for Studies and Publications, during 1971. The first part dealt with *Man and God*; the second with *Man and God in all Religions*, and the third with *Man, God, and the Christian Religion*.[2] The first of these three parts, somewhat more developed later, became the content of the course I gave at the Faculty of Theology of the Gregorian University in Rome, in November of 1973.

---

[1] [This book was never published in Zubiri's lifetime. Most likely he is referring to what became the present book.—trans.]

[2] [The first book is the present volume; the second is Zubiri's posthumous work, *El problema filosófico de la historia de las religiones* (1993), and the third, also posthumous, is *El problema teologal del hombre: Cristianismo* (1997).—trans.]

Index

A

Absolute:
  restlessness as problematism of, 46
  characteristic of being, 49-50, 56, 106, 239-240; cf. relatively absolute being.
  voice of conscience and way to, 83; cf. voice of conscience.
  God as absolute possibility, 117.
  fatigue of, 123.
  characteristics of God qua,, 125-130, 133, 136, 165.
  analogy of, 129.
  God as ground of absolute characteristic of man, 142, 171, 175, 177.
  personal truth of God as, 144-145, 161, 176, 255; cf. real truth.
  spirit in cf. Hegel, 172.
  individual, social, historic experience of, 244; cf. experience.
  experience of God as absolute for Israel, 248.
  experiential realization of person as, 238-239, 276.
  cf. also absolutely absolute reality, relatively absolute reality, and relatively absolute being.
Abraham, 245.
Acceptance:
  of divine occurrence, 172.
  and cf. surrender, 179.
  as cf. choice, 192.
Access:
  of God to world, 136, 140.
  of being of man to God, 136-137.
  to God, and cf. remission, 137-138.
  to God, and cf. fontanal transcendence, 140-141.
  things as concretion of access to God, 140, 145-146.
  to God manifestatively, 142-143, 145; cf.manifest-ation.
  truth as culmination of accessibility to God, 143-145.
  inchoate access to God, 146, 147-148, 150, 164; cf. inchoate.
  to God in cf. dragging, 146-147.
  to God for St. Augustine, 147.
  full access to God, 147-149, 150-151, 153, 164-165.
  to God, and cf. inter-personal causality, 152-153.
  radical access to God, and cf. faith, 157, 165.
  atheism, theism, agnosis, access to ground, 274.
Accident, and cf. note, 26.
Act:
  for classical philosophy, and metaphysics, 28, 235.
  unity of potency-act, and the "of", 40.
  subject of acts, and being person, 44-45.
  and definition of the *I*, 46, 122, 190.
  and will to real truth, 85.
  being as ulterior act to reality, 109.
  cf. action, activity, actuality.
Action:
  and making oneself person, 63, 66-67, 86.
  and the individual, social, historical dimension, 64.
  man as cf. agent, actor, author of his acts, 64-66, 85.

reality determines me in my, 71.
we are with *cf.* things by, 85, 136, 272.
of man in *cf.* St. Thomas, 95.
God as agent and human, 121.
of God, and constitution of the "in its own right", 151-152. *cf.* activity, act, actuation.
Activity, human, 40-41; *cf.* actions, dynamicity, self-giving, dynamism.
Actor:
Humans as actors of their actions, 65, 66, 85.
God as actor is the outline of my life, 121.
cf. agent, author.
Actuality:
what is, 28-31, 43, 47-49.
as moment of *cf.* body, 39.
the *I* as worldly, 43, 49-51, 54, 91, 105,
as subsequent to *cf.* actuity, 48.
I as actuality of persons, 54.
as *cf.* fruition, 128.
God as absolute, 128-129.
of reality in *cf.* intelligence, 128, 143-144, 182, 183, 209, 228; *cf.* real truth.
cf. intellection as actuality of that known, 174.
of *cf.* reality-ground in intellection, 175.
cf. actualization.
Actualization:
worldly actualization of the person, 49-51.
of things in their notes, 77, 144.
of reality-ground and reality-object, 83, 184-186.
of reality in *cf.* real truth, 84, 128, 143-144, 160, 182-184, 209-210, 228.
of the power of the real as something enigmatic, 86.
absolute actualization. of God, 144.
dimensions of, 144, 161, 228.
as "towards", 186.
and *cf.* will to real truth, 183.
of real truth and *cf.* donation of God, 228.
cf. actuality.
Actualness:
what is, 31.
as anterior to *cf.* actuality, 48.
Actuation:
of *cf.* potencies, 179.
of humans in a real manner, 228.
cf. action, activity.
Ad extra: 227, 241, 258, 274, 276, 277; *cf.* creation, God.
Adherence, personal, and *cf.* faith, 162-163, 165.
Admission as mode of *cf.* surrender, 159.
Adopt a form of reality, 65, 78-79, 81, 83-85, 240, 272-274.
Adore, 149-150; *cf.* acquiescence.
Adventitious, 25; *cf.* notes.
Affection:
as moment of *cf.* impression, 33, 36-37.
as moment of sentientness, 41-42.
Age as zone of *cf.* time, 59.
Agent:
Humans as agents of their *cf.* actions, 64-66, 85.
God as, 121, 234.
cf. author, actor.
Agnosis:
as mode of *cf.* access to ground, 274.
as mode of ground, 275.
Agnosticism:
as mode of resolving *cf.* problem of God, 19-20, 250, 270.
a. as form of conceiving *cf.* transcendence, 132; *cf.* pan-

Index

theism.
  as will to grounding, 198-200, 212.
  intellective justification of, 199-200, 207-208, 211-212; *cf.* option, choice.
  and indifference, 201, 250.
  and *cf.* atheism, 204.
  as *cf.* will to search, 208.
  as attitude facing the *cf.* experience of God, 250.
Aitía as production of reality, 70; *cf.* Aristotle, cause.
Ambit:
  of stimulation and reality, 41-42.
  and *cf.* intellection, 174-175, 178-180, 209-210, 240.
  of possible faith, 175-176.
  of possible *cf.* surrender to God, 177.
  terminus of, 179, 183.
  of *cf.* dynamic tension, 191.
Ambivalence of reality, 78, 110-111, 113.
Amphictyony as mode of historical experience of God, 247.
Analogy of the *cf.* absolute, 129-130; *cf.* anthropomorphism.
Analyzers of *cf.* sensing, 168-169.
Anánke, 30; *cf.* necessity, forcefulness.
Anaximander, 31; *cf. arkhé*.
"And", 20, 224, 276; *cf.* experience of God.
Anguish and *cf.* restlessness, 80-81.
Animal:
  having *cf.* impressions as something essential to, 32-34.
  man as animal of realities, 42-43, 49-50, 52, 55-56, 82-83, 229, 238, 241.
  humans as personal, 46, 52.
  grouping of animals, 55-56; *cf.* society.
  humans as diverse, social, and historical, 57, 59-60; *cf.* dimension.
Animist:
  interpretation of power, 31.
  God is not an animist ground, 130.
Announcement:
  reality as, 35, 82-83, 143, 167.
  presence of God as, 142-143, 145; *cf.* presence.
  as manifestation of the *cf.* personal fontanal transcendence, 143.
  and *cf.* faith, 174.
Anthropology:
  anthropological ways of existence of God, 96-99, 115.
  the *I* is not an anthropological structure, 262-263.
  cf. theology is not, 278.
Anthropomorphism:
  and characteristics of God, 129.
  and *cf.* inter-personal transcendence, 141.
  and the *cf.* Trinity, 262-263.
A-personal, 55-56; *cf.* person, impersonal.
Apprehension:
  of stimulity and reality, 24-25; *cf.* "in its own right".
  of *cf.* meaning-thing, 24.
  of the "in its own right", 33-34, 42.
  of things as real, 33-34, 78, 143-144.
  and *cf.* impression of reality, 36-38.
  of reality as *cf.* "towards", 35-36, 82, 167, 183, 254, 231.
  reality beyond, 38.
  of the *cf.* will to real truth, 86.
  of the different modes of *cf.* creation, 227.
  of *cf.* grounding reality of God, 239.
  cf. intelligence, reason.
Appropriation:
  of notes of reality by *cf.* soci-

ety, 55.
of possibilities, 84.
virtue as appropriation of possibilities, 155.
and *cf.* surrender, 179, 184, 188, 210, 213-214.
and determination of my *cf.* being, 179-180, 240.
and *cf.* volition, 183-184, 187, 209.
of the *cf.* dynamic tension, 191.

Aristotle:
the *cf. Theós* of, 20, 115, 126, 136, 191; *cf.* otiose.
idea of substance and accidents, 26; *cf.* substantivity, note.
idea of *cf.* "taxis", 28.
and the *cf.* pre-Socratics, 30-31; *cf.* truth.
idea of *cf. autós*, 33.
act and potency in, 40, 235.
idea of *cf. dýnamis*, 58.
idea of *cf. aitía*, 70.
idea of experience, 77, 246.
and *cf.* St. Thomas, 93-96.
metaphysics of, 95.
and distinction between *cf.* cosmos and world, 126.
four causes of, 154, 255-256; *cf.* cause.

Arkhé, 31; *cf.* power, Anaximander.

Articulation of reality, 85, 86-87.

Aspectualism and God, 219; *cf.* inter-personal causality.

Assyro-Babylonian, 31; *cf.* mathematics, *anánke*.

Atheism:
as way of resolving the *cf.* problem of God, 19-20, 204-207, 250, 270.
as *cf.* distancing from God, 123; *cf.* fatigue of the absolute.
nowadays as a theism of an *cf.* otiose God, 190-191.
as form of *cf.* will to grounding, 195, 205-206, 212.
and agnosticism, 204.
as way of *cf.* life, 204, 205-207.
as *cf.* faith, 206.
and *cf.* auto-sufficiency, 206-207, 212.
and *cf.* will to be, 208.
as a "covered up" experience of God, 250.
as mode of *cf.* access to the ground, 274.
cf. theism, agnosticism.

Attitude:
human attitute and articulation of reality, 86.
in front of God and *cf.* unity of knowledge-faith, 177.
and *cf.* will to grounding, 188-189, 192, 195, 196-197, 199-200, 212-213.
of the reasonable, 193; *cf.* reason.
to reach God and unity of intelligence-faith, 213.

Augustine, St.:
idea of restlessness, 80, 112, 265.
point of departure in the *cf.* problem of God, 96-99.
idea of God, 98-99.
idea of the access to God, 147-148.
idea of faith, 159.
reason and faith in, 176.

Authenticity as will, 84, 183-188; *cf.* Nietzche.

Author:
Humans as author of *cf.* actions, 65, 85.
Humans as author of their own *cf.* being, 240.
God as, 121.
cf. agent, actor.

Auto-actuality of God, 128-129.
Auto-fruition of God, 128; *cf.*

fruition.
Auto-possession:
  cf. life as, 32-33, 49, 63, 91, 127, 196, 242.
  God's absolute, 127-128; *cf.* dynamicity.
Auto-presence of God, 128.
Auto-sufficiency and *cf.* atheism, 205-207, 212.

B

Baalism, 244-245, *cf.* Elijah, historical experience of God.
Balance, 35, 82.
Being (*Sp. ente*):
  for *cf.* Parmenides, 48.
  God is not supreme, 48, 101, 218-219, 225.
  cf. entification of reality.
Being (*Sp. ser*):
  subsequentness of, 29, 34, 48.
  and *cf. autós*, 32-33.
  as worldly actualization of *cf.* substantivity, 43, 49-51.
  absolute characteristic of, 46, 106, 239; *cf.* relatively absolute being.
  degrees of in *cf.* St. Thomas Aquinas, 94.
  and reality, 46-47, 50-51, 60, 109.
  access of to God, 136-137.
  metaphysical modes of constitution of by God, 152.
  possibilities of, 179-180, 183-184.
  will to "be", 180, 209, 211.
  dialectic of in *cf.* Hegel, 234.
  cf. relatively absolute being., *realitas in essendo, esse reale*, being (*Sp. ente*).
Being, relatively absolute:
  acquired characteristic of, 46, 66, 102, 106-108, 190, 260.
  cf. restlessness of, 46, 265-266.
  cf. personality as figure of, 50.
  domination by reality over, 71.
  religation of to the power of the real, 75-76, 77, 80-81, 91, 99, 102, 108, 115, 118, 119-120, 130, 146, 171, 189, 223, 265, 270, 276.
  search for the ground of, 86, 192, 240, 274.
  terminus of the figuration of, 102, 138.
  making "with" things "in" reality, 87, 108, 110, 209-210, 229; *cf.* real truth.
  the enigmatic of, 102, 111.
  ground of, 122, 122, 145, 171, 175, 189-190, 191, 229, 239-240, 243.
  life and constitution of, 137.
  and *cf.* His-ownness, 141.
  cf. choice as possibility of, 180, 240.
  atheism as form of, 206-207, 250.
  will to grounding as will to, 207.
  to be free "in " reality as root of, 241.
  cf. relatively absolute reality.
Being here-and-now (*Sp. estar*):
  modes for the *cf.* real of, 29, 47.
  modes or forms of reality, 58; *cf.* actuality.
Belief:
  idea of in St. Augustine, 159.
  in the person, 161; *cf.* surrender.
  in what one does not see is not *cf.* faith, 167-170.
Benevolence as form of *cf.* donation, 261.
Bergson and metaphysical experience, 85.
Berith, 234-235, 244; *cf.* Israel.
Biogenetic as moment of history, 57-58.
Biography:
  the "biographic" as element of

history, 57-58.
of Christ and *cf.* docetism, 242, 242, 263-264.
Biology and *cf.* enigma, 170.
Body, 38-39; *cf.* organism, soma, psyche.
By:
  we live "by" reality, 69, 106-107.
  and God as impellent, 137; *cf.* impellence.
  access to God by the world, 140.

C

Capacity as *cf.* possible, 58-59; *cf.* talents.
Cappadocian, 235; *cf. hypóstasis, hypokeímenon.*
Causality:
  what is, 29-30, 70-71, 72, 116, 151, 154-155, 255; *cf.* functionality of the real.
  God is not efficient, 93-94, 117, 223, 225-226, 239.; *cf.* St. Thomas.
  classical causality not *cf.* personal causality, 154-155.
  moral causality and personal causality, 155-156; *cf.* moral.
Causality, personal:
  personal and *cf.* interpersonal, 151-153, 161, 219.
  what is personal, 152-156, 255-257, 258-259; *cf.* moral, friendship, love, surrender.
  personal causality in *cf.* open essences, 256.
Cause:
  idea of in *cf.* Hume, 70-71.
  of everything created and *cf.* ground, 70-71, 86, 115-116, 225-226; *cf.* creation.
Characteristic(s):
  of history, 57-59.
  biographic as characteristic.
  of concept of history, 58.
  of reality, 68-69, 85-86, 107.
  of the *cf.* ground, 69, 101, 117, 137, 149-150, 191.
  of *cf.* power of the real, 76, 78, 83, 86, 100, 114.
  of *cf.* religation, 76-79, 81, 86, 102, 108, 143, 149, 170, 190, 223-224.
  reality as physical characteristic of things, 107.
  of God, 125-130.
  ground as characteristic of *cf.* absolutely absolute reality, 129-130, 225.
Christ:
  crucifixion of,, 219.
  and the presence of God as *cf.* donation, 232-233.
  historicity of, 235.
  and *cf.* biographical docetism, 242.
  messianic secret of, 242.
  as subsisting experience of God, 243.
  as founder of *cf.* Christianity, 248.
Christianity:
  God of as Creator, 116; *cf.* creation.
  Christian God as definitive revelation of God, 121, 248, 277.
  non-demonstrable elements of, 173-174.
  and different ideas about God, 218.
  and *cf.* Incarnation, 232, 248.
  historicity of, 235.
  Christian thought and the concept of "person", 236.
  foundation of, 248; *cf.* Christ.
  as molding of *cf.* religation, 277.
  theological transcendence of, 277.
Choice (option):
  what is, 65, 165, 240, 273.
  and *cf.* appropriation, 179-

Index 287

180, 210, 213-215.
history as choice, 57; *cf.* invention.
to choose a *cf.* form of reality, 85, 273; *cf.* adopt.
and *cf.* faith, 165.
and *cf.* intellection, 180.
and *cf.* will, 180.
and *cf.* science, 184-185.
to choose a *cf.* reality-ground or reality-object, 188-189, 191-192.
and *cf.* acceptance, 192.
and *cf.* agnosticism, 199-200, 207, 211-212.
and *cf.* unconcernedness, 202.
cf. atheism, 204-207.
of *cf.* will to grounding, 211-212.
and *cf.* realization, 274.
Closed; *cf.* closed essence.
Co-determination:
of *cf.* persons, 51, 53-60; *cf. I.*
Coherence:
the *cf.* notes of a system are coherent, 26.
coherential unity, 41; *cf.* system.
animal groups are coherent but not *cf.* societies, 55.
Contemporary, 59-60; *cf.* temporeity.
Communality, 56; *cf.* community.
Communication:
cf. transcendentality as, 27.
is grounded on *cf.* communality, 56.
Communion:
personal, 56; *cf.* turning.
as mode of *cf.* personal causality, 155.
Community:
cf. transcendentality is not, 27.
human, 56; *cf.* communality, society.
Concretion:

of God, 126-127, 136, 165.
things as of the *cf.* accessibility to God, 140, 145-146.
"my" as mode of concretion of faith, 208-213.
monotheism and concretion of faith, 218.
Condition, 25; *cf.* things.
Configuration:
of the *cf. I*, 91, 99, 105-107, 148-149, 151, 190, 204, 224.
of the individual, social, historical dimensions by actions, 64.
Consoling as mode of constitution of being, 152.
Constitution:
of *cf.* things, 25-29.
of *cf.* dynamic tension, 152.
unity of God and man as constituting causality, 255; *cf.* personal causality.
Constituting as characteristic of *cf.* tradition, 57.
Constitutive:
and constitutional notes, 25-27.
environment of man, 42; *cf.* reality.
cf. phylum as constitutive of my reality, 54.
faith as constitutive of believing person, 215-216.
presence of God as constitutive of *cf.* things, 226-228.
cf. essence.
Content and *cf.* affection, 33.
Continuating as a characteristic of *cf.* tradition, 57.
Control over the *cf.* surroundings, 32, 46; *cf.* independence.
Conviviality [living in society], 55-56; *cf.* impersonal, society.
Corporeity as principle of *cf.* actuality, 40.
Cosmos:
what is the, 28, 47, 126; *cf.* respectivity.
implantation of the living be-

ing in, 46.
"cosmic" ways to reach God, 93-96, 115.
man as open "cosmic" reality, 228.
cf. world.
Creation:
  to be ground is not to be creator, 116, 225.
  as truth of faith and not of reason, 116; *cf.* Duns Scotus.
  what is, 226-227; *cf. ad extra.*
  of man, 241.
Credibility, 193.
Credentiality, 193.
Cro-Magnon, 59.

D

Deity, 118-119; *cf.* God, things.
Delphi, 78; *cf.* Heraclitus, enigma.
Demonstration of God and *cf.* intellective process, 200-201; *cf.* justification, ways, problem.
Dependence, unconditional, and religation, 76, 97, 99; *cf.* sentiment.
Depths:
  of oneself, 81; *cf.* voice of conscience.
  transcendent, 152; *cf.* surrender.
Descartes, 236.
Determination as moment of *cf.* sentient volition, 83.
Dialectic and history, 234.
Dictates of the *cf.* voice of conscience, 81, 86.
Difference and *cf.* phylum, 53.
Dimension:
  what is, 26.
  referring dimension of *cf.* respectivity, 28.
  individual, social, and historical the human being, 53-60, 64, 217-218.
  dimensions of *cf.* actualization, 144, 160-161, 228.
  moral dimension of man, 155; *cf.* personal causality.
  individual, social, and historical dimension of faith, 217-219.
  social, and historical dimension of *cf.* donation, 234-236.
  social, individual, and historical dimension of *cf.* experience, 234, 240-243, 266-267, 275, 277.
  dimensions of *cf.* personal truth, 160-161, 185-187.
  cf. religation as dimension of personized nature, 91.
Distinction between things, man, and God, 121-131; *cf.* transcendence.
Diversity:
  and *cf.* phylum, 53.
  man as diverse animal, 57, 60.
Divinity:
  man is implanted in, 123.
  acceptance of *cf.* divine occurrence, 172.
  finitude of divine life, 227.
  divine filiation, 242-243; *cf.* Christ.
  Baal as, 244-245; *cf.* Elijah, God.
Docetism and *cf.* biography of Christ, 242, 263.
Documental: history is not, 58.
Dogma, 241.
Dominance:
  of the *cf.* power of the real, 30, 71-74, 86, 107, 265.
  not all is *cf.* forcefulness, 30.
  not all is causal, 71, *cf.* cause.
  of my personal reality, 71, 86.
Dominion:
  what is, 71; *cf.* power.
  of power of the real, 71-74.
  cf. dominance.
Donation:

God as donor of *cf.* possibilities, 116-117.
God as donor, 152, 228-229, 235, 253.
reality as, 144.
cf. inchoate, 149.
donation-surrender as form of *cf.* personal causality, 151, 255.
experiential character of donation of God, 229-231, 234, 252, 260.
forms of, 231-236.
"not" as form of, 258.
as aspect of the *cf.* tensive unity, 262.
of God *ad extra*, 258.
Dóxa as mode of *cf.* tensive unity, 264.
Dragging, 146-147; *cf.* pretension, access.
Duns Scotus:
idea of God, 95-96, 101.
idea of *cf.* creation, 116.
Dynamic: reality is dynamic in itself, 151; *cf.* dynamicity.
Dynamicity of God, 127, 151-152, 226; *cf.* dynamism, unfolding, self-giving.
Dýnamis, 36, 58; *cf.* Aristotle, potency.
Dynamism, religating, 121; *cf.* religation, dynamicity.

E

Each-quality, 54; *cf.* individual.
Effectivity (facticity) as moment of *cf.* real truth, 85, 86, 144, 161, 182, 185, 187, 229; *cf.* manifestation, fidelity.
Egyptian mathematics, 31; *cf.* forcefulness.
Eidos, 35, 82; *cf.* sight.
El, 245; *cf.* anthropomorphism.
Elijah and his argument with *cf.* Baalism, 244-245.
Elohim, 245; *cf.* monotheism.

Enigma:
as mode of signifying the real, 77-78, 170.
enigmatic as characteristic of *cf.* religation, 77-79, 86.
ambivalence of, 78; *cf.* ambivalence.
enigmatic as a characteristic of *cf.* power of real, 78, 83, 86.
reality as, 78, 111-113.
cf. will to real truth as something enigmatic, 86.
grounded upon reality of God, 205.
as form of *cf.* hurling us "towards" root of things, 170-171.
Entification of reality: 48, 101; *cf.* being.
Esse reale, 47; *cf.* being.
Essence:
as structural principle of *cf.* substantivity, 26.
open, 57, 137, 141, 170, 227-228, 256; *cf.* man.
closed, 141, 227, 256.
cf. metaphysical e. of God, 96, 125-126, 239.
God is in things through, 136; *cf.* St. Thomas.
religated, 132; *cf.* religation.
theological e. of religation, 147, 265, 275.
Euclid, 31.
Eudokía, 261, 264; *cf.* benevolence.
Eudoxus, 126.
Eusébeia, 261.
Event, 58; *cf.* history.
Evolution: history is not, 57.
"Ex", 26; *cf.* "in", structure.
Exegetes, 242.
Existence of God in *cf.* classical theology, 125-126.
Experience:
of God, 20.
theological, 20, 85, 276-277.
and *cf.* religion, 76-79, 81, 86, 143, 223, 238-239, 275-

276.
as *cf.* physical testing of reality, 77, 118, 223, 246, 252.
for Aristotle, 77, 246.
manifestative of power of real, 100-101, 253, 255, 275.
individual, social, historical experience of God, 119, 152-153, 217, 234-235, 240, 244-249, 266-267, 277.
humans as experience of God, 224-225, 238-239.
"experiential" character of *cf.* donation of God, 229-236, 252, 260.
fontanal and fundamental experience of God, 238.
of God and life of Christ, 241-243, 263.
of the *cf.* ground, 248, 275.
forms of experience of God, 243.
indigence not principle in experience of God, 121, 123, 251.
cf. tensive experience of God, 259, 263-264, 266-267.
Extra-worldly: God is not e., 132.
Extrinsicism:
of faith, 216.
between man and God, 258.

F

Fact:
what is a historical, 58.
analysis of facts of human reality, and *cf.* theologic dimension, 271.
Facticity: life as auto-sufficient, 206-207; *cf.* atheism.
Faculty:
of the real, 34; *cf.* intelligence.
sentient intelligence as, 36-37, 58.
as possibility, 58-59.
of man, 64-65; *cf.* potencies.

Faith:
truth of *cf.* reason and of, 116, 121, 166, 189.
difference between intelligence and, 157, 166-178.
unity of intelligence and, 178-189.
what is, 158-159.
difference between knowledge and, 158, 172-173.
unity of knowledge and, 174-178, 180-181, 189-194.
in St. Augustine, 159-160.
as mode of *cf.* inter-personal causality, 161.
as *cf.* acquiescence, supplication, refuge, 161-162.
three characteristics of, 162-165.
as inspiration, 163.
as *cf.* surrender, 165.
and *cf.* freedom, 165, 180.
is not to believe what one does not see, 167-170.
and appropriation of *cf.* grounding, 175.
and *cf.* reason in St. Augustine, 176.
and knowledge for theist and agnostic, 197-198.
and *cf.* the intellective process, 198ff.
indifferent, 202-203.
atheism as, 205-206.
in the believing person, 214, 215-219.
extrinsicism of, 216.
individual, social, historical dimension of, 217-219.
Incarnation for Christian, 232-233, 248.
Fatigue of the absolute and the theological, 123-124; *cf.* atheism.
Feeling: see Sentiment
Fidelity:
as moment of *cf.* real truth, 84-85, 160-161, 185-188; *cf.*

firmness.
- concreteness of the lived, 219.
- God gives Himself in, 229-235; *cf.* donation.
- experience of, 245.

Figure:
- of *cf.* time, 59.
- of reality, 272; *cf.* form.
- of the *cf.* ground of power of real, 275.

Filiation, divine, of *cf.* Christ, 241-243.

Finality in *cf.* St. Thomas, 94; *cf.* order.

Finitude:
- of *cf.* divine life *ad extra*, 227.
- man as finite way of being God, 238, 241, 277.

Firmness:
- as moment of *cf.* real truth, 86, 144, 161, 182, 228; *cf.* fidelity.
- as characteristic of faith, 163-164.

Fontanal:
- transcendence as essence of grounding, 133, 226-227.
- experience of God, 238.

Forcefulness:
- and necessity, 30; *cf. anánke*.
- can be *cf.* powerfulness, 30.
- God as ground of forcefulness of being my *cf. I*, 117; *cf.* impellence.
- involves choice, 180.
- forced to proceed "towards" God, 200.
- of power of real, 272.

Form:
- of reality, 27.
- man as form of reality, 46.
- personhood as form. of human reality, 44.
- of being in reality, 57-58.
- to adopt a form of reality, 76-79, 81, 83, 85, 240, 272-273.
- *cf.* reason as form of apprehension of *in its own right*, 34.
- agnosticism as form of conceptualizing *cf.* transcendence, 132.
- donation-surrender as form. of *cf.* personal causality, 151, 255-256.
- enigma as form of being hurled towards things, 170-171.
- atheism as form of *cf.* will to grounding, 195, 206, 207, 212.
- atheism as form of life, 204, 205-207.
- atheism as form of being relatively absolute, 207, 250.
- grace as form of *cf.* donation, 232, 235.
- benevolence as form of donation, 261-262.
- to love God as form of *cf.* personal causality, 256.
- "no" as form of donation, 258.

Formality:
- what is, 33-37, 78.
- of the real, 24.
- of reality and animal groupings, 55; *cf.* society.
- of reality and *cf.* Hume, 70.
- *cf. in its own right*, reality.

Freedom:
- what is, 165, 240-241.
- and *cf.* personhood, 45.
- and *cf.* cause, 70.
- God as ground of my, 161.
- and *cf.* faith, 165-222, 243.
- and *cf.* option, 188.
- "free" option facing God, 191ff.
- and *cf.* surrender, 211.
- and *cf.* experience of God, 240-241, 243, 252.
- as moment of *cf.* theological unity, 243.

Frivolity, 200, 203; *cf.* atheism.

From: we live from reality, 69, 107.

Fruition, 35, 128; *cf.* will.

Full:
- God as full in His own right, 125-126.

what is the "fullness" of the real, 127; cf. "self-giving".
full access to God, 147-148, 150, 153, 164; cf. inchoate access.

Function:
 organic function and cf. schema, 52.
 of intelligence, 174-175.
 of God in life, 119-124, 137, 173.

Functionality of the real, 29-30, 70-71, 72, 116, 151, 154, 255; cf. causality.

G

Genesis and cf. species, 52.
Genetics and history, 56-57; cf. transmission.
Glory and life of cf. Christ, 242.
God:
 idea of, 19-20, 101-103, 121, 196, 218-219.
 problem of, 19-20, 263-271.
 intellection of, 142, 169-171, 175, 177, 196-198, 200-201, 211-212, 273-275.
 access of to cf. world, 136.
 access of man to, 136-141, 143, 144-145, 150, 157, 165, 200, 274.
 cf. inchoate access to, 146-148, 150, 164.
 plenary access to, 147-149, 152, 164.
 access to God for cf. St. Augustine, 147-148.
 donation of, 116-117, 153, 228-231, 234-236, 240-241, 247, 252, 253, 258-260.
 surrender of man to, 148-149, 152, 159, 173, 177-177, 193, 214, 219, 266-267.
 surrender to, individual, social, historical, 157.
 surrender to, knowledge and, 191, 193.
 experience of, 85, 89, 173, 229, 231, 234, 236, 238-241, 251-252, 260, 263, 266, 275.
 experience of, cf. individual, 119, 152, 218, 224-225, 235, 238-244, 250, 266, 275, 277.
 experience of, historical, 119, 217-218, 234-235, 244-248, 249, 267, 275, 277.
 agnosticism, theism, atheism and, 19, 123, 190-191, 204-207, 201-203, 250-251, 270, 274, 275, cf. Theós, deity.
 ways to, cosmic and anthropological, 93-99, 115.
 way of cf. religation, 99-103, 115-116, 119-120, 172.
 justification of, 104, 114, 133, 136, 194, 271, 274.
 demonstration of reality of, 172, 200-201.
 function in life, 119-120, 122-124, 137, 145, 173, 186, cf. I.
 vinculation of man and, 20, 129-133, 150-153, 200, 219, 254-259, 261, 264, 266-267, 273-276.
 distinction between man and, 116, 122, 131, 243, 258.
 man as small, 117, 238, 241, 260-261, 264, 277.
 different modes of presence of, 128, 141, 143-146, 148-149, 169-171, 186, 177.
 presence of in things, 113, 114, 116, 118-119, 131-133, 136, 138, 140-141, 145, 151, 224-228.
 presence of in man, 120-121, 141-146, 224, 228, 232-233.
 presence of in cf. history, 234.
 presence of for St. Thomas, 136.
 transcendence of, 131, 132-133, 136, 141-142, 145, 147, 151, 223, 226-227, 253, 277.
 as ultimate, possibilitating, and impelling, 69, 87, 100,

117, 119, 133, 137, 149-150, 192, 253.
is not *cf.* efficient causality, 116, 223-224, 226, 239.
supreme reality not supreme being, 101, 225.
essence of, 125-126, 133.
different characteristics of, 125-130, 131, 137-138, 140, 141, 144, 151-152, 159-161, 205, 225-226, 234, 239, 257.
as reality-ground, 87, 120, 190, 193, 238-239.
as reality-object, 120, 171-172, 190ff., 200-201, 245.
as absolutely absolute reality, 119, 125-126, 136, 140, 144-145, 148, 161, 165, 226, 229, 239, 274.
in *cf.* classical theology, 125, 173.
theology of the historical experience of, 247.
problem of in St. Thomas, 93-96.
problem of in Kant, St. Augustine, and Schleiermacher, 96-99.
idea of in Duns Scotus, 95-96, 101.
idea of in Pascal, 116.
idea of in Aristotle, 115, 126, 136, 191.
hypothesis of in Laplace, 154.
idea of in Hegel, 234.
search for in St. Paul, 263.
of Israel, 234-235, 244-248.
and *cf.* Christ, 232-233, 241-243, 258-263.
and *cf.* Christianity, 116, 121, 218-219, 248, 277.
Yahweh, 234, 245-247.
Theós, 20, 115, 126, 136, 191.
Baal as divinity, 244-245.
gods as *cf.* real things, 73-74.
Grace:
as form of *cf.* donation, 232, 235.

as mode of *cf.* experience of God, 241.
as moment of *cf.* theological unity, 243.
in *cf.* Old Testament and St. Paul, 261.
as *cf.* tensive unity, 261-262; *cf.* theological tension.
Greeks:
cf. forcefulness for, 30-31.
idea of *cf. phýsis* among, 30, 118, 226; *cf.* nature.
idea of *cf.* truth among, 84; *cf.* Semites.
"To know is to see" among, 166-167.
interior religion for, 261-262; *cf. eusébeia.*
Green, 27.
Ground:
power as ground of my *cf.* personal reality, 69, 73, 74-75, 86, 99-100, 102, 204, 274.
of the power of the real, 76, 86, 101-102, 113, 114, 115, 118-119, 133, 137, 146, 190, 192, 223, 265, 273-275.
of things, 87, 114-116, 119, 130-133, 144, 225-227, 274.
for being a person, 115, 116-117, 121, 192, 224, 225.
of *cf.* relatively absolute being, 119-120, 121, 123, 145, 171, 175, 189-190, 229, 239-240.
characteristics of, 87, 117, 133, 137, 149-150, 191-192, 265.
of the *cf.* enigma, 171.
is not a *cf. phýsis*, 226.
ways of experiencing, 250-251, 275.
cf. reality-ground, fundamentality, ultimateness, possibilitating, impellence.
Grounding character (fundamentality):
what is, 69-72.
characteristics of, 69, 186.
is not *cf.* causality, 70.

of my *cf.* personal reality, 73.
hurls me to *cf.* adopt a form of reality, 84, 87.
constitutes power of real, 86.
taking a position confronting, 91.
God as, 126, 130-133, 226.
making mine, 175.
my possibilities and, 184-188.
and knowledge-faith, 191.
hurling "towards", 196.
indifference facing, 203.
ambit of, 240.
cf. ground, grounding.
Grounding is to be self-giving, 144; *cf.* fundamentality, ground, self-giving.
Friendship as mode of *cf.* personal causality, 154-156. *cf.* love.

H

Habitude of personal otherness, 56; *cf.* community, turning.
Happiness, 80.
Hearing, 35, 82, 142-143; *cf.* announcement.
Hegel: idea of God and history, 234, 248-249.
Help as metaphysical mode of constituting being, 152.
Heraclitus, 78; *cf.* enigma.
Heredity, history is not, 57.
Hesed, 261, 264; *cf.* mercy.
Héxis, 56; *cf.* affection, community.
His-ownness or its-ownness [*suidad*]: what is, 44-45; *cf. in its own right.*
of the *cf.* real, 28.
man as his-own reality, 44, 51, 63, 105, 227, 272.
and *cf.* individuality, 54.
of God, 127, 128, 141, 144.
as ground of life, 128.
open essences, God makes-them-their-own, 141.
and self-determination, 214.
of *cf.* Christ, 262-263.
cf. person.
History:
historic dimension of the human being, 57-60, 64, 218; *cf.* temporeity, stature of the times.
there is no natural, 57.
as transmission of *cf.* possibilities. 58-60, 234.
testing of power of real, 77.
historic experience of *cf.* religation, 102, 276.
profiles the figure of *cf.* deity, 119.
experience of God in, 119, 234-235, 246.
tensiveness, 264.
dimension of *cf.* faith, 218.
dimension of the experience of God, 218, 234-235, 242-249, 267, 275, 277.
for Hegel and *cf.* Kant, 234, 248.
of religions, 234, 264.
and *cf.* Christianity, 235. *cf.* tradition, surrender, invention.
Hittites, 245.
Hosea, 261; *cf.* mercy.
Human being(s):
as reality, 23, 42.
implantation of in reality, 27, 57, 75, 128; *cf.* implantation.
is in reality, 66-67, 78, 87, 107, 108, 272.
as *cf.* system of notes, 38-42; *cf.* note.
as *cf.* animal of realities, 42, 43-50, 52, 83, 229, 238.
as formality of reality, 55.
as *cf.* substantive reality, 51, 104, 208, 260.
as *cf.* open essence, 57, 137, 141, 170, 227-228, 256.
as its-own reality, 63, 105-106; *cf.* its-own-ness.

as agent, actor, and author of actions, 64-66, 85.
life of as something enigmatic, 80-81; *cf.* enigma.
and *cf.* voice of conscience, 83.
must adopt a *cf.* form of reality, 83, 85.
as personal reality, 85, 91, 99, 208, 229, 260.
how does one become, 85, 91, 151, 208-210.
religation of to *cf.* power of the real, 91-92, 130, 223.
actions of for *cf.* St. Thomas, 95.
segregation of with respect to cosmic reality, 98.
distinction between and God, 116, 122.
as finite God, 117, 238, 241, 260-264,
implantation of in divinity, 123.
access of to God, 136, 141-143, 144-145, 200; *cf.* access.
surrender of to God, 148, 152, 159, 173, 193, 214, 219; *cf.* surrender.
God as strength of man, 150.
moral dimension of, 155-156; *cf.* personal causality.
and *cf.* will to real truth, 210.
as experience of God, 224-225, 238-239.
as author of his own *cf.* being, 240.
God gives Himself to as *cf.* real truth, 228-235, 247, 253; *cf.* donation.
concern of with God, 243.
cf. animal, person, I.
Hume and his idea of *cf.* cause, 70-71.
Hurled (or thrown):
and *cf.* intellection, 79, 170, 175, 178-179, 196, 200, 273.
towards enigma of the real, 79, 83, 112-113, 170.
and *cf.* adopting a form of reality, 83-84, 87.
"towards" the real and *cf.* real truth, 85.
towards *cf.* ground of power of the real, 137, 183, 190, 196, 273.
Hypokeímenon, 235; *cf.* substance, *hypóstasis*.
Hypóstasis, 235; *cf.* Cappadocian.

I

I:
configuration of, 53, 91, 99, 105-107, 114, 148, 151, 190, 204, 224, 239; *cf.* acts.
as worldly activity, 49-51, 54, 105-106, 262; *cf.* myself, my.
reality makes me be, 108.
co-determination of, 55-56.
as communally absolute, 56; *cf.* community.
religation as root of the construction of, 104, 118.
ground of, 115, 171, 175, 184, 190-191, 214, 240.
forcefulness to make, 117.
construction of the *I* as experience of *cf.* deity, 118.
function of God in the construction of, 119-124.
theological tension as constituent of, 122.
access to God insofar as, 137.
I-You in problem of God, 141.
ambit of *cf.* ground of *I*, 175.
is not *cf.* personeity, 260.
as metaphysical structure, 262.
and the *cf.* Trinity, 262-263; *cf.* anthropomorphism.
Idea:
of God, 19-20, 101-103, 121, 196, 218-219.
will to truth of, 183-184, 187; *cf.* will to real truth.

idealism and the *cf. I*, 51.
Ililim, 245; *cf.* monotheism.
Impellence:
    as a characteristic of reality, 68-69, 85-86, 107.
    as characteristic of the ground, 69, 87, 101, 117, 133, 137, 149-150, 192, 253.
    as characteristic of power of the real, 77, 100-101, 108, 114, 149, 266.
    as characteristic of surrender, 108, 149.
Imperatives, categorical, and *cf.* voice of conscience, 82; *cf.* Kant.
Impersonal, 55-56; *cf.* a-personal.
Implantation:
    of human beings in reality, 27, 75, 128.
    of the living being in the *cf.* cosmos, 46.
    of humans in divinity, 123.
Implication of humans and God, 257-260, 266-267; *cf.* personal causality.
Impression:
    what is, 33; *cf.* content, formality.
    of reality, 34-36, 37, 67, 82, 105, 112, 167; *cf.* apprehension.
    transcendentality of impression of reality, 47, 70-71, 108-110; *cf.* transcendentality.
    of reality and *cf.* Hume, 70.
In:
    Humans are in reality, 66-67, 69, 78, 87, 107, 108, 272.
    making the *cf.* relatively absolute being in reality, 87, 108, 110, 209.
    making the relatively absolute being in *cf.* true reality, 209, 229.
    God is in *cf.* real things, 132-133, 142-147; *cf.* transcendence.
    ground of the *cf.* enigma in things, 170-171.
    access to God in the *cf.* world, 140; *cf.* access.
    transcendence of God in the *cf.* person, 151-153, 224, 228, 277.
    freedom in reality, 241; *cf.* freedom.
"In," 26; *cf.* "ex," structure.
In its own right [*de suyo*]:
    what is, 24-25, 36-37, 82.
    moments of, 30.
    apprehension of, 33-34, 42, 82.
    and open essences, 227
    things as worldly, 48.
    power as moment of, 73.
    God as fullness, 125-126.
    constitution of, 133, *cf.* reality, formality.
In themselves, 140; *cf.* open essences.
Incarnation:
    in *cf.* Christian faith, 232-233, 248.
    and history, 235.
    as mode of *cf.* tensive unity, 263.
Inchoate:
    access to God, 146-148, 150, 164; *cf.* access.
    donation, 149; *cf.* surrender.
    progression, 274.
Independence from the *cf.* surroundings, 32, 46; *cf.* control.
Indifference, 201-203, 250; *cf.* agnosticism.
Indigence and *cf.* experience of God, 251.
Individual:
    dimension of human being, 53-55, 64, 217.
    testing of *cf.* power of the real, 77.
    experience of *cf.* religation, 102, 136.

concretion of the *cf.* surrender to God, 157.
dimension of *cf.* faith, 218-219.
dimension of the *cf.* experience of God, 232, 239-243, 266, 275, 277; *cf.* dei-formity.
Inspiration, 163; *cf.* faith.
Intellection:
what is, 33-34, 38, 41-42, 84, 174, 180.
and *cf.* hurling, 79, 170, 175, 178-179, 196, 200, 273; *cf.* towards.
of the "more" in things, 108-110.
of God, 136, 169, 170-171, 175-176, 211-212, 273-275.
types of, 167-169.
and *cf.* choice, 180.
and *cf.* real truth, 182-183.
of Baal as divinity, 244-245; *cf.* Baalism.
intellective surrender to God, 266-267.
and *cf.* progression towards the ground, 273-276.
Intelligence:
as *cf.* note of human reality, 34-38, 42, 104, 137, 253.
and *cf.* actualization, 38, 84, 128, 143-144, 160, 174, 182-183, 209, 228-229.
and *cf.* hurling, 112-113, 178, 186.
in the human embryo, 45.
difference between intelligence and *cf.* faith, 167-178.
unity of intelligence and faith, 178-213.
in *cf.* anthropological ways, 97.
in God, 128-131, 133, 140, 225.
and *cf.* transcendence, 70-71, 108, 110.
ground of, 129.
in *cf.* Christ, 242.
Intelligence, sentient:

moments of, 30-31.
as *cf.* faculty, 36-37, 58.
and *cf.* unveiling, 142-143.
and *cf.* sentient will, 83.
cf. intelligence.
Interdependency, 38, 40; *cf.* system, notes.
Inter-worldly: turning of God to world as, 132, 140; *cf.* transcendence, world.
Invention in *cf.* history, 57.
Israel:
people of, 234-235, 244-245, 247-248.
history of, 234, 246-248.

J

Járis, 261; *cf.* grace.
Jesus-Christ, 232, 263-264; *cf.* Christ.
Judge, to:
faith is not the acceptance of a judgement, 158-159, 215.
Justification of God:
not speculative reasonings, 104, 114.
intellectual, 133, 137, 172, 194, 199, 199, 211-212.
cf. ways.

K

Kant:
categorical imperatives, 82; *cf.* voice of conscience, subjective.
the problem of God in, 97-99; *cf.* anthropological ways.
volition in, 214; *cf.* auto-determination.
person in, 236; *cf.* Descartes.
history for, 248; *cf.* Hegel.
Kénosis, 242: *cf.* Christ.
Kinesthesia: 35, 82; *cf.* "towards".
Know, to:
and seeing for the *cf.* Greeks,

166-167.
scientific knowledge, 184.
Knowledge:
difference between knowledge and *cf.* faith, 157, 172-174, 177, 189.
unity of knowledge. and faith, 174-178, 180-181, 189-194.
of reality of God, 171.
of God without *cf.* surrender, 191, 193.
cf. intelligence, reason, towards, search.
Kósmoi, 28, 126; *cf.* cosmos, world.

L

Laplace and hypothesis of God, 154.
Law, 29; *cf.* causality, functionality.
Liberation, 240; *cf.* freedom.
Life:
as form of reality, 27.
as *cf.* self-possession, 33, 49, 64, 91, 127, 196, 242.
uncertainty of, 46, 79.
as *cf.* restlessness, 46, 79-81, 86, 106, 112.
as constitution of the *cf. I*, 99, 105, 114.
as something enigmatic, 80-81, 111; *cf.* enigma.
making with things, 114.
another life as matter of faith and not of pure reason, 121.
absolute, 127-129.
as ground of intelligence, 129.
access to God through, 137.
strength of life of man, 150.
atheist, 204-207.
divine life and finite nature, 227.
of Christ, 241-243.
cf. living.
Living:
what is, 66.

ways of life *cf.* restlessness, 80-81.
will to, 84, 203, 208, 209-211.
cf. life.
Lógos, 34; *cf.* to judge.
Love:
and faith, 160.
as *cf.* choice, 165.
of God as form of *cf.* personal causality, 256.
of God as *cf. eudokía*, 261.
cf. friendship.
Luke, St., 262; *cf. eudokía*.

M

Manifestation:
as characteristic of religation, 77, 84, 253.
of reality as something *cf.* enigmatic, 78.
as moment of *cf.* real truth, 84-86, 143-145, 160-161, 182, 185-188, 228; *cf.* patency, ostensive.
experience and occurrence of power of the real, 100-101.
access to God insofar as, 142, 143, 145; *cf.* unveiling, interpersonal tension.
Mark, St., 242.
Mathematics, Egyptian and Assyro-Babylonian, 31; *cf. anánke*, forcefulness.
Matter and *cf.* body, 39.
Mercy:
of God, 244, 261; *cf. hesed*.
is not the *cf.* ground, 117.
Metaphysics:
idea of act and potency in classical, 28-29, 36, 40, 59, 235.
idea of *cf.* cause in classical, 70-71, 154-155, 255-256.
in *cf.* Aristotle, 95.
essence of God, 96, 125-126, *cf.* Scholastic.
idea of *cf.* transcendence in

classical, 109.
idea of *cf.* friendship in classical, 155; *cf.* personal causality.
cf. personeity as a question of, 45, 50.
notion of *cf.* individuality, 53-54.
experience of God, 85; *cf.* Bergson.
to be "metaphysically" immersed in *cf.* divinity, 123.
modes of constituting my being in God, 152.
structure of *cf.* self-giving, 253.
I as metaphysical structure, 262-263.
unity of man and God, 263-264.

Mode:
Agnosticism, atheism as modes to resolve problem of God, 19-20, 204-207, 250, 270.
person as mode of being in reality, 27.
of presence of real, 29, 47.
causal production as mode of ground of real, 29-30.
"myself", "my", as modes of worldly actualization, 49-50; *cf. I.*
enigma as mode of signifying the real, 77, 170.
capture by the real in an ostensive and experiential mode, 80.
occupation and preoccupation as modes of living *cf.* restlessness, 80-81.
of God making Himself present, 91, 141, 142-146, 148, 169-171, 174, 177.
transcendence as mode of presence of God, 131, 138.
metaphysical modes/forms through which God constitutes my *cf.* being, 152.
friendship and communion as modes of personal causality, 155-156.
admission as mode of *cf.* surrender, 158.
faith as mode of interpersonal causality, 161.
towards as mode of surrender, 174.
"my" as mode of concretion of faith, 215-218.
apprehension of different modes of *cf.* creation, 227.
will to truth as mode of experiencing God, 240, 251.
grace as of experience of God, 241.
amphictyony as of historical experience of God, 247.
of tensive unity, 263-264.
modes of *cf.* access to ground, 274-275.

Moment:
"of" as physical moment of the real, 25-27, 39.
more as moment of reality, 27, 30, 71, 78, 108-110.
of the *cf. in its own right*, 30-31.
naked reality as moment of the real, 30-31, 168.
of sentient intelligence, 30-31.
of *cf.* impression, 33-35, 37.
functional position as moment. of the psycho-organic system, 38-40.
co-determination of moments of a system, 40.
of *cf.* sensing, 41-42.
biogenetic as moment of history, 57-58.
of *cf.* sentient volition, 83.
of *cf.* real truth, 84-86, 144, 161, 182, 186, 187, 228.
of *cf.* power of the real as more, 110, 114.
of the *cf.* surrender, 148-151, 161-162.
intellective process as momo-

ment. of *cf.* will to grounding, 192, 195, 200.
cf. human nature as moment of finitude of being God, 238, 277.
grace and freedom as moments. of *cf.* theological unity, 243.
real truth as moment of theological dimension, 267.

Monism, pantheist, 225; *cf.* cause.

Monotheism:
and concretion of faith, 218.
in the experience of God by Israel, 244-248.

Moral:
as mode of *cf.* personal causality, 155-156.
dispositions and religious truths, 166.

More:
as moment of reality, 27, 30, 71, 78, 108-110.
as moment of the power of the real, 110, 114.
cf. transcendentality, communication.

Moses and *cf.* monotheism, 245, *cf.* Israel.

Motion in St. Thomas, 93; *cf.* dynamicity, self-giving.

Mover, unmovable, of Aristotle, 126; *cf. theós*.

Multiform social experience of God, 244.

My:
as mode of *cf.* worldly actualization, 49-50.
reality-ground as reality "for me", 184-186.
and *cf.* volition, 214.
as mode of concretion of *cf.* faith, 215-219.

Myself as mode of *cf.* worldly actualization, 50;

N

Naked:
reality as moment of the *cf.* real, 30-31, 168.
presence of God, 143, 145.

Natura naturans, 223-224, 226-227; *cf.* efficient cause.

Nature:
for the *cf.* Greeks, 30, 118, 226; *cf. phýsis*, ground.
no natural history, 57.
personized, 91, 155; *cf.* religation.
human as moment of the *cf.* finitude of being God, 238, 277; *cf.* deiformity.
in *cf.* classical Theology, 93.

Necessity:
and *cf.* forcefulness, 30-31; *cf. anánke*.
the "necessary" in St. Thomas, 94; *cf.* possibility.

Neurotic, 217; *cf.* faith.

Newton: his idea of force, 30.

Nietzche, 84, 182; *cf.* will to authenticity.

"Not" as mode of *cf.* donation, 257-259.

Note:
cf. otherness of, 24; *cf.* apprehension.
note-of, 25-27; *cf.* "of".
not Aristotelian accidents, 26.
and *cf.* form of reality, 27.
of the real and *cf.* thisness, 27.
life as note of human reality, 32.
cf. sensing as note of human reality, 33.
cf. intelligence as note of human reality, 33-38, 42, 104, 137, 253.
of the *cf.* system, 37.
other notes of *cf.* human reality, 38-43.
give the form and *cf.* mode of reality, 43.
appropriation of notes of the

O

Object:
"objectum", 120, 188.
objectifying of God, 123; *cf.* "reality-object".
Occurrence:
of the power of the real, 100.
of the reality-ground, 172, 187.
as *cf.* function of God in life, 173.
"Of":
as physical moment of the real, 25-27, 39.
system of, 37; *cf.* system.
and *cf.* human substantivity, 39-40.
notified presence of a thing, 168.
Old Testament:
historical experience of God in, 217-218, 234-235, 244-248.
"grace" in, 261; *cf.* St. Paul.
Omnipotence is not the *cf.* ground, 116.
Open:
reality as, 27-30, 47; *cf.* transcendentality.
societies open to reality, 55.
man as open essence, 57, 137, 141, 170, 227-228, 256.
cf. aperture.
Openness:
of the real, 27; *cf.* transcendentality, open.
medial, 49.
religated, 137; *cf.* religation.
of the *cf.* ambit of the possible faith, 176.
cf. open.
Order in St. Thomas, 94; *cf.* finality.
Organism:
real by *cf.* society, 55.
cf. properties.
as *cf.* system, 26.
body, psyche, 38-39; *cf.* soma.
Ostensive:
seizure by reality in an ostensive way, 79; *cf.* experience.
as moment of *cf.* real truth, 86, 223; *cf.* manifestation, patency.
Otherness:
of *cf.* notes, 24.
as moment of *cf.* impression, 34-35, 37.
reality as formality of, 37, 78.
of God as ground of *cf.* respectivity, 132.
Otiose: God, 190-192, 201; *cf. theós*.

P

Pantheism:
agnosticism and, 132; *cf.* transcendence, fontanality.
pantheist monism, 225.
and the *cf.* "no", 258; *cf.* donation.
cf. deiformity.
Paradise, 235.
Parádosis, 57; *cf.* history, tradition.
Parmenides: his idea of *cf.* being, 48; *cf.* entification.
Particles, elementary, 167.
Pascal, 115.
Passing of time for the living, 33; *cf.* life.
Patency: as moment of *cf.* real truth, 144, 160-161, 182, *cf.* manifestation, ostensiveness.
Patriarchs, 245; *cf.* Israel.
Paul, St.:
idea of *cf.* grace, 261.
idea of *cf.* search for God, 263-264.
People of Israel; *cf.* Israel.
Person:
as mode of being in reality, 27.

as *cf.* subsistence, 44.
as *cf.* form of reality, 44-45.
co-determination of, 53-59.
humans as personal animals, 55-56.
cf. I as actuality of, 54.
history as capacitation of, 59.
personal reality, 70-71, 73-75, 86, 99, 102, 206, 274.
becoming a, 63, 67, 77, 86-87, 214, 224, 239, 277.
personal theological tension, 137.
transcendence of God in, 151-153, 224, 228, 277.
God as personal reality, 129, 141-143, 257.
personal truth, 159-161, 186-188.
cf. transcendent depths of, 152, 162, 211.
transcendence of the *cf.* power of the real in, 211.
faith of the believing, 214-219.
remission of the person to the *cf.* ground, 223.
unity of God and through *cf.* religation, 224-225, 238.
donation to be, 228, 231, 233-236, 258, 261, 264.
introduction of concept of, 235-236; *cf.* Christianity.
and *cf.* personal causality, 255.
of the *cf.* Trinity, 262-263; *cf.* anthropomorphism.
cf. its-ownness as formal reason of, 272.
cf. personality, personhood.
Personality:
what is, 44-46, 50; *cf.* personhood,
and *cf.* faith, 217.
Personhood:
what is, 44-46, 127, 260; *cf.* personality, its-ownness.
as *cf.* metaphysical structure, 105.

in God, 128.
and *cf.* faith, 217.
Philosophy, classical:
act for, 28-29, 235.
reality in, 47.
species in, 51.
and *cf.* entification of reality, 101.
analogy between God and man in, 129.
faith for, 159.
God in, 172-173.
will in, 181.
Phyletic, 52; *cf.* phylum, species.
Phylum, 52-60; *cf.* species.
Physical:
characteristic of the *cf.* "of", 25-27, 39.
testing of power of the real, 77, 86, 143.
testing of reality, 77, 118, 223.
we are physically thrown towards reality, 79.
testing of religation, 77.
reality as physical characteristic, 107-108, 110.
to be physically real, 144.
cf. morality as physical dimension of man, 155-156.
forcefulness to opt for a form of reality, 273.
Physics:
of elementary particles, 167.
Theoretical and the *cf.* enigma, 171.
Phýsis:
for the Greeks, 30, 118; *cf.* nature.
cf. ground is not a, 226.
Pinnacle of time, 60.
Plato:
and *cf.* truth for St. Augustine, 97.
participation of some realities in others, 235.
Plotinus and his influence on

St. Augustine, 97; *cf.* Plato, truth.
Pluriverse, 126; *cf. kósmoi.*
Polytheism, 132, 218; *cf.* monotheism.
Position, functional:
  as moment of the *cf.* body, 38-39.
  as moment of the *cf.* psycho-organic system, 40.
Possibilitating:
  as characteristic of reality, 68-69, 86-87, 107.
  as characteristic of the *cf.* ground, 69, 87, 100, 117, 119, 133, 137, 149-150, 192, 266.
  as characteristic of power of the real, 77, 100-102, 108, 114, 149, 266.
  as characteristic of *cf.* religation, 108, 149.
  of *cf.* surrender, 149.
  of *cf.* faith, 176.
Possibility (ies):
  history as delivery of, 58-60, 234.
  appropriation of, 84, 179-180, 183-184, 187; *cf.* volition.
  God as donor of, 116-117.
  my, 179-180, 183-188; *cf.* ambit, ground.
  and *cf.* real truth, 183-184.
  cf. potency, possibilitating.
Possible:
  in *cf.* history, 58-59.
  in *cf.* St. Thomas Aquinas, 94.
  cf. possibility.
Potency:
  idea of in *cf.* classical Metaphysics, 28-29, 36, 40, 58, 235; *cf. dýnamis*, act.
  of man, 36, 64; *cf.* faculty, intelligence, sensing.
  presence of God by, 136; *cf.* St. Thomas Aquinas.
  actuation of and *cf.* possibilities, 179, 235.
Power of the real:
  what is, 30-31, 73-74, 108-110; *cf.* forcefulness, dominance, powerfulness.
  as ground of my *cf.* personal reality, 69, 73, 74-75, 86, 99, 102, 204, 274.
  is not *cf.* causality, 70-71, 107.
  reality as, 72, 107.
  seizure (take hold) of, 75, 76, 79, 86, 272, 276-277; *cf.* religation, dominance.
  religation to, 75-76, 79, 91, 102, 146-147, 201, 204, 250, 253, 265, 267, 272-273, 277.
  cf. ground of, 76, 86, 101-102, 112, 114-115, 117-120, 133, 137, 146, 190, 192, 223, 265, 273-276.
  physical testing of, 77, 86, 143, 275.
  experience of, 76-77, 102, 223.
  religation as manifestative of, 77-78, 223; *cf.* manifestation.
  enigmatic character of, 77-79, 83, 86, 253, 272-273; *cf.* enigma.
  is in *cf.* things, 78, 117, 223, 253, 272-273.
  actualization of, 86.
  problematism of, 91, 274-275.
  occurrence of, 100; *cf.* experience, manifestation.
  as vehicle (transport) of power of God, 118.
  is not a *cf.* deity, 118.
  hurls us towards its ground, 137, 190, 273.
  facticity of, 205-206; *cf.* atheism.
  as *cf.* transcendence of God in things, 223-224, 274, 277.
  manifestative experience of, 253, 255.
Powerfulness:
  as moment of *in its own right*, 30.
  cf. dominance of the real, 30,

73; *cf.* power of the real.
animist interpretation of, 31.
as real things and *cf.* gods, 73-74.
Prayer, 149-150; *cf.* donation, adoration, supplication.
Preoccupation:
  as way of living the *cf.* restlessness, 80-81.
Presence:
  and *cf.* actuality, 28-29.
  of reality in senses, 167-169.
  of the *cf.* enigma in reality, 171.
  of reality and will to real truth, 183.
  of reality in reality-object and ground, 184-186.
  of things in the *cf.* world, 47-48.
  of God in things, 115-117, 119, 131-133, 138, 140-140, 145, 151, 224-228.
  of God in my substantive reality, 119-121, 141-145, 146, 224, 225, 228, 232.
  of God for St. Thomas Aquinas, 136.
  of God *cf.* as "towards", 142-143, 146-148, 175.
  of God, 143.
  modes of God making Himself "present", 169, 171, 177.
  of God in *cf.* history, 234; *cf.* Hegel.
  cf. grace is not, 241.
  cf. being *here-and-now*
Pre-Socratics and *cf.* truth, 31.
Pre-tension, 146-147, 259, 265; *cf.* dynamic tension.
Principle:
  structural of *cf.* substantivity, 26; *cf.* essence.
  indigence is not principle of *cf.* experience of God, 121, 123, 251.
  corporeity as principle of *cf.* actuality, 40; *cf.* body.

real truth as principle of intellectual acts, 183-184.
will to truth as principle of *cf.* attitude, 192-194.
Probing:
  as manifestation of *cf.* interpersonal transcendence, 143.
  march towards *cf.* ground in, 275.
  individual, social, and historical of the ground, 275.
  experience of the history of religions as, 277.
  Christianity as, 277.
Problem of God:
  19-20, 265-271; *cf.* agnosticism, theism, atheism.
  for Kant, St. Augustine, Schleiermacher, 96-98; *cf.* anthropological ways.
  for St. Thomas Aquinas, 93-96; *cf.* cosmic ways, demonstration, justification, intellective process, access.
Problem, theological, 180, 271, 278.
Problematic of making oneself a person, 86; *cf.* actions.
Process, intellective:
  as moment of *cf.* will to grounding, 192, 195-200.
  and *cf.* will to truth, 195-196.
  towards God, 196-197, 200.
  and *cf.* faith, 198ff.
  agnosticism as, 198-199, 208, 212.
  suspension of, 201.
  indifference to God and, 201-203.
  and *cf.* ambit of grounding, 240.
  atheism and theism as conclusion of, 250.
  cf. demonstration, justification, search.
Processual: character of *cf.* history, 59; *cf.* progressive.
Production:

causal, 30; cf. functionality, of reality, 70; cf. cause, *aitía.*
Progression of humans to God, 266, 375-276; cf. towards, reason, search.
Progressive as characteristic of cf. tradition, 57.
Projection of the "in" into the "ex", 26; cf. structure, dimension.
Properties, 24, 26; cf. notes.
Prospectivity of cf. history, 59-60.
Providence is not formally cf. ground, 116, 235.
Psyche, 39-41; cf. soul, body.
Psychology: the *I* is not a "psychological" structure, 262; cf. metaphysical.
Psycho-organic, 39ff; cf. substantivity, system.
Pythagorean theorem, 31.

R

Ratio essendi, 130; cf. *ratio cognoscendi,* grounding.
Ratio cognoscendi, 130; cf. *ratio essendi.*
Real:
　formality of, 24.
　physical moment of, 25-26.
　aperture of, 27-28; cf. transcendentality, open.
　functionality of, 29-30, 70-72, 116, 151, 154, 255; cf. cause, causality.
　faculty of, 34; cf. intelligence.
　apprehension of, 36, 78, 143-144, 169.
　appropriation of notes of by cf. society, 55.
　ultimateness of, 68, 116, 250, 271; cf. ultimateness.
　signification of and cf. enigma, 77, 170.
　ambit of cf. possibilities of 178-179, 210, 240.

activity of man, 227-228. cf. reality.
Realitas in essendo, 47, 122; cf. being.
Reality:
　what is, 24-31, 79, 105, 108; cf. *in its own right.*
　humans as, 23, 32, 44.
　humans as substantive, 56, 104, 388, 356; cf. substantivity.
　personal, 69, 71, 73, 74-75, 86.
　its own, 105; cf. its-ownness.
　unity of reality in Aristotle, 28; cf. *táxis.*
　is not a sea, 71, 108.
　as physical characteristic of a thing, 86-87, 107-108, 110, 113.
　unsubstantive, 26; cf. substantivity.
　implantation of man in, 27, 57, 75, 128; cf. seizing.
　man is in reality, 66-67, 78, 87, 107, 109, 272.
　cf. intelligence as note of human, 33-38, 104, 137, 253.
　formality of, 34, 36, 55.
　impression of, 35-37, 70-70, 105, 108, 110, 112, 167.
　awareness of, 180.
　as cf. "towards," 35, 82, 167-168, 186, 197, 231; cf. kinesthesia.
　and formality of *in its own right,* 36-37, 78.
　actuality of in intelligence, 38, 84, 128, 143-144, 167, 182-183, 209, 228-229; cf. real truth.
　ambit of and cf. stimulation, 41-42; cf. ambit.
　hurling towards by intelligence, 79, 178, 186.
　form and mode of, 43-46.
　cf. being of human, 46-50.
　actualization of human, 49-51, 105, 186-187; cf. *I,* "my-

self", "my".
and being, 51.
unity of being and human, 51-60, 109.
human societies are *cf.* open to, 55; *cf.* appropriation.
forms of being in, 57-58; *cf.* history.
characteristics of, 67-69, 85-86, 107.
physical testing of, 77, 118, 223, 246, 252; *cf.* experience.
cf. enigma of, 78, 83, 111-112.
seizing by in an *cf.* ostensive and experiential mode, 79.
humans as voice of, 83; *cf.* voice of conscience.
as *cf.* announcement, 35, 82, 142-143, 167-168; *cf.* hearing.
in *cf.* classical Theology, 93.
ground of, 116-118.
God as substantive, 128; *cf.* substantivity.
of humans and *cf.* access to God, 136-137; *cf.* to be.
as *cf.* donation, 144.
types of metaphysical, 227-228; *cf.* open and closed essences.
humans as *cf.* absolute, 272; *cf.* relatively absolute reality.
cf. naked reality, *res*, being.
Reality, absolutely absolute:
discovering, 115, 136, 266.
God as, 118-119, 125, 136, 140, 144, 148, 161, 165-165, 225, 229, 239, 274.
as reality of absolute concretion, 126-127, 136, 165.
as *cf.* absolute its-ownness, 127, 141.
and its characteristic of ground, 122, 130, 225.
surrender to, 149.
and *cf.* option for grounding, 192.
and *cf.* intellective process, 212.
Reality, relatively absolute:
being as mode of reality of *cf.* humans, 46-47, 49, 51, 65-86, 189, 239-240, 261, 271-272.
worldly actuality of, 49-51, 54, 91, 141; *cf. I*, relatively absolute being.
as my radical depth, 81; *cf.* voice of conscience.
God as grounding, 83, 115, 258-355.
Reality-ground:
actualization of, 83, 85, 175, 185-187; *cf.* real truth.
as solution to the *cf.* enigma, 87.
God as, 87, 119-120, 190, 193, 238-240.
and *cf.* knowledge-faith, 174.
and *cf.* life, 175.
surrender to, 172, 191, 200.
objectualization of, 188, 190, 193; *cf.* reality-object.
and *cf.* intelligence, 201.
Reality-object:
is not terminus of *cf.* volition (willing), 83.
God as, 120, 171-172, 190ff, 200, 238.
and *cf.* knowledge-faith, 173.
actualization of, 185.
as reduction of the *cf.* reality-ground, 186, 188-189.
Realization as *cf.* person, 272, 274, 277, 386; *cf.* option.
Reason:
as form of apprehension of *cf. in its own right*, 34.
truths of reason and truths of *cf.* faith, 116, 165-166, 176, 189; *cf.* creation.
commencement of, 167.
and faith in *cf.* St. Augustine, 176.
discovers the *cf.* ground, 263.
attitude of the "reasonable",

192-193.
absolute reason in *cf.* Hegel, 234; *cf.* history.
reasoning and *cf.* access to God, 274,
cf. march, hurling, towards, search, ways, demonstration, justification, knowledge.
Reflection and *cf. autós*, 32.
Refuge as moment of the surrender, 216.
Relation:
and *cf.* respectivity, 27; *cf.* relationship.
Relationship:
and *cf.* respectivity, 27; *cf.* relation.
and *cf.* religation, 100.
Relativism and God, 219.
Religation:
as *cf.* seizure, 75, 79, 86, 272, 276-277; *cf.* power of the real.
as root of the *cf.* relatively absolute being, 75-76, 81, 91, 99, 102, 108, 115, 118, 119, 130, 146, 171, 189, 223, 265-266, 276.
as a verifiable, total, and radical fact, 75, 99.
is not obligation, 76.
is not a feeling of unconditional dependency, 76, 97, 99; *cf.* sentiment.
to *cf.* power of the real, 76, 86, 91, 99, 102, 108, 119, 130, 143, 146-147, 170-171, 189, 223, 250, 265, 267.
experiential and ostensive characteristic of, 76-77, 80-81, 86, 143, 223-224.
to make oneself a person by means of, 77, 223-224.
enigmatic characteristic of, 78-80, 86, 102, 170-171, 189; *cf.* enigma.
is not something merely intentional, 79.
as root of the choice confronting *cf.* grounding, 91, 192, 219, 266.
does God manifest Himself in? 91.
way of and justification of the existence of God, 99-103, 123; *cf.* anthropological and cosmic ways.
and *cf.* respectivity, 100.
through reason we reach a God *qua* God, 101-102, 115-116, 119-120, 172; *cf.* ultimate, possibilitating, impellence.
social, individual, and historical experience of, 102, 276-277.
as something physical and not mere vinculation, 104, 107-108.
as something problematic, 111, 189-190, 273; *cf.* power of the real.
religating dynamism of the *cf.* ground, 120.
religated aperture, 137; *cf.* open essences.
theological essence of, 147, 150, 265, 275; *cf.* dragging, pre-tension.
cf. surrender as unfolding of, 150.
God grounds me in, 224, 229, 266,
Christ and *cf.* subsistent, 243.
we find God in, 254, 273-275.
as *cf.* probing, 275.
religion is molding of, 276.
Religion:
as *cf.* choice, 165.
and *cf.* otiose God, 190.
and grounding God, 191.
history of, 217-218.
interior, 261; *cf. eusébeia*, Greeks.
and *cf.* religation, 276; *cf.* sacred.
and *cf.* dei-formity, 277.
Remission:
remitting (referring) dimension

of *cf.* respectivity, 28.
and *cf.* access to God, 137-139.
and *cf.* unveiling, 142.
Repentance, 50.
Res naturalis, 93, 95, 98, 236; *cf.* Descartes, Kant.
Respectivity:
what is, 27-28, 47, 126, 132; *cf. táxis*, world, open.
and *cf.* impression of reality, 47.
and *cf.* religation, 100.
otherness of God as ground of, 132.
Restlessness:
of *cf.* life, 46, 80-81, 86, 106, 112, 122; *cf.* anguish.
idea of in *cf.* St. Augustine, 80, 112, 265.
as expression of *cf.* tensive unity, 265-266.
cf. uncertainty.

S

Sacred, 276; *cf.* religion.
Scheme, replicative, 52-60; *cf.* species.
Schleiermacher: the problem of God, 96-98; *cf.* sentiment.
Scholastic idea of *cf.* metaphysical essence, 96.
Science:
idea of *cf.* cause in, 154.
knowing is not seeing in, 167-168; *cf.* Greeks.
and *cf.* choice, 184.
birth of, 184; *cf.* real truth.
Search:
and *cf.* will to real truth, 85.
for ground and making oneself *cf.* person, 86-87, 192, 239; *cf.* ground, enigma.
for ground and *cf.* will to grounding, 192-194, 199, 211-212.
cf. will to search, 199, 208, 210.
for God in St. Paul, 263-265, *cf.* reason, towards.
Seat of God, 118-119; *cf.* things.
Secret, Messianic, 242; *cf.* Christ.
Seize (take hold of, capture):
by the *cf.* power of the real, 75, 76, 79, 86. 272, 274, 276-277; *cf.* religation.
by reality under *cf.* ostensive and experiential mode, 79.
of man by God, 274.
Self-expression, 127, 130, 133.
Self-giving:
dynamicity as, 127; *cf.* dynamicity.
to ground is, 130-131, 144, 226.
as *cf.* transcendence of God, 226, 253.
cf. self-expression.
Selfness, 40.
Semites: truth for, 84; *cf.* fidelity.
Sense(s) (*Sp. sentido*):
and *cf.* otherness, 33.
and *cf.* impression of reality, 34-35, 82-83, 167.
and presence of reality, 168.
and *cf.* intelligence, 168-169.
cf. sense, to.
Sentient:
apprehension and *cf.* impression of reality, 36-38.
intelligence, 30-31, 36-37, 58, 83, 142.
cf. to sense, intelligence.
Sentiment (or feeling):
and *cf.* affection, 42.
of unconditional dependence, 76, 97-99; *cf.* Schleiermacher, religation.
in God, 129.
Sense, to (*Sp. sentir*):
and *cf.* impressions, 33ff.
human sensing, 34ff; *cf.* impression of reality.

Index

as *cf.* potency, 36; *cf.* faculty.
moments of sensing, 41-43.
analyzers of sensing, 169.
cf. sense.
Sight, 33, 35, 82, 142.
Social:
  dimension of the human being, 54-56, 64, 217-218.
  dimension of the *cf.* faith, 217.
  experience of God, 234, 244-246.
  cf. society.
Society:
  human, 55-56; *cf.* affection, community, turning.
  and *cf.* world, 164.
Solidarity as moment of the *cf.* body, 38-40.
Somatic: function, 38-39, 52.
Son of God, 241-242; *cf.* Christ.
Soul and psyche, 39; *cf.* body, soma, psycho-organic.
Species, 51-56; *cf.* phylum, schema.
Spirit:
  cf. psyche is not, 39.
  God as absolute spirit in Hegel, 234.
Spring, 127; *cf.* concretion of God.
Stimulation:
  apprehension of stimulation, 24, 41-42; *cf.* apprehension.
  formality of 33-34, 36; *cf.* formality.
  as moment of *cf.* sensing, 41-42.
Strength of life of man, 150.
Structure:
  structural principle of *cf.* substantivity, 26.
  cf. theological as human, 20.
  metaphysical structure of *cf.* personhood, 105.
  of *cf.* possibilities, 179-180.
  of *cf.* faith, 215-216.
  of *cf.* power of the real, 223.
  of humans, 238-239.
  metaphysical structure of *cf.*
self-giving, 253.
Subject of *cf.* volition, 214; *cf.* subjective.
Subjectum, 82, 235; *cf.* subjectual, Kant, *hypokeímenon*.
Subjective in *cf.* Kant, 82.
Subsistence, 44, 243-263; *cf.* person, Christ, religation.
Substance, Aristotelian, 26; *cf.* substantivity, *hypokeímenon*.
Substantivity:
  what is, 25-26; *cf.* substance.
  structural principle of, 26-27; *cf.* essence.
  unity of human, 38, 43.
  substantive system, 39-49, 64, 82; *cf.* constitutional sufficiency.
  coherence of, 41; *cf.* coherence.
  cf. being has no, 47.
  worldly actualization of, 49-50, 261; *cf.* "myself", "my", I.
  humans as substantive reality, 51, 104, 128, 208, 260.
  and *cf.* schema, 52.
  and *cf.* figure and zone of time, 59.
  of God, 128.
  cf. constitution.
Subsystems, 38-39; *cf.* system, body, psyche.
Suchness, 27, 77, 126.
Sufficiency, constitutional, 25-26; *cf.* substantivity.
Suicide, 68.
Supplication as moment of *cf.* surrender, 149-150, 162.
Surrender:
  as *cf.* tradition, 57-58; *cf.* history.
  as *cf.* plenary access to God, 147-152, 164-165.
  what is, 148, 159, 210, 214-215; *cf.* volition, appropriation.
  how does man surrender to God, 148, 152, 159, 173, 193, 214, 219.

moments of, 148-151, 162.
and *cf.* personal causality, 151-153.
individual, social, and historical to God, 157.
and *cf.* faith, 157, 159-165, 172, 213, 215-218.
personal in *cf.* St. Augustine, 159.
to *cf.* personal truth, 161.
and *cf.* acceptance, 172-173, 179.
knowledge-surrender problem, 172-174, 177-178, 193-194.
towards as mode of, 174.
as appropriation of possibilities, 179, 184, 193, 210, 213-215.
knowledge of God without, 191-193.
cf. indifferent to grounding, 203.
free, 211; *cf.* freedom.
to reality-ground, 167-188.
intellective surrender to God, 266-267.

Surroundings, control and independence from, 32, 46; *cf.* life.

Syllogism and *cf.* experience of God, 244.

System:
what is., 24-31.
man as system of *cf.* notes, 32-43.
substantive, 53, 64, 82; *cf.* substantivity, structure.
of principles, 164.

T

Talents, 59; *cf.* capacity, possibility.

Táxis, 28; *cf.* Aristotle, cosmos.

Temporalness, 60; *cf.* history.

Tendency:
as moment of *cf.* sensing, 41-43.
as moment of *cf.* sentient volition, 83.
tending will, 180.

Tension, dynamic:
and *cf.* kinesthesia, 35.
as *cf.* function of God in life, 122-123.
and reality of God, 137.
as *cf.* fontanal presence of God in man, 141, 145-146.
and *cf.* access to God, 143.
and *cf.* inter-personal causality, 151-153, 161-162.
ambit of, 191.
cf. inter-personal presence.

Tension, inter-personal:
what is, 142-143; *cf.* access.
and *cf.* dragging, 146-147; *cf.* pre-tension.
tensive inter-personal unity, 259.

Tension, theological:
what is, 121-122, 133, 258-259.
and *cf.* grace, 261-262.
and essence of *cf.* religation, 265-266.
cf. tensive experience of God.

Tertullian, 176.

Testimony:
history is not, 58.
faith is not, 158.

Testing:
physical testing of *cf.* power of the real, 77, 86, 143.
physical testing of reality as experience, 77, 118, 223, 275.
physical testing of religation, 104.
cf. experience.

Theism:
as a way to confront the *cf.* problem of God, 19-20, 250, 270.
and present day atheism, 190-191; *cf.* otiose God.
and faith without knowledge, 197-198.

as mode of *cf.* access to the ground, 274.
as *cf.* experience of the ground, 275.
Theological:
as human dimension, 20, 266, 271.
is not the theologic, 20, 85, 278.
experience, 20, 85, 278-278.
fatigue: *cf.* atheism, 123.
as problem of man, 180, 271, 137.
unity, 243.
transcendentality of *cf.* Christianity, 277.
Theology:
the "theologic" is not the *cf.* theological, 20, 85, 278.
and *cf.* monotheism, 246.
is a theory, 271.
and anthropology, 278.
reality and nature in classical, 93.
existence of God in classical, 125.
analogy between God and man in classical, 129; *cf.* anthropomorphism.
presence of God in classical, 136; *cf.* St. Thomas Aquinas.
surrender in classical, 159.
intelligence-faith problem in classical, 165, 167-168.
God for classical, 173.
creation for classical, 227.
cf. grace for theologians, 241.
of the *cf.* historical experience of God, 247-248; *cf.* Israel.
Theory:
theological considerations are a theory, 271.
cf. religation is not a theory, 272.
Theós:
as divine reality, 20.
of Aristotle is not God, 116.
as unmovable mover, 126.
as inaccessible reality, 136.

as *cf.* otiose God, 191.
cf. Aristotle, God.
Thing:
meaning-thing and reality-thing, 24-25.
the "of" as that which is primary in real things, 26.
real thing as constitutively *cf.* open, 28, 47; *cf.* respectivity, aperture.
every apprehended thing is real, 34, 78, 143-144.
reality and being of each real, 48.
man is with, 66-67, 78, 87, 108, 272.
unity of things by *cf.* impression of reality, 70-71; *cf.* transcendentality.
real things as *cf.* power, 73-74, 108-110; *cf.* gods.
transport the *cf.* power of the real, 78, 86, 118, 223, 253, 272-274.
articulation of things in reality, 85, 86-87.
God as *cf.* ground of, 87, 114-116, 119, 130-133, 140, 142, 144, 146, 226-228, 274.
as *cf.* entities, 48, 101.
God as *cf.* transcendent in, 113, 131, 136, 223-224.
as *cf.* deity or dei-formity, 118-119.
distinction between things and God, 121-122, 131.
unity of things and *cf.* cosmos, 126.
as concretion of the accessibility to God, 140, 145-146.
and the *cf.* enigma of reality, 170-171.
and the ambit of *cf.* possibilities of the real, 179.
as *cf.* closed and open essences, 227.
difference between power of the real and, 273-274.
Thomas Aquinas, St.:

ways of for the existence of God, 93-96; *cf.* Aristotle.
and entification of reality, 101.
presence of God for, 136.
Time, 59-60, 78; *cf.* height of the times, zone of time.
Tone, vital, and *cf.* stimulation, 41.
Towards:
apprehension of reality as, 35, 82, 167, 168, 183, 186, 197, 231.
intellection hurls (throws) us, 79, 170, 175, 178-179, 196, 200, 273.
presence of God as, 146-148, 175.
as mode of *cf.* surrender, 174.
cf. hurling, search, reason, march.
Tradition and *cf.* surrender, 57-59; *cf.* history.
Transcendence:
what is, 131.
of God in the *cf.* world, 133.
as mode of *cf.* presence of God, 131, 138.
of God in *cf.* things, 145, 224-225, 233, 253, 274-276.
of God in the *cf.* person, 151-152, 224, 228, 277.
ground or depth of the person, 152, 161, 211.
self-giving as transcendence of God, 226, 253-254.
theological transcendence of *cf.* Christianity, 277.
cf. fontanal transcendence, transcendentality.
Transcendence, fontanal:
of God, 133.
and *cf.* access to God, 140-141.
and *cf.* notification, 143.
Transcendence, interpersonal:
and *cf.* access to God, 141-142, 145.

and *cf.* anthropomorphism, 140-141.
and *cf.* groping, 143.
Transcendentality:
is *cf.* communication, 27; *cf.* aperture.
of the *cf.* impression of reality, 70-71, 108-110.
of *cf.* things, 71, 79, 108-111.
and composition, 109.
Transcendentifying, 147; *cf.* transcendence, God.
Transmission:
genetic, 57.
tradition, 57, 59; *cf.* history.
Trinity:
and *cf.* grace, 241.
and *cf.* anthropomorphism, 262-263.
Truth:
and pre-Socratics, 31.
what is, 84, 181-182.
for Greeks and Semites, 84.
and problem of God in St. Augustine, 97-98.
of reason and of faith, 116, 165-166, 176, 189.
God as, 143, 232; *cf.* Jesus-Christ.
as culmination of the *cf.* access to God, 143-145.
personal, 159, 161, 185, 187; *cf.* surrender, real truth.
Truth, real:
what is, 143-144, 160-161, 181, 183, 228.
moments of, 84-85, 86, 143-144, 160-161, 182, 187, 228.
as *cf.* actualization of reality, 84, 128, 143-144, 160, 182-184, 209, 228.
as principle of every intellective act, 182-184.
surrender to, 184.
as birth of science, 184.
God gives to man his, 228-235, 247, 253; *cf.* donation.
cf. will to real truth.

Turning:
  between man and God, 20.
  and community, 56; *cf.* society.
  to the power of the real, 56.
  to *cf.* reality-ground, 240.

U

Ultimate (supreme, final):
  as characteristic of *cf.* reality, 68-69, 86, 107.
  as characteristic of the *cf.* ground, 69, 87, 101, 117, 119, 133, 137, 149-150, 192, 253.
  as characteristic of power of the real, 77, 100-101, 108, 114, 149, 266.
  as characteristic of *cf.* religation, 108, 149.
Ultimateness of the real:
  of the *cf.* real, 68, 271-272.
  God as ground of, 116.
  atheism and theism as conclusions confronting, 250.
Unveiling, 142-143; *cf.* manifestation.
Uncertainty, 46; *cf.* restlessness.
Unconcernedness about God, 202-203, 208.
Unfolding: history and society not unfolding of God, 234; *cf.* Hegel.
Unique: *cf.* human substantivity is, 38; *cf.* subsystem.
Uniqueness of God, 126; *cf.* polytheism.
Unitariness of *cf.* human activity, 40.
Unity:
  of the *cf.* notes, 25-31; *cf.* system, "of".
  of reality is not a *cf.* taxis, 28; *cf.* Aristotle.
  of *cf.* human substantivity, 38.
  of the "of" and act-potency, 40.
  of *cf.* sensing, 41.
  phyletic, 52; *cf.* phylum, species.
  moments of the social, 56.
  of reality and being, 60.
  in *cf.* ground, 69.
  of the power of the real and religation, 76.
  of tendency and determination of the real, 83.
  of man and God as *cf.* personal causality, 150-153, 219, 255-259.
  of the modes of *cf.* presence of God, 168-169.
  of knowledge-faith, 180, 193-194; *cf.* will.
  of intelligence-faith and attitude of reaching God, 213.
  of faith, 215-217.
  theological, 243.
  tensive inter-personal, 258-259, 261.
  tensive, 261-266; *cf.* dóxa, eudokía, hesed.
Universal history, 59.

V

Vector: things as vectors of reality, 78, 85-86, 273; *cf.* vehicle, seat.
Vehicle:
  each thing transports *cf.* power of the real, 78, 110, 118, 274.
  things as vehicles of God, 119, 273; *cf.* seat, vector.
Veneration:
  as moment of *cf.* surrender, 149-150, 152.
  as mode of *cf.* inter-personal causality, 153.
Vicissitude: history is not, 58.
Virtue as *cf.* appropriation of possibilities, 155.
Vocation, 65, 165.

Voice of conscience, 81-83, 86, 106.
Volition (willing):
  how it emerges, 42.
  what is, 83-85, 179-181, 210, 213, 215; *cf.* self-determination.
  sentient, 83.
  and adopting a *cf.* form of reality, 83-85, 273.
  of *cf.* real truth, 85-86.
  as appropriation of *cf.* possibilities, 183-184, 187, 209.
  as surrender, 210, 213.
  as act to realize oneself as person, 214.

W

Way:
  cosmic way to reach God, 93-96; *cf.* St. Thomas Aquinas.
  anthropological ways to reach God, 96-99.
  of religation to reach God, 99-103, 115-116.
  cf. justification, intellective process.
"Who", 256; *cf.* open essence.
Will:
  and *cf.* personhood, 44.
  sentient, 83; *cf.* volition.
  to reality, 84.
  to authenticity, 84, 184; *cf.* Nietzche.
  to live, 84, 208, 203-211.
  in the *cf.* anthropological ways, 96.
  as *cf.* fruition, 128.
  and intelligence as the "factum" of substantivity, 128.
  of God, 130.
  and choice, 180.
  to be, 180, 208-209, 211.
  to *cf.* search, 199, 208, 210.
  to be relatively absolute, 207.
  to put oneself in the hands of God, 262; *cf. eudokia.*

Will to grounding:
  what is, 187, 189, 192-195.
  as attitude of surrender, 188-189, 192-193, 213.
  as attitude of search, 199, 211, 212.
  as attitude of the *cf.* intellective process, 192, 195-200.
  lack of, 193.
  and unity of knowledge and faith, 193-194.
  life without, 200-203.
  atheism as form of, 195, 206-207, 212.
  and *cf.* faith, 215.
Will to truth:
  what is, 84-87, 181-189, 266.
  as principle of attitude, 192-194.
  in human reality, 194-213.
  and *cf.* intellective process, 195-196.
  and *cf.* author of one's own being, 328.
  as mode of *cf.* experience of God, 240, 343.
  as moment of the *cf.* theological dimension, 365.
  will to real truth and search, 108.
  apprehension of the will to real truth, 86.
  will to real truth, 182-189.
  will to real truth as condition of real truth, 183.
  will to real truth and science, 184.
  of ideas, 183, 187.
With:
  Humans are with reality, 66-67, 77-78, 87, 107, 108, 272; *cf.* "in".
  making the *cf.* relatively absolute being with things, 87, 108, 110, 209.
  making the relatively absolute being real truth, 209, 229.
  God as possibilitating, 137.

Word, the, 235, 262-263.
World:
  what is, 28-47, 126, 132; *cf.* cosmos, taxis, respectivity.
  worldly actuality of the relatively absolute reality, 43, 49-51, 54, 91, 105, 141.
  other world as question of faith and not pure reason, 121.
  presence of God in, 132-133; *cf.* transcendence.
  access of God to, 136-137, 140.

society and, 164.

Y

Yahweh, 217, 219, 234, 245-247; *cf.* God, Israel.
You:
  "You-ness" of God, 141; *cf.* I.
  and *cf.* Trinity, 359-263; *cf.* anthropomorphism.

Z

Zone of time, 59-60.